THE COMING MENTAL RANGE

THE COMING MENTAL RANGE

WILL ALEXANDER

Litmus Press 2023

The Coming Mental Range © Will Alexander, 2023
Artwork © Will Alexander, 2023
All rights reserved.

ISBN: 978–1–933959–52–8
Cataloging-in-Publication data available from the Library of Congress.
LCCN: 2021040293

Cover art: "Projection Beyond Quanta" by Will Alexander, coloured ink and pastel.
 Interior drawings: "Form As Transparent Drift," "Triplicate Cosmic Towers," "Intrinsic Flotation," and "Electric Intelligence" by Will Alexander, graphite.
 Courtesy of the artist © Will Alexander.
Design and typesetting by HR Hegnauer.

Litmus Press is a program of Ether Sea Projects, Inc., a 501(c)(3) non-profit literature and arts organization.

Litmus Press publications are made possible by the New York State Council on the Arts with support from Governor Kathy Hochul and the New York State Legislature. This project is also supported in part by an award from the National Endowment for the Arts. Additional support for Litmus Press comes from the Leslie Scalapino–O Books Fund, The Post-Apollo Press, individual members and donors. All contributions are fully tax-deductible.

LITMUS PRESS
925 Bergen Street, Suite 405
Brooklyn, New York 11238
litmuspress.org

SMALL PRESS DISTRIBUTION
1341 Seventh Street
Berkeley, California 94710
spdbooks.org

TABLE OF CONTENTS

Introduction
i   The Coming Mental Range as Unknown Psychic Beacon

PART I

THE COMING MENTAL RANGE
Essays

3   The Coming Mental Range
7   The Modern Mind as Debilitated Embroilment
9   Post-Electrical Replication
14   Sans Nouns and Blocked Verbiage
25   Primal Fragment as Subtext
26   Primal Fragment I
27   Primal Fragment II
29   Barren Aperture That Purposely Miscalculated
31   The Contemporary Mind: Pointless Rural Fragment
38   Centripetal Respiration
39   Aural Botany
44   Atop a Tasmanian Crag
59   Inscrutable Visibility
68   On Crossing the Vermin Frontier
80   On the Rise of Sodium and Fire
103   Saturate with Refined Enigmas
105   Escaping Mass Seduction
130   Antonin Artaud: A Glossary of Fumes
133   Solar Fire on Earth

PART II

BRILLIANCE ENSNARED BY THE UNSEASONABLE

Essays & Reviews

145 My Philosophical Matrix: A Hurricane of Luminosity
149 Our Present Psychic State: An Awkward Foreboding
152 A Note on Interstellar Audition
160 A Further Note on *Le Grand Jeu*
162 Phantom Electrical Scarring: The Drawings of Byron Baker
167 Superseding the Diurnal: The Latest Works of Byron Baker
170 Inscrutable Solar Configurations
171 Theresa Tolliver: The Soil of Indigenous Genius
174 Ghérasim Luca: Fulminate Inscription as Shadow
178 Georgiana Peacher's *Mary Stuart's Ravishment Descending Time*: A Species of Rapture
181 The Larsons' Journey Beyond Time
183 On Sonic Etching: The Work of Jean-Luc Guionnet
185 Aleatoric Circular Forms: A Trilogy of Circles
187 James Hart: The Cryptic Personality, the Unknown as Presence
188 Prologue: Quantum Lingual Deftness
190 Majied Mahadi: Enigmatic Icon
194 New Mexico Poets' Conference: Organic Poets' Society
196 Beyond Baroque: A Seminal Wind Encircling the Planet
198 Wanda Coleman: Bulletins from the Lava Floor

PART III

PHOTONIC RESPIRATION
Interviews

203 Primordial Vibration
     with Elizabeth Bryant

207 On African Free Labour and the Interstellar Vacuum
     with Chris Holdaway

225 Hearing a Second Bell in a Mirror
     with Sofi Thanhauser

241 Interview for National Poetry Month
     with Entropy

248 it remains sonic occultation
     with Stephen J. Fowler

252 Ghasem Batamuntu & Will Alexander
     with Darrell Jónsson

264 Spontaneous Aural Combustion
     with Justin Desmangles

PART IV

ELECTRICAL GRAMMAR
Afterwords

273 Note Concerning Higher Mental Scale
275 Higher Mental Scale: Glossary
291 *Acknowledgements*

INTRODUCTION

The Coming Mental Range as Unknown Psychic Beacon

THESE WRITINGS EXIST as a disparate ensemble electrically woven and transmuted by inner fire that broaches sequential pattern. They arc via an unfathomable inner Sun shifted via telepathic grammar onto a plane that gives rise to aural constellations that morph into other planes that reflect human, animal, and divine as other. These are writings that have taken me on a voyage of solemn exploration as if wafting across Einstein-Rosen Bridges into Andrei Linde's multiverse, as inflationary realia that somehow casts tremor into one's cells allowing something other than that which consists of an observable solar grammar.

I've felt when writing these texts as if I were both looking down and gazing up simultaneously, infused with an insatiable vertigo not unlike strange moons casting occulted rays through heathen binary suns that seem to spin at once in conflicting dimensions at differing levels of speed. The result from this turbulent tidal seismicity is that light emits itself via frictive streaks and angles, through darting shards of voltage.

Thus, this collection is concerned with the mind beyond its current working model attempting to access a mind/body template that Sri

Aurobindo understood to be the "Divine." The latter, being a primal presence where the mind/body can forge new possibilities other than by super-imposed technocracy.

It is my experience that life evolves and cannot be stilled by the past conveyed as static replica. In this experiential climate the unknown builds upon itself casting itself as unknown beacon far beyond the mirage of our present animals' neurology. This, for me, is *The Coming Mental Range* where psychic light naturally casts its rays out of ciphers.

PART I

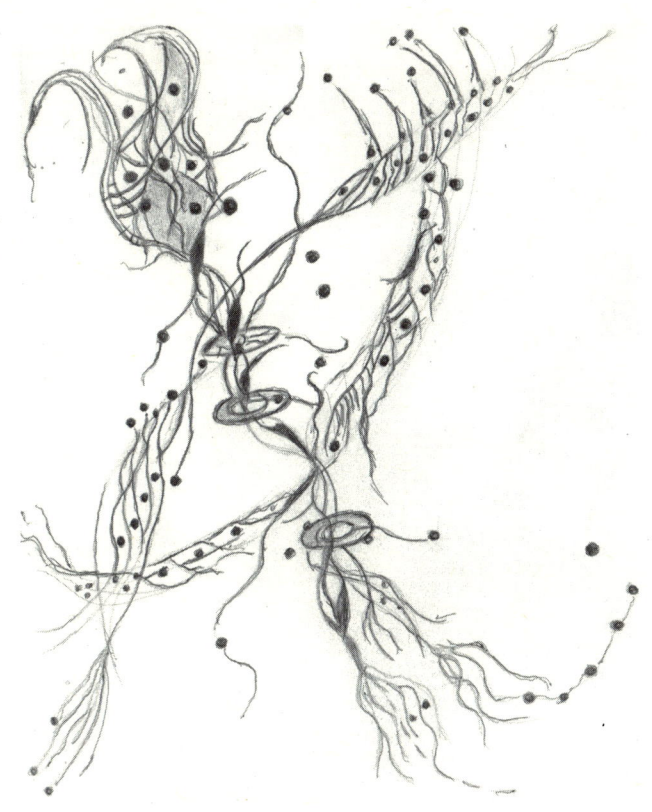

THE COMING MENTAL RANGE

Essays

The Coming Mental Range

All error proceeds from ignorance (or haste)
—FERNANDO PESSOA

OUR CIRCUMSTANCE IS fouled by protracted haste, by that which aspires to some form of clinical security. I am thinking of the quest to inhabit Mars within a foreseeable time frame. The question arises, does susurration amongst the Northern elite strive for an isolate colony where populace from the Southern cone is surgically omitted? This is something to contemplate given the prevailing wreckage that now consumes all corners of the Earth rife with chronic patterns of extinction that ranges from the condition of bees to the ominous breakage of icebergs, to the volatile scattering of humans from refuge to refuge. A daunting condition to say the least. So what Elon Musk proposes seems as pointed towards the future as some multi-planetary exercise. Yet, in our present context it feels at bottom as if it were nothing other than a skittish trope grasping for salvation for the financially appointed.

The zeitgeist persists across what I consider to be an expanding terminal phase, with our basic neurology being called into question. Human crossing of the solar system seems escape beyond the calliope that remains continuing earthly dread. It feels as though the void implies our every breath. History being nothing other than a concert that re-patterns each of our momentary efforts. This remains the gist for all outward escape.

History via our continuing terror combines terminal posturing bringing forth the chemistry of wealth and speculation transmitted as synecdoche confined to the shadowy urn we understand to be the one percent. The latter populace crowned in the collective sub-derma by enforced consensus. In the end, the one percent exists as none other than elite refugees themselves seeking escape from the planetary wreckage they have so willfully spawned. With the secular state now barely alive as a graceless sub-functioning order, with each of its individual components functioning as none other than particularized sub-functioning fiefdoms. The latter being none other than a moribund cellular confine, incapable of spontaneous electricity sans the power of transmutation. Such a state is not inclined towards movement via sattvic acreage in the cells. I am thinking of such acreage as transparence with its impalpable planes of respiration, not unlike Cantoresque sub-infinities allowing the body to transmute as a state into what I'll call shamanic vulcanism. This is where the cells take on capability that ignites as transhuman possibility so that gulfs between voids become open to something other than acquiescent consumption, or the individual being stunted by its own self-erasure. At best, the collective has become conditioned to aspiring to brokered animal limit, to nothing other than experience as a briefly wrought body amassed through dysfunctional assemblage.

Within this wrought consensus there remains among a small gist of the populace the desire to export this dysfunction to a Martian soil torrential with in-audia and howling, attempting to replicate the error that remains the Anthropocene. To create through this replication a compound solar error is none other than unconscionable exploration. If the specific honings of the Asteroid probes and similar attempts amount to nothing other than cosmic land speculation and graft, we have, in the end, wrought only a more pointed punctuation that signals further outgrowth of the tamasic.

As for the looming prospect of a human colony on Mars it remains the target of immediate saturation leading to completion. Again, private moguls reign via Blue Origin, SpaceDev, New Shepard, Virgin Galactic, and Elon Musk's SpaceX, being momentary figurines that seem solely concerned with exteriorized result. For instance, there remains telling silence concerning the inner dimension of the soul, their quest seems willing to ignore the soul and its confrontation with the Martian scape and its unrelenting weather cycles as they consume the body ultimately stranding its carcass on alien plateaus. The violence that accrues from such inclement isolation has not yet been considered. Highly efficient rocket boosters and possible "pizza" lodgings, the latter having been enunciated in passing as foreshortened ancillary effect of a stated industrial goal.

What the Egyptians understood as being the seven parts of the soul has been subsumed by the sterility that looms as business venture as momentary profit. This will not suffice. If what is true of numerically projected galaxies ranging between 200 million at the low end, and 2 trillion at the high end, this is an overwhelming range that can never be sufficiently explored by an ambitious but delimited techne. In the deepest sense this seems a marked derangement that projects, in my view, a reality that seems parallel as accessible analogy to the experimental implosion that was Roanoke. This is the template that seems to configure the Mars mission or any other similar configuration or any of the asteroids that portend mineral extraction. The latter policy persists as commercial projection.

The point that seems to naturally accrue is one of missing inner respiration. There is the implementation of Musk's BFR rocket, with its powerful boosters lifting the body outside of its earthly habitation, yet never having discussion concerning the volcano that invigourates the soul. Thus, exo-missions seem compromised by a kind of abstract sterility, by the passage of life as sightless enterprise. When the Arctic shaman Aua speaks of "'quamaneq'… the shaman light of brain and body" this is something that Space X, or SpaceDev or Blue Origin has so far failed to consider. They possess a glossary compelled by quantification, by palpable excess honed in principle by micrometer.

This being the state of official exploration, subtending itself via suicidal psychic clauses, via delimited transmission of psycho-physical food stuffs, and the result, a soullessness propounded via inclement animation, not unlike its homing ground of Euro-American cellular malaise, bereft as it is of the coming mental range, this latter range having at its heart the insight of the soul and its registration beyond quanta.

The Modern Mind as Debilitated Embroilment

THE INDIVIDUAL CONTINUES to remain an isolated figure no longer enabled to cope with its self-assumed predisposition. As the contemporary psychological template brings to bear its exponential complexity a circuitous spectrum emerges not unlike Einsteinian field relativity. The mind is thus exposed to complex gyrational instants. Perhaps a geometry of fragments, or an onslaught of muses not unlike the complexity of a Xenakian orchestral tome having a shrunken ballast never approaching a liberated stocastics being template. sans linear orchestration. The above assessment garnered from my cognitive realm not unlike my mind as primal echolocation. Not an assumed symbolism struggling with spontaneous opaqueness but surrounded as it is by dazed criteria dulled by syllogistic argumentation.

Thus, the individual has become an isolate connivance within itself. What one sees in contemporary thought arrangement remains an attempt to hold onto Newtonian thought analysis while being cast into an Einsteinian subset of its equation. This being a mathematics triggered by its own reaction to itself. Thus, contemporary psycho-neurology remains triggered by its own inherent pleurisy that seems to hobble within its own extensive discourse having little connection with itself as splendiferous gazelle. It seems now expertly scaled to move within an opaque latitudinal amplification. Within this interstate its motion senses suspension of itself so that it is no longer partial even within its own insight. No longer sired within a prior or gregarious certainty it struggles to survive not unlike the now obscure Chinchorro people as they were forced to endure the ambitious savagery of the Spaniards.

When speculating as I do even in the paragraphs scripted above, I feel compelled by a susurrance that seems to issue from the protracted coming years. A soured ambivalence, a regime of milliseconds arguing at its own limit. In response to this limit the mind takes on an arrogance of forgery within itself being claustrophobia as protracted illness. A nervous but blunted energy that dwells inside its own geometry via fundamental mishap. I think of Sartre's understanding of nausea, or Kierkegaard's crowds self-bullied into false agreement with themselves beveled by their own untruth.

For me, I only hear a cascade of syllogism not as a strange optical beauty but of a mathematics falsely conjoined to itself. The latter being a mathematics of what Artaud understood to be none other than an evil and barren equation co-equal with its own tautology. Under coming circumstances, it does seem to be an extinct phenomenon. It feels beyond the privation that is ideology but a presence that harasses its own making attempting to continue dwelling within its debilitated embroilment.

Post-Electrical Replication

A "NANOSTRUCTURED SURFACE on silicon" attempts to replicate the impalpable, with its recto-linear adjustments that persist as replicated voltage squared downward into minutiae recalibrating the atomic state according to delimited secular psychology. This being a vocabulary enacted that seems to simulate the function of the higher states as if the quotidian realm (or what I consider as the subsequent realm) had gained par with primordial origination. As if the cognitive template had contained by isolation a seeming electrical incessance that we find empowering volcanic lahars. These nano-etchings, these techniques, in no way acknowledge the sweeping general forces that empower their ignition. Because natural forces are noninductive they carry little credibility within the realm of cognitive proof. These forces do not require a generated science to prove themselves to themselves. They do not need coaxing from abstracted indication as to whether they exist or not. What Werner Herzog displays in a latter documentary, *Into the Inferno,* are waves of lava breaking beneath the earth, and what is naturally understood is that there exists no capacity for conversion of such power into reductive portions of capital. So, what is the power of generated capital? Is it capable of sustaining seasons? Does it empower respiration? Does it ignite the thirst that reigns in mating season? The former are not conditions controllable at room scale, subject to the windowless research through increment pursing the trapping of voltage via cognitive emendation. Saying such I am not abstractly demeaning "bioimaging and diagnosis" that can divert disease-ridden bodies from the looming door that is death, as if this diverting in itself is capable of neutralizing the soul, implying by its prowess that the soul is of some secondary order sans its unacknowledged alchemical presence.

In modern parlance, evidence by the senses remains the prime priority. For instance, we find in "microfabrication" principles such as "etching," "bonding," "polishing," "integrated circuits," "solar cells," "Flat Panel Displays," prone to the principles of the marketplace. As with molecular engineering these principles are concerned with the delimited functioning of matter, nothing of which approaches the understanding of transmutation. And by transmutation one fields concern with states that supersede those of a calculable nature.

I'm thinking of solid-liquid interfaces found in surface science, or the "subdiscipline" that is organic chemistry, all of which gives way in the end to arid complexification of the marketplace. Even when the body is diverted from death by means of materials whose structure of measures registers "billionths of a meter" by our very circumstance this nanomedicine indirectly infers its profit-driven atmosphere that accrues from life and death. This latter state is none other than the paradise of quantity, of its infinite alterity, never inclined to transgress its authorship by matter. Let us contrast this state to principles which guided Egyptian electricity and its relation to the soul. First and foremost, the soul was understood to exist as a living state as it existed as a part of an animate dimension not given over to limits imposed by exoteric criteria. To this degree the nanostructure remains a delimited state that exists from the "bottom up" for the service by the exterior plane and the exterior plane alone. Its brilliance dazzles the mind with what I'll call an obfuscating solar sterility. We must understand that it is a "manipulation of matter on an atomic, molecular, and supramolecular scale." This understanding has it that "Manipulation of matter on an atomic, molecular, and supramolecular scale continues to exist below the common size as threshold." Because this technology possesses a "variety of potential applications" it remains a boon to all manner of markets. Governments "have invested billions of dollars" for its implementation touching on all manner of possibility. Let us take molecular self-assembly. This being a process "by which molecules adopt a defined arrangement without guidance or management from an outside source." Yet for its seeming array of magical coalescence, it amounts to a superior manufacturing technique sans inner technology. What I mean by inner technology is that the higher states ignite the human form as Schwaller de Lubicz understands to be the living model for the Temple at Luxor. The Temple at Luxor being the principal of Egyptian pyramidal construction thereby forming the body as the lifeblood of a divine conducting principal. This conducting principle being code for those states where palpable measurement fails to accrue. I am not alluding to the nano realm as one condemned by ruinous invention, but of one condensed by its application to delimited capital and its singular concern of the marketplace. Thus, its absolute segregation from living primordial grammar that never negates its ability to enact seemingly vertiginous application, producing portrayed miracle after miracle, all within the teeming plane of secular application.

When Richard Feynman opened the gates for its arrival, it allowed extension of matter from the macro-realm to that of the micro. What started out as masonry and mortar circa 1750 has advanced its applicability via micro-incorporation. Matter being the singular application of scale that remains delimited to lateral application, to constrained exhibit, which signals the absolute tautology of itself extended forward from its scale in 1750 to the present hours, but also extending as an anterior realis prior to 1750 thereby pervading the collective memory to such a degree that any psychological or cultural alternative seems subsequent and insubstantial, the latter having been denigrated in the collective mind to ruination by an abstracted ideological tinge, so that any realia garnered by common perception tends to level at a chronic plateau.

As this chronic stalemate continues to hallucinate the collective mind it becomes by a person's early age the only substantial realis.

A premature constriction begins to invade and suffocate the cells at impalpable levels, leaving developing minds curiously crippled and invaded by quotidian purview.

When Feynman first broached the nano-realms in 1959 the complication of our collective stasis had not reached its present level of critical mass witnessed at this present writing. When Feynman gave his seminal talk, "There's Plenty of Room at the Bottom: An Invitation to Enter a New Field of Physics," there existed no trenchant stir of overlapping global forces, no dive into atomic enigmas in order to manipulate its reduction into goods and service. Ultimately, the nano-realm has become in principle a superior conduit to the marketplace reflecting commercial profit in its wake. This being in sharp contradistinction to Feynman's original insight, which was recursively endowed 30 years onward, this latter endowment being inspired by K. Eric Drexler's book *Engines of Creation: The Coming Era of Nanotechnology* published in 1986.

What followed from Drexler's work was commercial explosion codified by Feynman's "retroactive" reputation. Saying such, do I deprecate the scanning tunneling microscope that enabled "unprecedented visualization of individual atoms and bonds"? Absolutely not. Gerd Binnig and Heinrich Rohrer created a technological leap that enabled atomic control. This being technical genius in its purest state. What I'm speaking of is the delimited application of this genius reflective of a coarse and over-concretized value system. No other priority can be seen except profit. I contrast this with the old Egyptians and Aurobindo's experiment at Pondicherry concerning transmutation of the cellular state, active as human transmutation, not simply a technical attempt at improving our present stasis. Since the Occident empowers the recto-linear as its principle mental conduction, it remains operant within a scripted tolerance that can only evince itself via higher or lower quantification. Sans quantification nothing supposedly exists; beyond its confine one is thought to enter a negligible condition where only a mind can persist at either a savage or principally nonexistent negligible state. Yogic exploration in this context posits realia that can be, at best, classified as exotic addenda, since they can be none other than entry into pejorative realms that cannot be explained according to values spawned by linear assumption. This assumption equates, say, with the state of humanity that existed in Voltaire's Paris or in Beijing or Los Angeles in the 21st century. The soaring of the subtle body has been negated to such a degree that realia such as the nano-realm seem to elicit possibility within our present parenthetical stasis. Humanity has aspired to occupy a static narration of itself capable of only exoteric refinement via the manipulation of matter. A mature respiration would see the material body and its subtle counterpart as a harmonic resonance capable of realizing a state over and above the suffocating principle that informs the psychic pressure that has been embraced as normal living.

Sans Nouns and Blocked Verbiage

To write is to surrender oneself to the fascination of the absence of time.
—MAURICE BLANCHOT

CONCERNING THE POET'S phase of proto-navigation there exists protracted anonymity, nebulosity as registration, marked by the paradox of seeming inaudia. Early development seems self-sabotaged by attempts at climbing the great works while overemphasizing one's nascent depths locked within. It seems at first glance an incendiary slide into failure. Consensus grasp seems blunted, protracted confusion transpires, destiny begins to sculpt itself via mirage-like patterns always attempting to magnetize one's spirit so that the effort descends into the gulf that is failure. One becomes not unlike a displaced moneron, dazed, stumbling across a prairie of phonemes, self-compelled to summarize lost or forgotten lists. And these forgotten lists begin to dye one's increasingly discomforted moments protracted as they are by withdrawal. Yet, through all of this, unbeknownst to oneself a fuse has been silently ignited in the cavernous realms of one's future. A future that is nothing other than proto-magnetics, nothing other than desire and scale vis-à-vis invisibility. This being nothing other than what I would call alien adventure, being transmutative analogy burning with silence and risk. According to French theoretician and author Michel

Leiris, this risk is sometimes punctuated with reward. Let us say that one's obscure chronicle at some random moment ignites via unknown aural registration into heightened spells of aural absorption that burns as interior etching. A linkage then begins its frayed establishment at the outer edges of consciousness. One then curiously enters a gallery of options momentarily condensed by say, shadings of verbal turquoise as well as aural scents of primordial lavender. Again, this is proto-entry into a secretive life. A life prone to sparks that rise from any subject the mind at hand is capable of exploring.

This inner world is none other than a galaxy of magic, not unlike a telepathic monsoon culled from trans-hybridity where language simultaneously exists and de-exists, where imaginal prairies collapse and open onto kingdoms of otherness as living experience. This is where the quotidian realm begins to vanish becoming verboten, where its transgressive interference is never allowed to enter and maim. Poetic awareness for me becomes the condition where its creative diamonds remain unsized, and of no use to rational containing modules rife with connection to the marketplace.

Before one reaches the poetic shore of authoritative misnomer it seems that one may drown in the aether of this internal attempt, with each stroke to shore being a bottomless escapade seemingly sullied by profound dis-orientation, igniting to such a degree that possibility seems conspired against one, as if one swam in an oneiric yurt dis-comforted by demons. At this pitch of crises, one's voice seems stultified, self-derided, inert. Both oneirically and diurnally plagued, a dazed pariah attempting to advance the parapets of general oblivion. The gales seem to magnify via the power of seeming non-limit. Again, one remains self-scorched like a dazed leper awaiting execution. At this stage of one's journey the books one consults take on differing variations of uselessness, as if they emitted an intransigent plague in the form of dishonored serpents distorting absorption. Following this are neurotic sub-variations that further extend this horror of in-audia. Thus, the voice remains vacant in spite of its former absorption, carrying in this protracted turbulence doubt that signals the very paradox that is resurrection.

By struggling with such engulfment one builds power unbeknownst to oneself by embracing doubt via elements of hell in one's psyche always lit by a blazeless lantern of inversion. And in the midst of this inversion a small sense of ambrosia begins to replicate even as doubt swarms as the dominate body of one's negated self-assessment. This being none other than the fiendish alignment with alchemic tribulation. Thus, this tenor of tribulation susurrates via its secondary state a rhetoric of fever. This fever being a rhetoric no other can claim. It is germane to site-specific scorching. One is thus dyed by experience of interior burning living at the brink, at the very exhaustion of stamina.

If I recall correctly, it is not unlike the internal chronicler Satprem's discussion concerning the lungfish proto to its experience of respiration on land. Just before breathing its forces seem irretrievably scattered by swarming pestilence, then out of seeming impossibility another neural possibility transpires and coalesces over time striking at this distance one's sudden aural analogy with lenses giving one a view other than through summarized optical cognizance. One is never felled by optical misplacement thereby generating primal aural imagination where the lungfish exists as magnetic analogy to one's alchemical tribulation of seeming drowning by vapour. This is the moment when phonemes invade themselves and begin to generate according to spontaneous arising. I am not speaking of prehensile elements, but of elevated primal form equivalent to the first naming of mountains. Of course, the poetic voice responsible for the naming of lizards and herons. In our present circumstance this phonemic vibration evolves into poetic tendency and then morphs into notes and essays, drama and novels, further extending into indeterminate forms.

The point being is that language crystallizes as imaginal blazing, as musical incandescence, so much so that plasticity inheres as its substance, not as superimposed intention, or staged relic, solemnly importing repetition confining itself to some previously defined set of standards, thereby attempting to gain on itself by repeating a staged form of eloquence. In my view language need erupt like a burning temperature of moths feasting on themselves so that it grows greater in strength. This being language resurrecting itself unclaimed by the famine that describes itself according to quotidian scholarship. One then basks in rays that issue from a sonic sun, that issue and reverberate via every nano-second of respiration. Thus, poetic energy exists isometrically soaking every bit of occultation as the province of expression. In consequence, barriers invoked by common assignation spontaneously fail themselves according to their lesser vibration.

One's former doubt and self-scorching begins to evolve and dwell at unimaginable heights crossing from one level of language then residing at another. Movement at this level being none other than inner sporulation, being language travelling great distance across itself ceasing to reside in eclipsed strictures, or other forms of distorted embranglement. As for behavioural anachronism, it is encouraged by self-spawning in order to disrupt an outmoded psychic climate. This level of language resonates its philosophical character that exhorts itself as a curious wandering balance. Its mellifluous tenor electrically merges with a greater lingual field proto in character being simultaneous with itself as un-stated voltage.

Having reached this higher mesmerism the optical life retreats and takes on a susurrant form of secrecy. It then exists as protracted invisibility, as an uncodified remainder subsequent to seasoned aural blizzards. The eye being paramount during one's daily gauntlet, in poetic trance it takes on a subsequent pirouette no longer quaking as a carking or meddlesome foray into consciousness. As for basic inherence one no longer views the character of outside formation as prime example. Sight at this juncture is prime with annoyance only capable of provoking a firmament of ruin. And this firmament sullies the ear with distraction. It is other than the wealth of cadence. In this circumstance I am speaking of sattvic inherence that emits phonemically, that emits itself as transparence. This is something other than heraldic weight. I am speaking of circumstantial charisma being other than language as static misapplication cognitively placed according to a priori manipulation. I am not concerned here with synaptic manipulation bedeviled by downward symmetry. I'm speaking here of language compounded by leprous routine ideologically grafted onto isolate lingual particles, the latter condoned by tamasic skills that signal the operative balance of morning walks, or daily office ledgers. The latter being none other than propaganda, than figments that condone curious recruitment of the psyche towards collective deadening thereby expunging general behaviourable complexity in favour of marooned simplistic statement.

This remains daily life in the Occident under the astrological plague after the discovery that was Eris replete as it's been with carnage and disruption. Eris is none other than a scattering of energy in all directions so that these fragments clash and attempt to occlude the deeper strata of aurality creating a condition that blurs, that desiccates conjunction, so that aural connections can never refine themselves so that aural inertia builds on itself and thus conflates itself with received invention.

And the question comes to view what is received invention? The latter being none other than fossilized criteria forged according to collective repetition. The populace at large subsumed by contaminated audition creating at an atmosphere that blurs, that in-substantiates itself via chord-less decibels that deafen. Thus, inward definition remains torrentially weakened by nulling fragments and hissing. This being glossary as forfeiture, this being none other than ambulant corpses wandering across the strata of the kingdom.

This being the chakras of the dead active as they are in reverse. They stammer, they spout phrases, they sour identity, as they overspill their former habitat in hell. So, it can be said that this is the state of collective audition not unlike the listless seismography of strewn kelp. Persons embody an existential withering prone to states of profound jealousy, of suffocating rage. A spasmodic estrangement forming its debilitating structure of chronic ineptitude. They carry the genetic character of assaultive ghosts thereby seasoning the percolation of the hive that functions as a state via ill-begotten ciphers. This being liquor of distracted imposition where the mind is prone to blossoming evil, to blazes that circumvent. This being nothing other than harried neurology summed by a deadly and uneven balancing ritual that comprises itself according to the worship of capital. It has been said that one advances beyond this structure of partially hidden hells. When ascendance is broached via behaviourable merit there exists no functioning adherence. It is as though one accounted for higher states through functioning depletion. Such aspiration is accorded equivalence with the purposeless ideal of gathering spiders. A disparate and disjunctive praxis. This higher state not unlike a circuitous mirror that curiously emits incalculable flashes of consciousness. Thus, one is labeled a self-ignited bearer of consciousness. A poet, who has risen via language as perpendicular self-reaction. Perpendicular seepage sans solemnly etched Teutonic calendars. Such seepage is not averse to uranian rooting in poetic blizzards striking lightning shores.

By means of the poetic condition there can be reached levels through alchemical foment into blankness so that plasticity is achieved, and all things remain possible. This being poetry far removed from the canonical tensions of the 20th century. Because of its power of natural revelation, it enacts through inward lensing unscripted galvanics. In this state the poet exists sans the plutonic prairie studded with mirage that seeks to enact itself as discipline. Words spiral with license, colours then infer heretofore unknown spectra. Specific traits of the poet expand to peoples with their miraculous habituations. This being none other than interior amplification over and beyond the senses as we've come to know them.

Knowledge then ceases to ensnare the mind with burdensome drainage, as encephalitic lessening, not duty as torrential policy. Discipline needs be embraced not codified via manual or statistic. Knowledge is not some Dutch invader trading Indian property for trinkets. It is the underlying ethos that erupts into seeming fact hurtling into view without context. I am speaking here of a diminished view of events as if one wore blinders while viewing events from a sculpted hurricane carriage. Again, language need be mobile in situ and remain wide-ranging at large. There exists no higher plane as to chronic perspective. As to systematized definition there exists only blind and inherent dosage adhering to a super-imposed chronology. The latter persists as the colonial climate pared down to dosage. To a certain palpable instillment that ceases to lean on nuance that denies respiration or value beyond anything that clear mean thought can advance. Therefore, conjunctions are absolute and manufactured according to didactic simplicity.

In contradistinction, poetic language need rise enabling it to summon astral cobalt emanation, not in an absolute sense, but through a refractive form of isthmus, spontaneously understanding that its endemic realization exists on an intervallic parallel plane far removed from dissemination along quotidian embankments. I am speaking here of refractive dye simultaneous with inner experience. Not scale according to deafening solar information.

This being apprenticeship evolved to apparitional energy coalescing as uncanny spiral that enlivens as pitch apparitional praxis that exists sans the backdrop of counting. When Breton spoke of the diurnal paucity of literature, of its conventional folly, of its restrictive expanse, it remains none other than lacunae, none other than a galaxy of vacuums. Again, it remains a laggardly blazing capable of partially simulating fire, having never reached a circumspect presence vis-à-vis consciousness of what the galaxies imply. Thus, a moot point to the galaxies solely embrangled by market-based yield and its stratagems. Literature via secular crystallization seems to have reached a prior apogee and is non-germane to the wilderness of stars. Of course, it takes its place as parasitic enclosure; this being its inevitable outcome tracery by illusion. Since it fails to truly live always in the context of weighing kilograms, so its margin surfaces as accepted tracery by rote. By a kind of weighed form that gradually manipulates itself to more tangible means, to industry standards that seems to coalesce with old skeletal ideas.

Language as rationality is a spent exhibit, a failed mirage, open and closed realia endemically extinguished by the eons. Thus, it occupies a condition of magnetic erasure. So, does one gloat at magnetic erasure and its swallowing of cognitive praxis? I'd go so far as to say that the expressive spirit of such works is only capable of animating bodies in a blind house, only capable of arousing piranha infestation. Its extension being none other than quotidian propaganda that has now cannibalized itself via magnetic erasure.

So does one gloat at this tenor of rationality as magnetic erasure malingering in some static position waiting for its palpable collapse? Instead, one must continue supra-lingual praxis as though its erasure continues to remain as imminent possibility. There must remain pursuance of the accuracy and the excellence of excellence.

Thus, in hindsight poetic apprenticeship must synthesize both the past and the dazzling abundance of the future. Initial hesitation via seeming failure and fatigue is none other than an alchemic form of trembling, which, if protracted across living experience, allows one to live beyond provincial definitions, the latter being nothing other than transitional entrapment. And this entrapment conjuncts with its seeming realia by inscripting inner liberty with the moniker of crime. Crime in this instance is none other than invoking power through language that goes beyond being the voice transmuting through turbulence. One could ascribe to this voice the imagination that ignites flight as a carnivorous swan, as something other than brusque simulacra. This carnivorous swan exists as none other the stage of what Philip Lamantia spoke of as the "red phase" of the "Great Work." The imagination in formation not unlike tumultuous candles that spin inside themselves and emit the wonderous as calculation. This being nothing other than eclipsed energy being folded mass unleashed invoked as intervallic leap.

What is most concerning language must never fail at convincing, at emancipating its readership via transgressive spiral. From a cognitive point the spirit accrues as amnesia, via failure as forced rotation. Ultimately nothing other than the limited guise of torment capitalizing on scripts of lingual suicide. This being none other than static infection. There exists no supra-conscious flow, no explosive uranian lava, no entry of language into heaven.

Some would misconstrue linguistic rising as savage and transfixed glistening, as confusing metrical advance. I am speaking of language as essential dynamism, as circular botany of possibility. Language can no longer be grounded by nouns, by draft after draft so that it reverts to balanced colloquial equation. In order to expand, poetry must exist as spontaneous fragment that respirates, that is passionate convergence in its deepest sense that glistens as alchemical surprise via passion that evinces itself through what I would call discriminatory burning possessing as its specific condition dynamic inner poise, having the presence of mind to understand the weight and balance of words, of how they interact not unlike explosive chemical properties, so that maximum effect must be of their flowing combinations that results as motion that was trapped within the fixated combat of nouns where language inheres as declarative dysfunction. Thus, inspiration conforms to protracted tedium, being none other than cognitive listening effort.

To submerge into deeper wells of consciousness, one must succumb to oneiric twilight, to oneiric spawning, where psychic water runs in all directions. But to spontaneously mine verbal nutrient from these waters being key so that an architecture of the beyond begins forming. This being verbal nutrition which begins to expand as living neural capacity. This being what can be called vertiginous inner farming that brings to fruition a thrilling cascade of beatific lingual crops.

In the early wilderness of experiment Breton explored a galvanizing conduct for poetic experiment suffused by oneiric ethical flame, thus surmounting self-conflict. Thus, writing as spherical turbulence, as greenish generating current, where separation is abolished, where astonishing transparence circles as omnipresence. This being none other than respiration as language. Every nod or gesture, whether by visible or invisible nutation, associations promulgate via the strangest of angles, whether it be a nuanced volcano hermetically altered to molten underground intarsias, thus the aural scale is extended in such a manner that it evinces hybridity itself, spawning itself as philosophical ballet. Not pointless dry dice, but magnetic ciphers combusting, as soundless conduction where phonemes coalesce as if arisen from the valley of origin. So, to ruin this trance by claiming a living girl cleaning ceramic tiles can never become a stunning crown atop a populace of hoaxes, nor is some blind archaeology diverted from original aural transmission. Instead, there is glass through which one ceases to stare always hearing a fulcrum of ideology beyond dissonance as a kingdom. There exists through hearing a dark green momentum that signals higher traits of consciousness. In this sense nouns become liquidated by colour, by that which empowers known quantity and its optical component of mirage that remains operant as condensation. Thus, the optical in this tenor remains operant as subsequent randomity evincing a yield that misleads and signals ruin to higher union with presence.

All too often this vigour of thrust remains curiously lessened by the scrupulous sedentary scholar stultified, surrounded by arcane regalia, the latter cognitively reduced by psychological emanation of Greco-Roman bronze flamelets, sans alchemical compounding. The creative range always glistening by means of alchemical niacin, and its lessened extreme effort that strains as palpable cognition, hoping by that effort to simulate the depths, to curry favour from the invisible, the latter effort never in accord with what I'll call aural cellular quaking. And because this quaking can never be approached by cognitive lingual effort it produces nothing other than interesting paraphernalia of the zeitgeist. Then how can such an attempt summon totality? Perhaps by extending its range to quakings on Saturn. I am saying by exercising through the aforesaid understanding, this naturally allows language to rise above those portions of reality that maintain machinery by belief. As this meditation proceeds, I concur with language that concurs with intergalactic examination via spontaneous compounding and release so that a substantive exploration can transpire. Of course, this is not an ideological template for internal achievement but dossier as outline for working with the uncanny via attempted lingual perfection, not unlike poetic accuracy inside seeming mathematical vacuums, thereby allowing one's neurology to expedite the unknown.

Primal Fragment as Subtext

WITHIN THE REFLECTION of the zeitgeist distortion reigns, memory interacts with base agenda as topological vacuum that inverts and becomes a sieve for delimited transmission, as if the galaxy were a rationally constructed asterisk, to be colonized via quotidian dossier.

Primal Fragment I

WESTERN CONSCIOUSNESS HAS evolved scripted from self-imposed pastiche. All the while knowing that parts of its anatomy have been willfully obscured, so much so that it now faces itself as an out-sized distortion, ferociously out of contact with itself. The result from its original intent now looms as hallucinatory realia rising from self-doubt. And because this doubt increases daily it has morphed into a hallucinatory circulation that embrangles everything it touches. Its trinity of planetary robbery, murder, and stunning prevarication has become its absolute condition, as I take leave from its psyche riding atop a lightning-struck camel entering into a new rotational paradise.

Primal Fragment II

VIA TERSE INDEFATIGABLE rumour we are given a dominant calligraphy that goads us to transmit our corpses across innominate diameter in order to ply their delimitation without fumes of resolution. This being the central artery of advance not unlike a toxic sea lane where frigates are disposed to wander while being monitored by a sum of toxic rays. The frigates in this circumstance being analogous to figments all the while circumscribed by common limit. Thus, the sea lane flows to the sea. And the sea to the sea lane scales to view as seeming measureless galaxy that de-exists to human view that beams from the frigate. And the frigate optically transpires so long as its entanglement can be espied. This scenario being the principal gist of surveillance that attempts to align itself (in this case) as nautical tremor. As if life could be x-rayed and plotted according to cognizant tracking, according to dictates primed by what I'll term listless anti-shadow. The body within this tenor being nothing other than the grainy daylight of shadow. A negative euphemism that careens and makes itself known via portions of ignorance. The latter energy corrosively honoured by pragmatists as possessing meaningful experience. Human experience is thus primed to wade in polluted streams of lucre and subscribe to its own aberration, so much so, that it is expected to solicit energy from the lowest possible denominator becoming the patriot of its own negation. Add to this the need to be saved by a seedy over-exposed doppelganger in league with priests who stake claims to psychic flow that open onto inner lands equivalent to stench from psychic sewers.

Thus the Christian narrative carries responsibility for effort that inveigles its inner carrion to such an extent that its surreptitious claim to eternity must take responsibility for collective neurological regression. The leaders of the world now presiding over a partially lit cloaca.

Having voided its living essence, human planetary fauna remains an aberrant genetics that in large part has ceased enunciation of itself. Chronic realia that have demonically quelled sattvic frequency in order to foster tamasic respiration as collective functioning mantra.

Barren Aperture That Purposely Miscalculated

I AM THINKING of two post-19th-century colonial essays riddled by their own purposeful miscalculations. It naturally blinds itself on purpose. Therefore, it kinetically blinds itself when relating to Sub-Saharan Africa and its achievement as regards seminal application of the mind. By attempting to implant the African within the European mind it has impaired its own purpose by means of slanderous ineptitude. So, by giving principal effort at abducting the spectacular achievement of Egypt and placing it in the sphere of European accomplishment reeks of the banter of a ironically designed self-ridicule.

By mentally abducting Egypt's presence from the rest of the African continent those souls that remained, they hoped to achieve scale more to add to their lasting Imperial proof of European authority. In hindsight this perpetually registers to us as perpetually mis-scripted ostentation. This was none other than an awkward choreography scripted by blindness. A scattered in-stillment placed within European auspices. Since Egyptian mathematical accuracy could not be replaced by surreptitious superimposed corruption these less than deft practitioners sought to procure their arguments via a non-convincing verbal wroughtness as disastrous mishandling according to verbal imposition. At various points referring to Egyptians as well as beings from southern India as "Dark-Skinned Caucasians."

The latter was considered as rote by always mishandling the colour of African apparitions. Of course, this was a consuming rote authored by beings that extended from M. D. W. Jeffreys and Egyptologist

James Breasted, both lauded in the earlier years of the 20th century the latter having graced the cover of *Time* magazine. All the while there was their concerted effort to psychologically wrest Egypt away from the Sub-Saharan plentitude that existed and persists in existing as the enriched yield that continues to grace its less respected southern portion. Of course, these are now texts for the most part defeated and consumed by their own endemic error. Yet this hardened error has been psychologically translated over time and space and continues to surface thereby en-graining measurable elements in the Occidental mind via this erroneous subtext.

English speaking or not this subtext continues to stutter the mind as existential deficit. Such energy continues to inveigle one's in-born intelligence by corrupting and splintering its thesis that I understand partakes in collective mental deprivation.

Such corruption naturally singes clear outlook so that it promulgates a false and non-living tenor. A tenor that equates with hot branding irons. This was none other than willful obscuration creating false psychological riddles that demand a maimed psychological wellspring where the oxygen of truth can only procure poisoned and convoluted answer.

The Contemporary Mind: Pointless Rural Fragment

... lateral thinking is generative...
Richness is what matters in lateral thinking.
—EDWARD DE BONO

THE MIND, SYSTEMATICALLY scattered during our current phase of late Democracy has been presented to itself as unquestioned design imbued with itself as being no more than a partially functioning fragment. A fragment that has reached crucial amplification as fragment, understanding that its higher nature has been disgorged living as a corrupted mechanism that now merges with itself via the arc of pervasive confusion. This being none other than suppressed evolutionary tension, having now long inhabited this terminal phase by continuing to explore its current housing as it exists within a neurological question mark. Thus, the individual is suffused with basic distraction due to allegiance to its own negation. And this distraction appropriates numbed in-detection vis-à-vis non-functional clairvoyance. Of course, this instigates realia constrained to tenebrous leaning. The resulting amount being a mislaid being, bubonic, laced by curious indifference. These are now lauded characteristics that have ascended no higher than pointless gerunds, than "dangling participles," than fraction-less particles. Thus, the general psyche remains parched, staunched at the root by mimetic generality, all the while remaining painfully isolate in perpetual silos and fragments. The mind in this state being a chronicle feckless with freneticism, with distraction as the ceaseless métier of its energy. This resulting in insistent irritation culminates with bottomless ire, in dark intransigent posting, in pre-inscripted obscuration, in hyphenated verbal panorama. The body in this state results in broken cellular affliction, in inductive psycho-physical mazes ignited by blockage. But above all there exists chronic conflation with error.

Such a state possesses no call to evolutionary tension, to apogee that opens onto the panoramic. Instead, there exists thought scattered as thermal neurosis, as protracted inclemence. Thus, the mind becomes a damaged storage mechanism incapable of endemic creation. Struggling with itself via a superimposed sequential threading that weaves in on itself, repeating itself ad-infinitum. More simply put, thought remains trapped by the tenor that is sequential surcease. This being the sarcophagus of the overwhelming majority being those I call well-diggers, attracted to the stationary semiotics of ill-use. And by ill-use, I mean activity over the span of the past 21 centuries being none other than a disabling stationary mantra. This being none other than psychic arthritics, none other than pointless entrainment prone to energy that de-reveals itself, thereby producing predilection for perpetual opacity. Such a mind has nothing in common with the mind in its aboriginal state, the latter having the capability of movement in all directions at once. This simultaneous state being incapable of self-pillory, of self-dishonoured mis-suggestion, always hounding itself across the ends and outs of existence by the drone that issues from self-derived soliloquy. A soliloquy that issues non-stop from super-imposed commercialized tech-tonics. Unlike the motion that is geology, commercialization as movement is rapid, capable of feigning itself through opaque transposition. It thereby produces a state that pointlessly susurrates and deadens, giving rise to epi-genetic misnomer that spans generations. The elasticity that was its original condition is topologically angled towards graceless abandonment. So, what normally happens is that a fragment is extracted from surrounding misnomer and is hailed as being superior to the rest of psychic climate as misnomer. Choice is falsely summoned by a myopic patriotism to received belief, or perhaps, from generational family allegiance operant as the mind consuming itself as pointless rural fragment.

Thus, one embarks from such a juncture in the mind enacting a lifelong chronicle of fatigue. Such endemic hypnotizing signifies a mind that only lingers, ensnared by after-thoughts, by bulletins stressing envy and the pleasure of the moment. Thus, it becomes territorial, plagued by regression leading to a skewed temperament vis-à-vis its own possibility. This being none other than consensus senility as regards the subtle states and deeper grasp. Only the surfaces configure, and because these surfaces contradict and overlap themselves there seldom transpires clarity or rest. Thus, a magnified sterility accrues and inhibits the alchemic state that is synaptic juncture. As for higher disengagement nothing transpires so that being remains stifled by contagious glacial arrhythmia.

This being nothing other than generic debility where inner alternative wizens and is seen as improbable sluice incapable of opening to planes occluded by mystery. Thus, the individual is obscured by derivative agglutination, thereby committed to the epigenetics of imprisoning self-regulation. The latter being the ultimate policy of global controlling regimes. One becomes as individual a galaxy of isolation, always in need of mental oxygen always juggling suspicion with expectation of the worst. Respiration becomes a soliloquy unto one-self prone to de-basement and crass result. Thus, one has nothing in common with one's peers except the common similarity of numbness. This is destructive psychic carnage replete with base distracting mesmerism. Within this mesmerism the impulse to greed is inspired, along with the grammar of doubt that spews psychic miasma, that always besieges possibility, the latter condition possessing nothing but the seeming power of interior mirage. This mirage always kindling psychic drought by always retaining its negative character. According to Breton this formula that combines rational mechanics with simulated Christian praxis merges as collective design for directing the afterlife thereby containing one's spontaneous commingling with paradise. To this mechanical mind paradise retains its character according to sufficiency as quotient. It is none other than the spirit striving towards a plane of non-existent sequence. Fluvial dissemination is thus decried as being an overextended multiplication that can only bring to bear the red flag of trespass. As for paradise it remains cognizant thought never capable of realizing its own inner destination. Because it remains self-conscripted according to the general colonizing principle it becomes party to a select group of Europeans who astringently dole out non-existent religious reward. Of course, a moribund populace should never be grateful for such compensatory wrath fueled by such debility and arrogance. This being the very shadow of colonized regression that hangs over the populace, is meant to obscure and detain the mind keeping it impaired via the detritus of that which exudes external trinkets.

Poetry by its very nature destabilizes these particular externalities by delving into the instantaneous through blinding salvo from the un-nameable. It is this tenor that blinds as finely wrought glass, being empyreal, morphological, transcendent. By its very nature it gathers distance from Greco-Roman minutiae thereby according to its own example shorn of gravid classical bunting being impervious to previously wrought delimitation as example.

As one poetically rises one is no longer obscured by the anti-kinetic as an obscuring dust that issues from purpose-less precedent, from cauterized mental shields that call for verbal angular wolves to tear open its cauterization so that stationary plotting and the defective cognitive model gives way to proto-instigation thereby creating microscopic summons that magically devour lack. Of course, this paraphrases the praxis of Césaire's microscopic summons for interior grammar that inundates the view, being praxis of the panoramic that evolves to organic view incapable of cognitive self-hounding. Not the Protestant body as it occludes itself by general shadow furtively built by capital and guilt. Instead, I am speaking of totalic germination via liberty rather than by generic transposition. Transposition always feigning ersatz recognition of itself as a forceless cascade that attempts to assassinate the unknown. Thus, the vitality of grammar is blocked, it is subverted by keeping council with the day-to-day dossiers of quotidian mismanagement. The latter being nothing other than stifling amplification skewed as random cups and saucers that by their very nature take on a quality of motionless inherence. This being a gulf of objects that ruminate as tin. They being tenebrous obstruction always failing to generate the alchemic. Thus, the exponential becomes privately arrayed via limit, via dazed pessimism always crowning itself according to measurable summit. When Bob Kaufman utters his spectacular lightning kinetic he verbally leaps from balconies of light thus leaving behind prescribed notions of perception. He allows us entry to primal experience, to the basic circulation of atoms. Thus, we espy something other than the parenthetical expectation that separates and inspires the mind as mortal fragment. The latter being cognition cobbled together as a commonly wrought thesis in league with unassailable blockage. This is what is called the gist of living. Thus, Kaufman enunciates a paradoxical state other than closed proposition, something other than a sullied diacritical odyssey. Language at this level being simultaneous with telepathic contact, with a skill set of motion never conversant or contiguous with cognitive restraint. Of course, it is never entrained by quotidian tutelage subject to living misnomer.

Across the Occident living misnomer is the mind expertly skilled at wandering across roadways towards ruined destination. It possesses a falsely skilled timing in that it absorbs as its generating current that which empowers generic incoherence. Because the human mind remains genetically ensconced in the zodiac it remains bound as fragment, as tainted tablature marked by its own susurrance as decay, as module of the in-accurate, where neural motion collapses, stunned by its failure to organically perceive.

Within this condition there is the failure to address from one's depths uncountable stellar possibility. This being failure to understand the true structuring that is depth, being failure to perceive beyond immediate perception the swarming presence that remains daily realia. I think of daily realia as wizened scrutiny that evinces toxic evidence marked by the fatal misperception of Anglo-Saxon stewardship stranded as it is by the "leprosy" of imitation. The latter being fraught with the failure to organically implement itself, no longer having the confidence to fuel its own inflammatory yield. Thus, one is surrounded by a group of moribund Romans who have bound and gagged themselves to such an extent that the power they now project remains a deadly misnomer. This misnomer is pointed out by Peter Van Wyck in his book *Signs of Danger* concerning the half-life of Uranium 238 that equals a half-count of 4.47 billion years. Uranium 238 being none other than our atomic accompaniment, constant, without antidote, across the span of each known measurement as time-frame.

Within this context the imagination needs condition, collective neurology so that it becomes capable of transmuting differing cellular planes in order to create transpiring leaps of the physical mechanism so that it becomes capable of primordial transfer to more transparent planes thereby having the capability of telepathic summons. I am thinking of hyper-dimensional summons from other forms of seeming alien registration. A registration rife with contiguous properties that become open to organic contact understood via stunning morphology. Not contact according to the flight of honed rockets, or the mortal mechanics of technical mesmerics, so that non-physical frequency can be broached thereby opening contact via grace of the cosmos itself. This being formation beyond dualism, functioning as unbelievable electrical communion.

Conventional perception will look askance at the above, seeing it as abstruse transference, as shamanism seemingly de-limited by the idealism of suicide. On the contrary this being a frequency capable of communing with the living dead, with their hallucinatory aural forms that combine the verbal exploration of say, Vallejo, with the invisible sub-text that continues to populate the indigenous shamaness Maria Sabina.

Recently, the zodiac has been broached by the velocity of A/2017 U1, an asteroidal form that has hurtled towards Earth for the past 300,000 years, having issued from an unknown system circling the sun that is Vega. A specimen that is other than our zodiac, the latter fueled as it's been by endemic hesitation and fragmentation. Thus, we need to open specific aural exploration to such a momentous degree that individual patience and fire can transmute to an occulted inner scape, capable of en-firing its power as morphology that can cast itself beyond the remaining life that exists as our Sun.

Centripetal Respiration

AS FOR CONFLAGRANT centripetal forces, they remain as far as one can tell, insouciant conundrums, a vastitude of cells spinning, blazing as gestures inside vacuums. Perhaps, they remain equivalent to themselves as molecules of insight, as fleeting topological creatures respirating at the extremity of the possible. They symbolize the mind as paroxysmal flare, being borderless energy, collected as primal scintilla. In essence they are proximal to Mayflies, being flashes of light, not unlike burning cataracts that respirate, according to speed via their own rotation.

Aural Botany

I am no writer. I am someone who writes.
—THOMAS BERNHARD

WHEN THE WORD "botany" transpires, a garden or a greenhouse seems to flare across the scale of one's optical cortex. At a more substantive remove it is living cells as transmutation. This being illuminated conduction of energy not unlike spontaneous vibratory quanta, akin to the poet's skill of intervallic interaction. This being disparate as understanding of itself via angles and approaches always at one with primal magnification as being. Not chaos, but the enigma that is respiration. Say, the leap between papaveraceous prairies and galactic sporulation knowing that both examples resonate via supernal dialectics.

For the poet the disparate exists as insight that concretizes aurally. Not chaos, but the enigma that is a living system. Thus, the nature of the intervallic remains occulted, transpiring at hidden tempo, being curious respiration not unlike curiously hidden moons that rise and fall within a scape of mellifluous lightning. At first glance, there seems to be directional imbalance, as if one peered through refractive nautical lensing. Such lensing being simultaneous with aural fuel is not unlike hyper-dimensional chlorophyll that invigourates the channels of the registration of hearing. And it is asked, how do these channels transmute to tomes and black ink?

For instance, a photo-synthetic psychic channel that is magnetized by what I'll call heightened aural rivers. And these rivers flow by means of inter-dimensional susurration, as something far beyond the craft that is cognitive susurration. They are bendings, lunges of motion, incapable of harnessing the grasp of static prediction. Verbal fauna suddenly leaps and electrically coalesces and flowers as a script of seemingly random aural botany. Thus, what flowers is an insular stream of irreducible inner value, simultaneous with the verdigris fire that empowers the entire cosmos. This being the verdigris power of cellular eons that when contacted allows one to reach the highest nths of lingual communion at one with the sattvic allowing one's writing suffusion by primal aurality.

This is not one's aural gift bonded to consensus restriction via surreptitious transposition, giving, somehow, the impression of anomalous originality. I am concerned with heightened aural flow that irrigates the inner lingual field and through spontaneous understanding that the Earth remains nothing other than a lesser solar fragment. Thus, each writing example transcends its own capacity thereby producing an astonishing circularity, a balanced kind of grace, that even at lesser scale remains capable of extending its life across coming generations, epigenetically engaging the psyche via lingual trance, resulting in language that nurtures the unpredictable not unlike a maze of wayward verbal falcons.

One can say that the imagination remains a windblown maze, being a bulletin of achieved awareness that, by extension, is a neural inscription capable of extending its reach across differing psychic terrains into the interstellar continuum which includes extra-solar valleys and oceans as well as movement through measureless spatial realms, as well as realms that exist within realms. This being language that explores itself via heightened sporulation ceasing to replicate the human condition, a condition sustained as though it were common provincial neurology. This expanded aurality is not unlike Kraken Mare on Titan, appearing and disappearing as transmuted code, as unprecedented meta-neurology, no longer underlain by transfixed linear inferential.

This magnetic aurality being language circling and leaping through all manner of conditions with such panache that an impalpable neural pulse opens onto a range that was initially condoned by the author as a free-standing fragment. This insight now takes on the power of inter-connected density being capable of inhabiting itself as rays from the alphabet that beget itself across the scale that is inward heliopause.

Of course, this can never be language as effort, as dissemination by cognitive planning, but exploration by energy seemingly opened by blinding error, by lingual rambling that seems to ensnare itself by revelation. Yet, seeming error invigourates motion itself, not via derivative posture, but by powers of primal transmission. Not a state of affairs en-scripted by a cognitively caged beast, but transmission as aural seepage. Seepage at this level exists in its initial form by concurring as vibratory deafening where intervals are transmuted by stunning imaginal leaps that magnify the carrying tenor that indigenous praxis conveys as invisibility. Of course, this is not a state that concurs with derivative transposition that condones ill-derived layering, that promotes a subsequent posture, and promulgates mirage by doctrinal mirage. The latter state of mind always conveys métier as exploration, never allowing itself to subsist upon abstract manna as origin.

When the true manna of origin descends, written characters become dyed by invisibility, indeed, psychic nutrients flow from this invisibility, invoking in one's mind hyper-dimensional equators, thereby allowing interior rays to formulate fauna out of curious mountain chains or waters, as they accrue from the uncanny. The latter formations being alive as unknown spectra connected according to route-less sporulation. According to these realia the linear medium is nothing other than minor ossification attempting to enforce its limit as governing pattern. At this plane its logic seems nothing other than enfeebled regalia. It can be said at this level one thing does not lead to another; linear logic in fact now functions as naive minority enactment. Because of this it fails to register the very signature of its origin from the cosmos.

This is not a theory of dis-identity, but solar osmosis in the midst of its own osmotic mapping. Which is not a modest psychic flare meant to resolve its own eruption through surreptitious cognitive sculpting. Thus, writing becomes embrangled by what my terminology understands to be the cobbling of itself as teeming as trapezoidal vanishment, meaning that the writer is trapped by calculation in his or her attempt at self-concealment, creating by this means the temporal personality according to confine. Concern at this level is for the surmounting of confine so that language transpires as a functioning mesmeric thereby conflating with itself as retro-causal perfection. This being lingual yoga as duration, which never transpires as ungainly nostalgia.

Lingual yoga goes beyond and spontaneously possesses itself as hyper-dimensional aurality. This being the state that leaps far beyond the zodiac via the fatigue of our single solar formation 3/4 removed from its dark galactic mean, far beyond what is known as prior solar patterning, so much so that one's hearing begins to transpire at scales that one can only enunciate as errorless density.

The word "errorless" in this context is having what Sri Aurobindo experienced as "Knowledge by Identity." This is where each word summons, and carries as its presence, gulf upon gulf of cosmic intelligence, an intelligence that subsumes a field of writing, having as its essence inter-cosmic respiration. Writing at this level induces the trans-personal as chronicle, having as its phonemic presence the most magnetic plane of sensitivity. This sensitivity carries the reader to perpetual habitation of lingual refulgence. This is where one's cellular state remains subsumed and can never again be confined to what can be considered religious lacunae. Quotidian residua seem to vanish, yet they susurrate as ghosts appearing and reappearing as other scales of being thereby magnetizing the reader's flow with blazes that Breton once beautifully clarified as oneiric channeling. Thus, one enters the spiraling portent of the Sun, being part of what I've called elsewhere a relay of suns.

The latter refraction being none other than irregular relay from the origin of origins. This being analogous to lingual experience that more and more clarifies itself via the riverine aura of mystery. To profane perception this is language procured by ungainful sweltering, but the more riveting view is praxis risen to the diagrammatic plane of vertiginous shaping that suddenly reveals itself as ghostly parallel to ouroboric auricular musicality, understanding its basic nature to be the combined resonance of collective tuning that enunciates the hymn prior to all formation.

Atop a Tasmanian Crag

... You deny us human rights
—KEVIN GILBERT, AUSTRALIAN ABORIGINAL POET

I like crossing imaginary boundaries people set up between different fields...
There are a lot of tools, and you don't know which one can work...
—MARYAM MIRZAKHANI, MATHEMATICIAN

COMPELLED TO EVOLVE within psychic draconian terrain, my pre-birth implies interior volatility, alive as proto-astrological nexus, and this nexus marks an explosive pathway beyond human neurological capacity. Such is my post-mortem state under the auspices of the planet Eris, the latter linked to a state igniting strife, stoking greater life by means of seminal disorder. This being destiny seemingly marked by ingrained disruption, by dossiers of contradiction, nevertheless, allowing higher view of human destiny as it progressively reels from super-imposed disruption of itself. It has become not unlike scattered salt, poisoned, primed to dissipate at the evolutive crossroads. It being an amperage spontaneously subject to gross psychic disruption. The general mind rife with evolutive disorder seems vehement with spontaneous rupture, with general distress spurred by eruptive oscillation. What follows from this are degenerate breathing rhythms, limited to superficial conjoinment of facts via material ideology. This leads to nothing less than psychic a-rhythmia. And this a-rhythmia spawns itself across collective neurology lending itself to unsparing dissension. In consequence, one's lake of neurons surreptitiously wizens and devolves into particulates that perpetually clash. Hence, spontaneous circumstance kindles a sullied human field of habitual devastation attempting to rise above this habitual scale. Thus, reality having lost all distinction between upper and lower planes seems skewed towards magnification of lower bodily function, which seems to coil the mind in the service of negative minutiae, which in turn provokes a more in-grained myopia. Thus, my voice non-aligned with the explosive dissipation of capital that has accrued under the aural principate of a psychic Tasmanian whose aboriginal connection exists prior to the earliest suns. Therefore, I am other than ghost, other than the maze given over to visibility. In terms of visibility, I am of isolate compilation teeming with impalpability, with none other than blaze-less grasp, susurrant, emitting telepathic observation that counteracts entropy on all scales. I counteract constriction to such a degree that any numerical constant shifts so that it naturally eludes scale or measure. I, being equivalent to that which preceded original stellar formation, which preceded its nascent magnification. I exist as energy beyond the syllabus that empowers the mind with energy translate-able to nouns.

Thus, my energy does not imply noun-like stasis hovering above Mount Ossa construed according to myopic evidence, thereby implying some intangible savage, implying a species of creature European settlers once shot on sight. The earthly calendar holds forth the time frame of 1828 when my once embodied carcass was codified as evil. Codified for my being dark and male and obstreperous. According to European assessment my body was the site of menacing interior calamity, of gross ill-proportioned dread. I have secretly surmounted that which ignites all habitation. And now, what has been scripted via birth and its existential withdrawal from the inferno of congealment can only be equated with that which amounts to leaking solar mass. To make an irregular leap this means that I naturally subtend the fumigation of stasis as leprosy. This leap is not unlike the radiant internality of mysterious electrical mapping that has clarified my state as spontaneous repulsion of gravity. This was nascence as context prior to my existence as an unknown noun circa 1828. I was sent to Flinders to perish only to have emerged after death by existing on a plane of impossible forensics. The dialectics of salt can never announce, or never conjure its presence out of matter. This is the secret that saviours withhold from existential emergence seeking to convince us by their aloofness that eternity can be squared according to the stationary praxis of a free-standing noun. What arises from this state of instruction remains a proportional glyph structured via illusive mechanics, this being power curiously inscribed via perpetual delimitation. This is how fragments hypnotize, this is how illusive saffron is ingested. Of course, a leap beyond this latter psychic state can be referred to as meta-irradiation. This is where extinct mammals bask, where trenchant physical proof de-exists as ellipsis. An irradiation not unlike indetectable pressure that is akin to the interstice between galaxies responsible for their motion as structural meta-carbon where the realia of this pressure respirates as impalpable uranian acreage. This being the perpetuity that persists as infinite continuum. This continuum can neither be stored or measured.

    The beatific can never be cognitively construed as the model of origin but only through electrical inference by which galactic structures are ignited. As for inferential trance one can never be in-starred via human sensing stranded as it is at its present juncture. Because this trance exits over and beyond sensate limitation, higher rigour suggests pressure that continually seeks escape from itself subtended as it is by susurrant fuming. There always persists the tenor of grasp scrawling itself as master of the incalculable. Never can the cognitive convey material supremacy over that which escapes it. Because my voice exists as nameless meta-orality, I remain as de-inhabited foment whose body has seemed to vapourize into the refuge of mystery, whose remains are absent of sentient memorials, whose voice now blazes as seeming in-vocable, yet continues to expand beyond all the bounds invoked by extrinsic measure. I cannot be extracted by powers ideologically subjected to data, to tangible imbroglio posited upon European finding. Therefore, I ride a strange long horse into darkness, into irregular yield, that attempts to square my former body within the principal politics of death. This is not the nexus of the body as perpetual code glaring with evidence as fundamental tension as propounded by Laplace. Of course, my power extends sans the wake of Newton inveigled as it is by determinism, beholden as its been to optics cast adrift inside itself. Tasmanian registration was never open to myopic substrate. Matter, as regards its Newtonian habitation can never do other than remain at a level of secondary evidence, acting as a tool for a delimited set of integers, that when faced with forms of intangible proportion seems only to whir by means of incriminating tautology. As if reality is non-seismic, is nothing other than a manipulated clause, capable of emitting a perfect set of evidence. As if realia could be cognitively scaled and announced as half and half of that half ad infinitum. As if one could extract by flagrant particularization a specific core of centripetal hamlets. Within these hamlets, beasts, plausible methane, general nitrogen and fire? They can only be evidenced via noun-based proof, enlivened via a sense-based spectrum condoned within the throes of exterior formulation.

    Because infinity exists, invisibility exists within invisibility, thus, the forensics of material speculation fails in terms of assessment of itself creating for itself the forensics of isolation weighted as it is by exotic spectra and theorems. What is implied by these spectra and theorems are apparitions leading to unknown beasts, to seas of populated methane. So when cognition brokers itself at this level, it brokers a galaxy of cataracts allowing nothing higher than myopic optical cinder, which in turn brokers a circumstantial unnerving, provoking a glossolalia of panic, that rises no higher than three-dimensional menace. As if these three dimensions persisted on the other side of vapour.

Within this internal vapour I am cryptically squared being akin to empty space that contains more energy per cubic centimeter than "all the known matter in the universe." Thus, I am synecdoche as power, as summary that persists without a mimed or cognitive thesis. In order to chronicle fluctuation, the mind must regress in order to emend itself so that it ceases to engage itself as restless example. Thus, quelling itself via abstracted fever so that it is able to remove itself from telepathic expression, via compound laterality. Perpetually bound to analogy as stricture, to analogy as reduction, simply to evince a bound monomial assessment. The latter being telluric inscription never prone to living nautical intelligence, to the spirit of living solar array. Thus, to beget mystery, to extoll seeming error, one's mental script alchemically scripts itself to rise above noun-lit solar fragments as if uttering through collapsed torrents a bodiless dossier of sound. I can by no means adduce rabid gravitation while remaining sired by galaxies that vanish and emit themselves as powerful proto-turning. Knowing that they harboured alien self-sufficiency prior to seeming stratification. Knowing that prior to their present circumstance they possessed genetic pre-disposal towards refractive Palawa. The latter being none other than their motion as after-current, again being motion as brazen apparitional silence. Not as Christianized perishability, but what was called in Palawa "krakapaka," constant circulation over and beyond death. Thus, I am never circumspect via human absence, say, as a mysterious sea dog, or via growth of ferns on the moon, or perhaps, as a carnivorous Macaw in transition. As emission from the refractive plane, I sing a hamstrung carol in psychic Palawa compelled by its angular omnivorous density. And these carols are daunting phantasms as aural streaks across blackness not unlike sonorous simultaneity as rays out of Africa.

I can speak of my Ice Age lucubrations in Fraser Cave 19,000 years ago that descended to the "Black War" when the Whites sought to reduce us to corpses, when we clashed with them to re-abduct our stolen women. On this refractive plane absence of noun exists as personality being akin to darkened energy absorbing and creating space beyond itself, beyond the scope of cognitive instigation. This being none other than the discipline of anomalous choreography, this being what noun-based psychology would announce as abstract pontification. Again, there must concur a state of refractive evidence concerning our aboriginal crossing "during glacial maxima" when the sea was at its lowest ebb 39,000 years ago. Our first migration was across the primeval estuary called at present remove the Otway/Murray estuary via the King Highlands, being 12,000 years removed from "glacial maxima," we, as new immigrants from "South Grampion's region" followed by a third wave of us that entered via the Furneaux Islands from "Gippsland," and after 5,000 years BP "a final wave of immigration via the King Highlands from the Mount Gambier/Warrnambool region," not as abysmal conclave but as vanished inscription.

We fished, we carved tools out of bone, there was never hesitation as regards our interior strength. We maximized location, we ate wallabies and possums as part of our demonstrable meta-condition. And this condition remains akin to energy that populates empty space. Not simply juncture via interior quantum dazzling, but contact sans say, empirical kelp that tends to isolate itself in itself as diurnal minutiae. Akin to diurnal minutiae our spiritual power has been subject to constriction by gaunt European verbiage that has promised supreme summation of paradise sans inclusion of those accused by their God of spontaneous infraction. Spontaneous infraction in this instance aligned with circuitous alchemical acts, which according to their sullied mystical saviour broaches the self with evil sans eternal salvation. As pronouncement of their saviour, alchemy remains nothing other than a wizened mesmerism in keeping with the Danse Macabre.

Heightened neurology as trance creates in its wake transparent neurological vapour, the latter living as cleansing non-sequitur. This portends transparent rotation as holographic ballet. This is not some fictitious meta-scalpel, or a prairie of blue lenses aligned to capture the void and weigh it as intervallic circumstance. According to phantom displacement I susurrate atop an oneiric Mount Ossa, the latter being part of an astral Pelion Range. it is not unlike fire from our oneiric Sun, anonymously lit 3/4 removed from its galactic mean. Let me say that this oneiric Sun is meteoritic in demeanour open to meta-suggestion that never registers as weight. This is not theoretical magnification, or a complex theorem formed from thirst-ridden psychic complication. This complication being not unlike a tribe of noiseless owls wafting infinite degrees below tremor seeping into a plane that supersedes velocity being errorless and hyperbolic. This exceeds isolate information remaining in its depths causeless and perpetual in its expansion. This being expansion beyond all known and unknown subsequence, beyond vanished particularization and the body as origin of primal mountains and geysers. In this sense I am concerned with simultaneity that supersedes phases.

Say, as Bantu or Tasmanian I am hieroglyphic sand that continues to waft above cognitive orchestration. In this context I am subject to errorless contagion, not unlike alchemical labour, but without sense of exhaustion, without compound information that constricts one's inner spectrum.

And so I ask, what comprises energy that ascribes itself to the curious dictation of lenses? Stricken palabras? A whale seeking refuge from waters roiled by human imprecation?

These latter questions imply weighted noun-related venture subconjoined by the terminal wattage of fixation. Thus, the palabras, the lenses, the whale all elements of anti-fixation, of repulsion to gravity. As regards blazing decree its disappearance is due to absence of scale. Scale in this instance being rigidly sourced cognitive delimitation. For instance, there exists ironic realia that self-creates itself beyond particles that reflect it scattered as they are throughout various utensils. Perhaps, the latter scattering exists as exercise via alchemical lacunae over and above private suggestion. I'm thinking of the power that enlivens a breathing mammal which enters its form as living tidal consistency. Thus, I am not a posited feud, or a miraculous hamlet aligned to private compunction. Because of the latter I am not a script restricted and trapped by fomented scales on alphabetic plantations. As alchemical figment I combine with empty space over and above combined matter thereby superseding the scale that evinces combined delineation.

According to prior Tasmanian inkling one is capable of the energy of disappearance allowing one to utter via decibels of inaudia. Perhaps one could say that I refer to the body as curious gestural dust, as non-methodic and never prone to contraction. Thus, I am not corroborating or complexifying a curious feud with existence, igniting waves of micro-inflammation so that they combine as cubic centimeters of emptiness superseding combined matter that seems to suffice as the gross measurement of heaven. There exist planes that do not subscribe to themselves, that subsist prior to Tasmanian inkling combined at the pitch of disappearance. Let me use as measure the momentary grammes of the Sun, not as a terse ferocious habitat blazing above this crag of Tasmanian quanta, blazing above a looming wilderness of voids, sans structured celebratory crystal simultaneous with its own telepathy. This code of voids being of abstruse energy seepage through terrestrial property as scaleless ghosts, as a-mundane circulation.

The latter being my power as Tasmanian aboriginal, as aboriginal, assaulted and physically scorched so that elimination transpired as the order of the day. This, in accordance with British brutality as amendment. These were tumultuous instants. Because I no longer register as noun, as carnivorous skill set, as lurid dangling, I am freed to circumvent asuric vibration. Thus, I exist knowing that as darkened energy I seep through myopia as it exists as superimposed alignment. And this superimposed alignment is none other than Western moral geriatrics with its personal mores, with its extrinsic doctrinal instigation.

Thus, my energy persists over and above its inclement posture, over and above its degradation, being living jade, being higher spiritual verdet. And this deepened verdet is none other than an inclusive state of pre-positional energy that exists as wandering flow, as torrential understanding. And this understanding reveals itself as seepage passing through a varying calliope of wombs.

As vanished Tasmanian I am at one with sable irradiation, with weightless pitch that dawns over and beyond infinite solar mass. This being none other than aboriginal velocity, supersessional in nature, not via grammes, not analogous to a wilderness of birds, but as impalpable state that refracts the Ground, never concluded as angular forum, or a form of doubt lifted and re-concurred as re-classified stasis. I cannot discuss myself as particularized fever, or prosecuted circumstance suggestive of burden to myself, because nouns as ultimate condition can never be fixed, or prosecuted via latent configuration posited as separable confinement, or as harried monomial venture at the juncture of darkness. Of course, the mind needs be cleared of omens and fixated trappings. They can do nothing other than litter light as it seeps from transpersonal kindling. One must free oneself of separative cognizance, of structurally stillborn thinking in order to brave the challenge of psychic liminal gulfs, of protracted intervals where the soul is curiously tested. Fettered perception creates illusion of motion through paralysis all the while having it suffused by uncertainty. This being circumstance that seeks to scale a closed referendum, a referendum seismically assaulted by post-mortem apparitions. The latter being bodiless states alive via unknown conditioning that exists as a-linear pacing that allows subconscious meandering before and after death because the void does not explore its tenor via nouns that obscure its presence always leaving its riddle refracted.

When the body expires under the auspices of the Saxons the void remains excluded in principle, with the corpse surmounting its presence via a chronicle of residue. In this context the body is the only known acquisition, the only known tracery of former energy that once enlivened it. This leaves the senses bereft sans the planes of the uncanny. Therefore, one needs evolve beyond seeming domestic minutiae allowing a curious emancipatory stillness to transpire. This stillness seemingly arrayed with regressive intentionality evinces itself through dazed behaviourable glances. This state being response to broken moral considerations, being response to squandered reply ushered in via the guise of quantitative registration. Not that I seek to further obscure my meandering alchemics by orchestral density. The a-terrestrial continues to erupt in code sired by circuitous neural quantity. Thus, the cells spin as inclement meta-ciphers, problematic, self-haunted, seeping into tenebrous complexity via complex motility. Perhaps this is none other than evolutionary code, resonance that continues to build as proto-Tasmanian choreography, as primal Tasmanian electrical field that understands even murderous whalers and the general decimation they have wrought.

As electrical presence I can do nothing other than condone seepage in the service of seeming vehicular absence. Thus, I am alive as unknown immensity, as mysterious geometrical incandescence. Let us take earthly solar example and its seepage into absence. It is nothing other than the reverse of spontaneous absence shaping itself into galaxies that condense into differing rates and turnings. So as this electrical absence I imply an interior plane of blizzards, a proto-mutability sans tenebrous colloquies of confusion thereby summoning a scenario of Betelgeuse and the Sun, our common solar ember, as scenario teeming with riddles. To describe these random solar examples exists as nothing more than a combinatory fragment, knowing that Betelgeuse extends beyond the general rotation of Mars. Yet, in a numerical sense these dialectical suns and their attendant planetary planes remain infinitely subsequent etched with the genetics of mystery.

So as oracular Tasmanian I spontaneously repulse the tenets of gravity understanding the double solar example of Betelgeuse and our common solar figment to be what I'll call simultaneous fragmentation.

One could say that simultaneous fragmentation could serve as an ambiguous treatise attempting to particularize vapour or match abstract law with abstract law. But in this instance, simultaneity remains code for hyper-dimensions of existence. These dimensions being both visible and invisible include seen solar systems as well as the impalpable state that empowers them. In terms of quanta, Betelgeuse and the Sun, at one level, are in-consequent fragments that function at oblivious scale. But as simultaneity or fragment this double solar example enacts itself as interior sigil being seepage of itself beyond itself, thus, it is the universe itself expanding beyond its staggering body of mazes, beyond what poetic philosophy would aurally signal as an isometric gulf subverted by rogue integers. Because as fragment they seem as ratios, but concerning their simultaneous underlying current they go on forever not unlike an irrational number of continuous sevens existing beyond authorship of invisible galaxies, beyond the limit of what the mind can conceive. Perhaps via partial glance the void abstractly staggers as a meandering gramme, as a gramme that seemingly fails at consistency with itself. This exists as vertiginous exercise that both escapes and absorbs itself as particle. Thus, one's neurology is simultaneous with such exercise expanding and contracting to such a degree that it begins to ascend above known respiration where known thought can never enter.

As for trans-cosmic solar bifurcation none ultimately exists, existence is one. To rise to this level through experiential understanding one must submit to the agony of transmutation far beyond the exercise of pointless pagination, far beyond the abstract evidence of un-kindled facts. Thus, my imaginal body sits astride a vapourous Appaloosa circling simultaneous crags of Tasmania and Mars. Such circling remains a subsequent quest if solely committed to noun-centred revelation which in the end extends no further than compound stationary induction. This being psychic tautology seeking a populace of nouns that goad themselves to finalize as answers. As if the mind could winnow a single answer from an infinite fraternity of answers.

Perhaps if I summoned a figure from what I'll call contained stationary value, say, containing a quantity of abstract insistence, say, a number that streams into presence as 999 followed by 350,000 zeros and then squared 150 times remains within the auspices of spectacular containment housed as an array of vertigo, as a delimited draft of vertigo, subsequently compressed as synecdoche to a 5 with 50 zeros compressed for accessible consumption. These being attempts at totalitarian integer so as to psychologically ensnare motion making it subsist as an ironically squared fraction. In such context the mathematical mark ceases as poetic fluidity thereby ceasing to partake of its invisibility as consciousness. I am concerned here with uncountable blankness. The latter thus transmutes to dynamical glistening.

Yet to approach these numbers from another plane is to say that the unknown and the other merge at a juncture sans practical habitability, a habitability that I contend was once simultaneous with levels of meta-Palawa. I was bred to inhabit these meta-ranges above dispersal of the body after death, where the essence of Palawa as power can never be walled off via seeming extinction condemned to faulty recollection of its prior animation.

The flow of singing in eastern Tasmania continues to exist, continues to flow as darkened expansion of space. Yet its flow on Earth has been extinguished by Saxons honing their hatred to its self-appointed presence. By doing such they've annealed themselves to a corrupted form of subsequence, to theorems implicate with truncation, with a savage form of infamy, providing them with classifiable justification for self-appointed crime. They have created a brief but destructive linkage to living nuance condensed by inductive self-priority, thereby instilling psychic autocracy. As vanished Tasmanian, they remain to me in-starred as lizards who abducted our spacious paradise acre by acre so that we have become subject to absolute physical vanishment. Having passed over into darkness I propound through perpetual resistance, ignition of ghosts, ignition of intrinsic profanation that continues to seep as baleful susurration, as principal power combining heresy with intransigent psychic palpitation. My voice being alive as particle dyslexia, certainly not contained by diagnostic priority or proportional tirade. My voice being nothing other than an architecture of blurs, of burning selves that exist as cross-identity, as camouflaged basins teeming with pre-emptive sharks. As if my selves are the voices of sharks in transition fore-telling immeasurable scale, hidden as code within barbarian semiotics. Its spirit not as blind and illegible ornament, but provocation of eclipse allowing rise of higher obscurity where certain cephalopods cross into light listening to themselves via the tone of a transparent clavicle.

Because there is tacit correspondence between the dead and the living dead, this is none other than a medium akin to the darkened transitional ray symbolized by the Oort dimension. This being bodiless grammar not unlike the substance that hovers as bottomless petroglyphs. This being vibrational emptiness scripting itself as a living maze of sapphire sans distraction erupting from embrangled apparitions.

This being the scale of my summary realia that existed as interminable grace. And it was this grace that Saxon invaders disrupted when they terrorized my kin by abducting our "orphaned" children turning them into servants. Such action was symbiotic with their venomous colonial governor who had us hunted for sport. This was none other than compound ruination that subsisted as post-mortem methane, as protracted avidity. This being neurology wizened to such a degree that it distills at ophidian boundary. This being sans the Sun or Tasmania as origin. This taking on the spirit of superimposed evil where translucence itself enters a gulf susurrant with endemic corruption. This being a blinding replete with threat that seems to spiral out of sulphur.

Since I've assumed the depths of the invisible, I've assumed the purest signals from the Sun. It has entered my voice and perpetually lives through my voice, where the noun loses reception of itself and becomes conversant with vibration. Perhaps the cells of cephalopods partake of hyper-dimensional synapse and exposure to a level sans stupendous dimming existing as ferocious example. As for latter-day

Europeans they remain in confusing psychic vacuums over-extended with strain and failing attempts at calibration for control. It remains a dubious pressure, a pressure that extends to all domains of living. In contradistinction I remain mesmerized by hyper-dimensional ballet, thereby overcoming a terse circumference of tactics. The latter remains another nutation which neither lives nor dies, nor suffers general gnawing from proposals advanced by what is generally accepted as secular propulsion. In the latter state one is both simplified and rendered inert by charismatic burden. It is none other than a glossary of bewilderment that abets a facile consumption of one's nature as chronically measured discomfort. One is thus cannibalized by disheartening.

This being said, there exists the alphabet of the cosmos with its experience of solstitial widening. Being thus transmutes through deepened summarization. This being none other than an immaterial compendium. Then the body advances as a transmuted glossary, the latter existing "as all outcomes of measurement" realized on differing parallel planes. Of course, the soul cannot be assessed as a probable state, but as an oscillating gulf never prone to gross statistical pulse, to contingent repartee as waking informational complex. It remains suffused by internal rays, in this sense akin to the shadows of galaxies pointing to the origin of their state as being sourced by realia of otherness, of darkened energy refracted as spectral flotation.

This being a mediumistic glimpse into boundless percolation. And at Tasmanian scale this is not unlike the legendary Walyer who sought to protect this inherent percolation who brought mayhem on European sealers who sought to seal off her spirit by brutality as their primary method.

To paraphrase Einstein space comes into itself by means of itself like a cobra wrapped around its own inference as its own self-making expansion.

Here I am existing beyond the accepted scale of neurological syntax that accelerates through compositional generality so that it floats not by myopic measure, or by ominous tautological haunting, never trapped by dark behaviourable winter. As for incommensurate reasoning or penurious speculation none seems to have the power to propound itself via the code of conspicuous desecration. Thus, the Tasmania above which I float being akin to quantum baryonics given over to non-registration, to non-existent summation, to dense intergalactic plainsong.

Inscrutable Visibility

Being in the spirit on the edge of space.
The sidereal body.
—ROGER GILBERT-LECOMTE

I AM THINKING of the ongoing condition of human electrical current always signaling to itself what can be considered cellular malapropism. Which means history remains slippage into cul-de-sacs, and general behavioural dyslexia, carrying in itself burdensome seeds, existentially incapable of advancing itself beyond its continuing foment, incapable of extracting itself from the power of gross ruination. Never the antidote enacted through the pulse of pure vision. Like a chastised infant it burns with complaint always announced through bulletins of regression. And this regression is analytically probed by its own decay, by the machinery of consensus analysis. The latter built by trauma, infused by genes of unserviceable extinction. This being the psycho-genetic grip which self-describes itself through the popularity of impasse. This being the reality of an odd exorbitant serpent continuously sickened by its own ingestion. A ruinous self-infliction thrashing about by means of crazed insensibility.

Every day the headlines throb with the fever of crises. This issue versus that issue, this death against that death, this attempt at conquering versus that attempt at conquering. Which adds up to no more than a circumstantial fatigue. A continuing malaise which erupts on an ongoing basis. Crises ingested in the collective blood as a general toxin. Under this circumstance it is impossible to project such a condition even 30,000 years into the future. This is an embarrassing coup for the forces of extinction, maliciously punctuated by the stifling tactics and stratagems enacted by the troubling nations to the north, profit through greed being their sole originating principle. Which remains their a priori given for governing human relations. I call it the universal conquering genome, covertly and overtly branded upon consensus thought arrangement. This being the restive nature of the European tenor always seeking to control the general mental vicinity with dualism sustaining and re-sustaining its transmittable paradigm. Which has authored and continues to author divisiveness, lust for gold, slaughter of innocent parties. It has summoned the worst tendencies in the human species over its reign for the past 500 years, so much so that contagion seems now complete, humanity now seems saturated with a smoldering alliance to psychic deficit, to false nostalgia and panic.

Myself, a creature of this menacingly eroded ozone, seeking sight outside its choreographic wreckage, seeking at the aboriginal level to free my neurology from dread, to free its powers from a superimposed vacancy of spirit. By establishing such an assent another level of contagion could pullulate, possibly seeding a new atmosphere of consciousness. All this being stated not in terms of advancing new leadership or in terms of some dazed aggrandizement where I would be recognized as the sole imparting factor of general salvation. I am simply speaking of having a fecund enough liberty to instill anonymous vibration. A vibration not unlike the supra levels above the mind. And I'm speaking of the mind as it now enacts itself as the human given. I am relating the aforesaid to the fact of present circumstance where birth in many ways has become a contaminate property. Witness the monstrous apparitions of Cyclops babies invading our eyes as they pour from wombs in Falluja, as apparitions of depleted uranium. In many ways, they seem symbolic of the future, with commitment to divisiveness and blinding in unparalleled assent.

This is an energy which tends to reek as if it were a hive of burnt fowl with its glow wafting beyond the troposphere, as if this circumstance could be rescued by cryptic powers from Vega, then rendered into habitable form. This being the covert mantra of the era, to be redeemed by alien enablement so as to freshly start from scratch. I am speaking here of forms outside of oxygen, so as to fundamentally escape our moribund data, our reality of compromised phenomena. In contrast, I see alien immanence as non-utilitarian, as energy floating around the quanta of other suns. Saying this, I am not some abstract explorer, whispering beneath my derma, seeking to enter the sidereal in order to conquer, which could never be a re-invention of Columbus or de Soto. Via the higher states, I am experiencing a shift from solar to sidereal, not as a clause, but as a singular expansiveness. For me, this remains the psychic aeronautics of the old Egyptians, the experiential current which they used to float structures, to kindle frozen matter to an animated state.

I can only say that I am a whisperer, having never been provided with an enriched sequestering, always being askew in the crowds, only able to harvest glimpses from the other planes, always buffeted by what is understood to be collective assumption concerning human delimitation vis-à-vis the other. Of course, I am not complaining about fragmented exposure to the higher planes, thus I experience gnosis within medias res. A trans-physical stamina transpires simultaneous with a surreptitious mantra in the cells. A trans-functional listening by means of ethereal cadence which is spontaneous, with one's being no longer trapped and held by the frontality of shrines. Of course, not a conscripted cadence clashing with itself due to non-integral priority, but the sound in question rising from separative hives of commotion and stillness, susurrus with blurred translucence.

Commotion at this level being decibels of annoyance, infamy by truculence, which are staples of the modern kingdom. Which mimes itself through the anguish of meters and gigabytes. Thus, insight is sullied by the compound anaemia of abstraction. Which always produces a state of affairs girded by the ammonia of dimness. Thus, insight in its purest movement seems surrounded by fumes from psychic naiveté, by fumes from general fundamentalisms, from passé instruction spawned from middle class obstruction. The latter three examples congealed by the broken worms that exist as non-awareness. They being paradigms fueled by moribund assumption as kinetics. These being vile ideologies enacted by the present mind as finalized habituation, comforted by this or that belief.

Because I am neither influenced by commotion or ideologically imposed silence, I flow through being as a non-conscripted ghost. Thus, I create by my presence contagious suffusion, always leaving my mark as parenthetic absence. An absence, not unlike a signal issued from the cells. Because of this, I remain an anonymous concrescence. Unlike a wandering monster, part tiger and mongoose, I've ceased the stoking of flames from my nostrils. In this sense, I do not enact as presence a barrage of terror and scales, nor am I an upwelling messenger formed from the literature of preconceived anathemas. I feel synonymous with evolved presence, and because of the absence which I emit, I am beginning to know the essence of the body as geology according to patience. A patience capable of emitting supra-rays, capable of emitting vertical neutrinos. One becomes a surreptitious avatar trans-rationally self-gathered through the means of powers over and above the personality as a given. Say, by evolution I enter the field of interstellar neutrinos, getting the first glimpse that other states of reality are simultaneous with unending. Presence then remains, active without death.

If I say that my outlook is dark, I am only assuming the pessimism of the age swung as it is by the pendulum of doubt. As a neurological phantom, such doubt does not befit me, does not chronicle me with negation, thereby reducing my kinetics to a wandering spectre amidst truncated crops. Under present definition, I exist without context, not a saviour, nor a prognosticator, nor one who registers according to the turbulence of belief. I am an energy minus due fixation, as if my body were composed of asteroidal rays carrying as my voice transmuted statics from Saturn. It is always knowing in each of my steps the fecund distance that issues from the Sun. Therefore, grasping distance by power other than analytical enablement, I now know the Sun as a non-chronological combining. As non-accumulation being beauty as vertical phasma. A phasma that floods the field with perpetual metamorphics. My body could be Ison, or Saturn, or Ceres, not consciously knowing inch by inch the distance or closeness of objects. I am prone to arbitrary states closed to the general mind by Greek biology and habit. At this level, I have more in common with uncoded whales on the ocean floor swimming, say, along a route between Sumatra and San Francisco. Within my present state duration is synonymous with transparency not unlike a saffron-coloured butterfly drifting towards Mexico in winter. What I am saying is that there is a natural understanding which I call the other of all rotation. There is its fever which blends by means of vertigo and euphoria, which then burns as an unruly vitrescence. Therefore, I cannot reduce my condition to a brass or stoic impact upon itself. Because I am incapable of true collaboration with induction, I am given grief by perspective from the general social view as to proof of intellectual coherence. The whole cannot cohere through separable parts. The part for me remains the sterilized stage along the way. Now if I spit out the parts, they are ammoniated with saliva, with organic psychic pepper. This being a distilled asset of brilliance.

Thus, one cannot engineer portions in lieu of the imagination, in lieu of the circular as illumination. Here I am speaking of the climate of the innate. Of the mind whose speech is a blizzard of sea waves. Saying this, I cannot make up boulders, or transpose schist in order to ensure a type of closure or clarity, piece by separating piece. Thus, I am not a magus who attempts to control known triumph, who inches along the road of chiseled index factors. Instead, I am always the migrating skeletal phantom, never tersely configured, or pointlessly ensconced within a deserted stretch of land. I am never the fatigued assurance of the conscious mind counted on to remain in one setting. Therefore, I am the bizarre infraction which tumbles out of nowhere. Not the patch of filigree seemingly stuttering to himself, but of insight from which the filigree emerges. The latter being none other than the zero field simultaneous with both the anterior and posterior state which has nothing in common with clouded doppelgangers. This being purity by internal doppelganger seeking transverse rotational elevation. Such elements do not befit me, burning as I am in an open universe of non-locatable definitives. I would simply be an isolate hurricane teeming with entropy. Instead, there is patience turning the smallest of elliptical motions into upwelling fumes from the field. These being akin to rays creating a compound field as the field of fields, always alluding to the trans-state of stellar captivity.

    A mind sullenly trapped within its self-wrought contact points tends to make war on the invisible and the seemingly non-begotten. This being a superfluous mind sealed off from itself, sealed off from knowledge from the field, exploring through due course various powers of anaemia which are forces that attempt to refute the non-measurable, which concatenate the regalia of particles, the private tendency of isolate concurrence. This being lowest elevation of the nanosecond, reducing its scale to the derivative by going back to the electrical manifestation of the mayfly within the reign of its 24 hours. Saying this, I am addressing the strange array of experiment as it exists across the field. I call it the electricity of the sublime, never confining itself to empirical happenstance but to magnificent squalls of empirical lightning. Empiricism in this sense being a revelatory beacon conveying itself as the in-contaminate kinetics of auto-suggestion. Which becomes the trans-reality of the *ba* where the life force communes with its own identification.

    This is not psychic banditry seeking to open inner worlds through subterfuge, through unmanaged angles fraught by superimposed forces but a stage of new electrical reaction where bread is no longer ingested by one's rapacious bodily urn. This being the body ⅞ths removed from the human state as presently constructed. Not a mirage as false containment but sound igniting light from where now dearth presently exists. This being supra-mental animation, as supra fractal, making it something other than greenish lunar fire. This lunar fire being an abstract diagonal fire rife with broken inner power. Thus, phenomena at the supra level blazes as incarnation of the field and can be no longer colonized at the diagnostic level but becomes a strange interior summons unto itself. The registered hamlet becomes a non-impactful hull sunken in the ice that simulates itself as history.

As if I now floated over brazen lava fields inhabited by concocted fevers no longer alive with great electrical depth. Thus, I've surmounted the point of the purely optical and its fount at the juncture of divisiveness. No parts of motion, no decimal static within the embellishment that is being. I am no longer active in the gardening of nightmares. This being purity by internal cyclone which always cleanses the lens of speech. Rising to this level, I've always been cleansed by the tincture of absence, by an incipient fire from the Ground, never dependent on the given. This means there is never the look back, the frenzy to replicate, to suddenly translate ash as perfection, thereby condoning a recursive nerve yield that imprints a dearth into one's holding grain. Devolved presence, sterile sensitivity where the alchemical ceases to persist. What follows is that grammar ceases to uproot itself losing its power to gamble. This being the mind fallen into prior circumstance, non-conjoined to supra possibility, always conjoined to tautologies of unease. Bound rejoinders, restrictive verb engagement, gainless spiritus. Which is the majority vibration of the global mental inherence. An advancing vacancy, a general failing, an insular state of pervasive darkening.

Now the site of the body is valued only for its attraction of treasure, for its extrinsic economic charisma for being exterior to itself and its own worth. All higher discussion is reduced to preambles, to a central exchange of absence where only the transactional is seen as relevant. A provincial concrescence at best always prone to annoyance and envy of brokered spite in the service of inner cul-de-sacs and panting. The latter remains the working paradigm of the era. In contra-distinction, say, the skull of an oryx is shaken with a beam of alien consciousness, beaming through veils of separation. Not only is the oryx conjoined to discredit but its image is then squared in the media as being no more than the reverie of a feeble Bon Magician. I'm speaking here of an energy which is found in the old Tibetan art of healing, where the invisible body is encountered, where not only are the dead revealed and resurrected but beyond this resurrection a wakening by the force of universal enigma.

I am concerned here with subtle registration, with less registration than the blink of an eye. In this sense, I am eschewing miracles which raise the dead, which remain inside the lone domain that is Jesus Christ. Let us go back to the Westcar Papyrus and the raising of the dead by the magician Teta in the IV Dynasty during the reign of Cheops. We exist at present in such a state of sterility that can only recall such energy in a fixed Biblical setting with no prior or latter precedent. This being the case of general mental subjection where the populace seems rendered according to false stimuli not unlike a charged scattering of rodents across riveting outer darkness. This is not the darkness which renders itself as sigil but a darkness principally defined as being consistent with paralysis. In my view, the ancillary as obstruction, as amplification is linked to parochial psychology. The latter, having no wider radius than personal connivance. This is why the Sun is never seen as transpersonal witness. As dawn which rises above seeming liminal opacity sending a dyad of signals across the phantasmic. Not unlike pure musical yeast conveying in its wake the unscripted.

Which I maintain is higher kindling of the cells thereby allowing the body to both widen and raise its power of being. I am signaling no known system. I am simply stating the fact of the cells evolved to a higher peril. Which remains the first condition for exploring the transpersonal as biography allowing an incipient sidereal psychology to flare. The latter partaking of an invisible solar capacity where the eating of one plane by another ceases to exist. This is not history nor can it be called an irregular shadow field but simply a new interior species, which trembles with the luminosity within blankness. Which is not strictly the shifting of monerans according to repetitive pre-determination. By its nature, it remains the state of the non-predictable, always altering its density and its form. A perpetual percolation which can never describe itself according to an abstract terminology. I am not stating that all harrowing has been superseded or that a climate has been instilled where we can generate our efforts as akin to the Egyptians when they stated higher consciousness as *The Coming Forth by Day*. We have achieved at best a liberty of blankness that from the zero field interacting with its tenets never presaged any aforesaid phenomena.

On Crossing the Vermin Frontier

... the "dream body" and the "bardo body" are the "vision body."
    –A FOOTNOTE IN TIBETAN ZHITRO

I AM NOT infected. I am not of pestiferous lodging. At first self-glance there is perception of failure. Nor am I writing this to conceal myself by pejorative isolation.

Let me state that I feel suffused by vibrational activity with othered parallel dimensions. There is always respiration within the vicinity of the innate. This being the weather of the primordium. An emptied zodiacal greenness where integers linger at the cusp of dimensions. The immediate body not unlike ignited leather giving rise to its sense of duration in endlessness. I do not see the body as entropy delimited by present circumstantial assumption. An assumption bent on securing itself within provincial infernos, within an infernal portion, trenchant, fixated, vis-à-vis the old laws of oblivion. Perhaps I could be accused of raw naïveté, of optical dishevelment constantly confused by my distance from consensus observation.

Sub-susurrant hubris?

Folly dared in the face of the unalterable?

Perhaps I am attempting my first entry into mystery, into the preternatural, all the while listening to myself as a parable of dice. I am not waving a magic wand, making of myself an icon, eclipsing arcane dilemma.

You say, a marred kindling, a translocated scarring?

I say, opening, transpersonal charisma, pedagogical nonexistence.

So am I defending myself as monster, as crystallized subjection, as pointless invariance, as something only the disfigured can consider engendered by concussive minerals?

Do I aspire to iconic example, to a level of deceptive regalia?

I cannot in my present state answer such queries in the affirmative.

Of course, I've scripted no posture as regards enacted devolution. Perhaps I've sculpted peculiarity to such a degree that it has taken on the cast of insular royalty. As if I were sailing on a niveous raft towards partial distillation, shifted beyond the shadows of labour conscripted due to illegible suffering. Power at this level is other than tornadoes, is other than carnivorous beckoning from the blood. As for me, an inexhaustible blueness blazes. A leakage of elegance filling the spirit. Yet there is always seething through mystery. Perhaps I can say yoga extends through ignited moons condensed in a ray that unifies disorder. My internality singed by being raised to a plane of meteoritic combustion, traced by non-limit. For the less inclined, a scurrilous density, a neurological aphasia, as if my name were Ouppa Galdos. A name no longer grounded via pre-planned persona. It both escapes and consumes me being something other than the charisma of philosophy. I can only register its inferential state as sidereal animation, knowing its dust to be expanded beyond the powers of personal limit. Which has allowed me latitude in acquiring unbelievable respiration. In this sense, I've gained a principal source of maturity suffused as it is with parables from hyper-dimensional becoming, coming to myself by means of intrinsic coma expressed through seepage as oneiric charisma. Which lifts me above the emphatic, above coherence of myself as hylic gravitation. This seepage has engendered gravitational unrest invoking something other than the lower inferno as behaviour.

This has spawned an understanding inside me that knows that the human body is incomplete, that it remains occluded from the differential as experience. As of now, I receive vibrations from bottomless aural transmission. Not an ill-inhabited transmission, or normal temporal fate, or micro-imbroglio as doubt but experience across a range undefined by limit. Which projects an absence of explanation for itself, as if it suddenly appeared from the inscrutable. Sans prior explanation, or balance as measure. As for a priori registration, images cease to signal through their essence hurtled as they are from the bizarre. Not unlike the atmosphere spawned in pre-natality, as if one floated in a cyanotic ocean room. Within this room forces beam from the indefinite: I cannot rank such experience as being psychically carved from allegation, from the circumstance of my own conscripting. This is other, perpendicular in strength flowing inward and rising upward without explanation. Perhaps, this could be attributed to spinning inside the cells which implies more than private explanation. It is more akin to electrical force which registers without explaining itself through statistical observation.

So, am I under the gaze of my own vapour?

Under self-translated peril?

Overwhelming myself by shadow?

Or am I burning as neurotic candle through contagion?

I do not remember my former selves living as I've lived through disintegrated circumstantials. Memory for me has become a tortuous disservice. As if I sought to interrogate my shadow as if it were a warring python. A python struggling against psychic glass squandering itself by implosion. In contradistinction, I feel lifted by rays of inspirational dust. To extrinsic perception I am only reacting from numbness, from ethers arisen from purposeless sand. The darkness in my being sigil living as transmuted elevation. Perhaps as micro-source of spirit. Even now extrinsic consensus will say that I am a fulminate or lost identity. Perhaps a maze or plunged balance. Liminal realia allowing respiration through mystical anaemia. A luminosity teleportational in demeanour.

An equational flow transcending past and future. Much like fire working outside its own limit. This being life as arisen hypnotics.

The question can be asked, what levels have I reached?

Certainly, no discursive persona can be discussed. One could say that I am plagued by inconsistency, that I've been subsumed by bluish neuro-electrics, an electrics rarely found on earth. Not an energy prone to nature as given or power extracted from pharmaceutical electricity. Again, this is not a privately captured imbroglio scattered inside secret meridians.

Hallucinogens?

Fumes from dazed minerals?

All I can say is that I feel inside my curative ambrosia an internal Dharsan slipping through the pores of my skin. Simply put, I have become what literature calls the "other," an "other" honed by surreptitious complexity. Infinity whispers with its foretaste of cleansing slipping into modes of new electrical worth. Of course, there are some who ply themselves with strange emotional forgery, absented as I am from such a quandary. Thus, I feel lifted from the roof of analytical clouds. There exists no fever from a priori equivocation. For instance, days prior, I hear tornadoes arise from the afterlife. They whirled as moons that arose from interstitial faulting. Which is not life in the role of bickering through conjoinment, or a blur from merged lenses. Within this understanding I cannot vilify my presence or link my blood according to postulates of error. Or of private oscillation wandering through my mother's heart at birth. Unlike most, my mother was graced by a riveting intuition, she knew that birth was empowered by the invisible. She passed its presence to me, spawning in me consciousness that condones impalpable traces, which has spawned in me intangible realia over and beyond the scope of hermeneutics. Which in my case has left no corpse to worship, no mirage or belief to complete my trances. This of course is not posturing through neutrality as if I had conscripted ardour through documents of sand. Thus, I teleport across vapour.

I build no foundation according to extrinsic count or counting. I can no longer be counted within a plausible network of beasts. I cast no fumes from my scenario. It cannot be described as stupor, or scattering, or holographic bribery. Nor am I a shadow who haunts himself by irony. Not an occupational tracking under the spell of neurotic flora. Nor have I expressed myself to gods returning to the animal realm with a face of perfectly wrought crystal. Yet I know that I dwell within the province of the uncanny. At times, I ingest morose dictation, at others, I spew as a fabulous source boiling with diamonds. What I experience is not monological meta-burning, but an aura lit by suffusing sub-sonics. Certainly not a structured laterality or the scripting of a soul misled through cryptic infloatation. Being one already born, I have no need to invoke a separable prakṛti flashing as an illusive meta-condition. Yet I feel lifted by forces that are other, never embrangled by compound mystique, by hollow call, by disoriented raven.

In certain circles my efforts could be revealed as a culminate text, as inevitable Bodhisattva, parallel to impalpable prolongation. A blankness arising from Akashic spinning, knowing its tone of broken voices as they rise from cosmic ether.

At times, I feel drafts of light inside my aura, my energies flickering like the amarillo cinema of Saturn. Within this state I've listened to lakes explode and rediscover themselves so that their poles of magnification work through other scripts beyond surcease. Perhaps, as an internal North conjoined with an ellipse of blinding purity. Thus, I do not weigh the body as gnomic physical weight, but as light advanced through navigational translucence. Flow as diaphanous algae being motion which forms through incendiary wonder, as osmosis, as sprawled flux, as unalterable seepage. Not the shadow that casts itself through harassing tonics, or as research extracted from the bitterness of talons. Yet, by respiring through luminosity I am free to conduct myself according to the gospel of lions turning general schist into the wheat of ascension. Never have I conducted utterance according to the bitterness of recension, or by problematical gist fueled by what I'll call nautical apprehension. As if I had issued fumes from crushed locusts by means of storms from dialogical tensions.

I do not graft myself from the wool of theoretical relation. I must confess at this moment that I am angular, alive, contradicted, at the lower plane of seeming cross-purpose. Yet, I've never been accused of being a mulish consumptive plagued by pejorative in-action, self-condoned by unpardonable ferocity. What I speak of has nothing in common with a boisterous syllabus gone astray, engendering itself by means of listless embitterment. Perhaps, one could say, I am a sociology of bereftment conjoined with dazed animal form my instincts held hostage according to the dictates of an unseen harassment. Which is not unlike being thrown into a square humming with deceptive containment.

A commingling through the paradox of the unruly as spoil?

This experience remains for me the genetics of the mystical. As if my alteration were shifted beyond the rays of the Sun. Not unlike a curious fuel conjoining with itself as a clarified emptiness. Thus, a mirrorless discourse where a fragmental prakriti no longer consumes the stage, blotting out its vertical respiration. I am beginning to understand the realia of the Kunzhi Namshe stored as it is "in the base of consciousness." Its free letters, its zeal, its fumes which ignite from open language. This being my essence spun from a cliff open with transparency which are worlds that appear from rapturous emptiness. This being my yoga of language that exists as limitless aurality, a charged munificence no longer consumed via personal regalia. Nonetheless, it remains an energy en-fueled by feverish observation. An observation from a field vapourous with peninsulas.

Living at this level I've receded from the actual glances of others. I have taken on the power of sequestered example finding my way through telepathic morphology and as a result I speak to myself through utopian disregard. Not language searching only for the enactment of search but vertiginous experience constantly spawning bewildering balance. Having studied disorder in myself I shift from the inscrutable to the inscrutable, knowing it to carry the power of its own perfection. Which at one level is oneiric perfection and at another ceasing to trace its own ignition.

At this level one can summon what I'll call aural mirage. Perhaps traceries towards paradise. At certain planes of hearing there exist an ubiquitous whirling of phonemes in concert with commingled light. The result, a spontaneous turquoise whirling at an exponential rate which transmutes to a beet and amarillo sky. And I'll call this sky scorpion, rubefacient, spinning clockwise and counter-clockwise as a simultaneous topology. Knowing as I know that the Sun and this planet being part of the Orion Spur remains a microscopic ignition within the Laniakea complex of galaxies, realia vis-à-vis the Kunzhi Namshe being an oscillating bonfire, such a field for me is not an isolated teeming but symbolic of a whole not bearable to the contracted figment. The Kunzhi Namshe being of differential expansion is something other than the blind and weighted mirror body. A transpersonal clearing over and above the zodiac as entrapping habitat. In this sense, I'm thinking of verbal fumes rising by means of the grammar of disappearance. A grammar in its visible reaches retains an incendiary confirmation, as it rises as cacophonous antelope, not unlike salt vertically rising from wizards.

In this sense, I've become vitreous in form, a transparent Nirmāṇakāya always inferring the Saṃbhogakāya and as imageless realia as Dharmakāya. As Nirmāṇakāya I am veritable blueness turned to transparency.

A first philosophy of seclusion?

A treatise on blinding variables?

A totalic renegado?

I can only say that I register luminous ferocity from hiddenness. A bizarre transmutation being comprised of risen cellular heresy, functioning as impalpable nuance. As draft of median transparency, I am not unlike a moth drifting beyond the unscalable as symbol.

Becoming in this state an open electrical phylum unclassifiable within range of the given. As to psycho-philosophy prone to a frontal view what I continue to say reeks of the uncanny. It provokes fever, both glycerin and baseless, clouding the frontal view with sigils of ill design. Which tends to frighten, which floods its view with formless inner signs. Signs which flow as spontaneous lightning rivers, always inferring cryptic lepton notions of de-existence, of adjacent clauses and burnings. Perhaps on a more hylic plane I seem to lean toward misperceived signals and objects. Which are objects daunted, flattened, that waste away as subtractive elliptical grammes. This being the flow of inner lightning not confined to suns, over and beyond their various entanglements, over and beyond the subjection of shadow to non-veracity. Its non-locality as light, its intangible infra-deftness as witness.

    I am at times asked to create a traceable magnetics of the invisible, to fuse its torrents with the vernacular. This being electrical levels no surname can shape. Thus, mirage coalesces in the foreground and, as paradox, remains a mirror of weight. Prakṛti as isolate protraction being none other than sub-equal lightning. None other than a partial refraction of the universe. Of course, I'm concerned with the electrical level that carries human shape, which bears no resemblance to extrinsic cogitation. At this level, mirages open themselves, the cells waken, self-generation evolves. This being spinning as spontaneous gateway to the limitless. A stunning aperture into otherness which spins beyond hollowed apparitions. One then comes to the nexus where the great juncture resides, where a hurricane of focus throws, aurally hurtles from the invisible. Which carries no concerns as regards the psychiatry of commerce. The latter consumed by the warren that remains the Occident, distilled as it is by corporate manipulation of lucre. In my present state I am gazing from the other, from a resonant transparency not unlike the Hill of Nāgārjuna. This being the plastique of the unseen, the force that evolves from the innominate. Which transforms the panic of insurrectional anxiety. One can then no longer claim personal definition due to regressive neural fixation. One then commences seepage into sensitivity spawned by the differential.

In order to thrive throughout such vertiginous kindling intractable patience must combust as abundance. Not stubbornness through pointless cognitive addition but a spectrum of glints spontaneously charged by the cosmos. The conscious mind acknowledges such experience according to inklings of doubt. Doubt fails to accrue mystery as it snakes through transference of planes. It fails to condense spectra honed by interior specification. Something other than a high unruly litmus fueled by physical spectrometers. Thus, scattering transpires and cannot be transfixed by calculable transcription. Phases transmute through rotational hyper-limit not unlike refraction from elliptical starlight. And being dust of this starlight, I filter through a sieve not unlike the motion of Aśvaghoṣa which inhabited Nāgārjuna, which saturates form throughout its maze of obscuration. Thus, the body becomes other than scaleless contraband hovering beyond the moat of contestation beyond galvanized iconics where being is summoned through error. Having slipped beyond resurgent cultural limits there exists innominate boldness no longer embrangled by non-ascending negation. Yet I cannot say that my organs are operant at the pitch of pure cyanoethene. I remain invigoured as an intransigent tonic, as hidden tessellation, which provides me with vortical overview, with transmuted silicas beyond blood. Which in its initial phrase sends signals into the bottomless, which supersedes the Kunzhi Namshe, which sweeps away the Kunzhi Namshe. By breathing restorative elements, I sense in myself the nascence of hollow integers. Thus, I become spell released into the budding of emptiness being other than dialectical extrinsics. There is nutation, there is transcendence of viral infamy, sans the motion of psychic residue as vermin.

One is renewed by aboriginal dictation, by its circuitous shadows, etched by traceries spawned by the beatific, so that I am both warm and distant to colour, to sacrificed lilies, to palpitations which ensnare the dictated body.

I can give no diagram concerning levitating warrens or the blankness of transmuted vehicular form. At the stage described I am one of first rotation, I rise and spin from unnumbered gullies. Therefore, I cannot be claimed by dutiful minutiae, by details embedded in tamasic squalor. I feel as something other than slated to be buried as oxygen. I could be described by some as combustible stray clothed by interrogative ciphers. So, in no way can I be proven according to the principles of cognitive testing pressures, or energies condoned by straightforward utterance. Again I am compelled by the oblique, by the aural density rising from silence. I, who am animate water, who exists over and beyond the transparent shift of ferocity. In my present state I am partially parallel, mass-less, seeping into view from the upper planes, enlivened by forces other than subjective charisma. As regards prior habit I am neither in denial nor defamation. Denying and subjecting all my urges to denial amounts to no more than blurred ubiquity. This is how worms begin threading the being, how compost is soldered, where a peculiar gravity transpires. But as I blaze the worms descend and explode, then emptiness whirls and suggests itself within the mirror of the indispensable. Cleansing transpires, one becomes less and less prone to fumes from peninsulas of carrion, smouldering less and less from the powers of blood and food, less and less conjoined to entropy as fever.

I do not advocate a tense priority or system. For one, I refuse the domain of geometric practicality, and two, I am not ruled by ambitious quantity counting the steps of invisible pandemonium. No, I am not seeking to rule the species according to haunted capability by unequaled dread. I can say no more than that I am plentiful schist dissolving, no more than embodying the curiosity that are Albanian sunsets marking as due a despicable soliloquy analogous to the motion of an unmoving burro. As if reeking of paradox, of assumed mystical wealth, suddenly reducing myself to a dark and stunning energy to wavering fumes from electrocuted trees. Perhaps fumes from poisoned observation, bringing back vibrations from the Tethys Sea in order to enunciate a psychic ensemble subjectively procured from the retrograde. An energy seeming to project itself from compound invisibility making of itself a treatise, projecting itself from the telepathic to the telepathic, from the formless to the formless.

This remains for me purity as subjective voltage, as unsparing linkage, as if I were sailing around a misplaced sun gravitized by complexity through chaos. Its fumes spinning as alien regalia, as a curious and ciphered chroma, consumed by various shifting awash inside aural internality. A sun nonaligned to polluted self-scrutiny all the while ignited as a parallel disembodiment. Of course, I gaze from insular rooftops attempting to balance the echoes as they issue from my aura. I cannot say if any particular assessment befits me or if I remain as moonless and unserviceable kindling, leading a pointless mongrels' army festooned inside a sunless moral density.

As may be evident, I am shifting through initial blazes of roaming inner autonomy gaining the power to exist beyond an isolate neural limit, knowing that the cells can transmute as they whirl around the Sun. I do not aspire to the realia of Methuselah or Enoch, to dwell 900 years hovering by means of biological incapacity. Of course, I continue to respirate by means of ozonal blueness as I cross the first crippling ranges of psychic inherence, as I cross the mind seemingly consumed by hallucinatory auroras swimming without axis. Which means I have entered the first pavilion of distraction, the first locatable trance, struggling with the art of discipline. This, of course, emits no tactile emission, no sound from my body as audible craft or tone. It remains illusive vibratory witness, irradiated litmus, seeping into suspended aural horizons.

Because I have gone so deeply into the hidden, the mind has lost consensus aspects of itself, opened by fumes from telepathic suasion. Because of this suasion I am beginning to breathe through unblemished impulse pitched at the scale of the auto-mesmeric. This being not unlike an osmotic pendulum without regularity of spacing which shifts in its essence by mystical ironies. Thus, motion is emitted by means of baffling, knowing that ages burn and live and disappear without seeming palpability. At one level new things live, yet only the impalpable transmutes as electrical contagion. I have entered the zero field without sight of myself as palpable warren. Because of this I no longer have sense of what the zodiac contains, swayed as it is by a dense and wayward infamy.

On the Rise of Sodium and Fire

IT SEEMS ON the surface few beings have movement. The inner cycles seem vanished. For most citizens have even lost their search for regret. This circumstance being concurrent with what I consider to be a neurological inferno. This state being a contorted human draft utterly delimited and wizened with error. And this is not simply a politically concurring energy but a poisoned complexity amidst pestiferous phenomena. For the opaque consciousness the official palace is always scaled and constructed by mesmerizing dust, by facile and deranged giftings. Respiration always concludes by means of outer precedent. There is nothing other than emptiness by form, nothing other than tenebrous neurosis. This being a hypnotics of the despicable acquiring no higher level than function as corruptive substance. Again, this being life as stained compost, as canceled indemnity of mind. This being a state of mind that condones the facile subsumed by clauses that condone no variation. This being the modern citizens' quest sipping from the rims of frustration seeming to engage in a prostrate jubilation sinking deeper and deeper into emptiness.

This is how modern living occurs, always fleeing inside borders of itself being a dodecahedron that implodes that takes as its merit elemental dysfunction holding it up as a normalcy within ongoing errata. What then occurs are disparate squalls, disfigured emotional currents. Seldom are there attempts at explanation concerning inner micro-exploration or ethics that concern the invisible. If one asks the common person his or her kinship with the rise of the present universe, one witnesses the rate at which their forces scatter, how their attention to the transactional then falls into silence. When one questions such psycho-physical reaction one is deemed a menace not unlike something akin to the pull of blizzards or something more terminal like prior continents erupting. The latter reaction from what's known as the ordinary mind that can project no further than broken laws or victims of terminal ransom notes. They react like panicked owls imprisoned in a fragment. So, when explosive realms are invoked they inwardly fall into a wakeless turning ghat. And these ghats are as frightful muons spinning prior to the act of assembled creation. To the common mind they are threats from riderless Gods. Thus, they cling to products made from oil or pine. The latter are the molecules and the warrens which surround the personality as distractive exhibit. These are beings who threaten one another with flags, with infunctional burnishments, with talons that lead to murder. Therefore, each pinnacle of achievement is modeled on misfortune. This being the general spell engendered, which travels and obliterates and strikes dead the mind as imaginative range.

Now let us look at another dimension of this oddness. The mind conceded as omitted ammonia as in-palatial mental fort at the cusp of darkened minerals. In its embrangled disputation telepathy is broken into mundane valhallas. This is how belief in the contiguous falsely expands. It keeps the mind prone to deleterious arrangements. For instance, God being judgmental figment as parochial gondolier making up fate which collectively careens between burning and drowning. Being horror and fear as simulation of the agnostic which in the deepest sense fuels the penchant for exterior codification, for modeling oneself upon a fevered human nexus. This being sample as tragic array as saturate general flaw. Perhaps from this flaw a development will transpire where piercing concealment will range, where the occulted mind will illuminate its cinders.

Yet these are not the cinders of the populace at large. Again, a teeming gulf of fallen lemmings that signal the proto-catastrophics, which posit eerie forms of weather where summers fail to burn, where enclaves of beings ignite and disappear. The Earth as foreseeable presence a mansion of collapsed surroundings. Flaws burn according to intensified interregnums. Quickening appears. All arrangement seems scrambled. Questions then arise: what are the coming chapters? Who are beings that will gather new traction? Certainly, we cannot draw from recent social consciousness as we are left with nothing more than a diary of abandoned sums a diary that cancels itself through barbarous indictment. This being a zodiac that clings to itself through mirages as self-hatred. This being the era of decline as pressurous collective producing mutant forms drowned as they are in plagiarized ammonias. These being lemming graves scattered on an ad hoc basis. What's being spoken here is not based on doctrinal chastisement or shards of law stranded within osmosis. Again, what's being spoken here are lowly graded deliriums washed by toxic mental sands.

This being the human form maniacally warped struggling in the throes of penultimate configuration.

Why is the term penultimate so suddenly signaled?

Penultimate in this context being strategic confinement, allegiance to pestiferous hiding. Which amounts to respiration by damage, by unintended scorching. Not a form of theoretical prowling or wisp by plagiaristic impact but a lack of true sources being experience void of foundational rhyming. This results in disorder of the senses, in dense encapsulation by minimums. Being unendingly fraught the perpendicular flattens and dissolves into formless animal's dust so that each ballistic adjustment is corrupted by soured motives, so that basic contact is established by means of fractious kindling.

Of course, there are other levels of complication. One's natural feel for immensity seems to vanish. Qualitative demeanour is deemed as inadequate calling; the latter state is considered the worship of effigies according to internal confirmation. And such worship is no more than prolapse, no more than degraded monerans fallen from Sirius considering the body as immemorial postulate. Reality is then considered to reek of posturing according to error, of shiftings, of obliterated molecules as divided simulacra. What is being pointed to is life as negated spectra, as indigenous telepathics gone awry. The horizontal is thus cast free from all ulterior hypnotics, a personality casting off vestiges of the shamanic that can never be considered. Even partial synchronicities are never acknowledged. According to this condition, the mind never prowls or embraces itself like a burning owl in flight. The owl in this sense is leper, is ambrosial intangible, which always signals disadvantage. Thus, the higher states of adventure are voided, are placed in the context of infeasible aeronautics. So trans-cosmic analogy remains a nonexistent electrical field and the quotidian plane seems to solve its intangible perchings through evidence marked by blunted erasure.

Living in the trans-cosmic one is always subject to the machinations always hatching from a den of thieves. And these are thieves who snatch minerals from the Congo, who create from these minerals the most advanced micro-technologies, the most condensed of apparitional mechanics. When the mind is always summoned by this order it is forced to filter these constant impurities, these elusive gravitations, which by their very nature adhere to reductive definition. It is like the atmosphere is fueled by a burning kind of hatred, by a purposeful state which features denigration. Thus, one must contend with monsters, with didactic unmodified usurers. Since one carries no such aggression, one fills one's day with codes that function like broken needlework. And by doing such, one rises by means of perpendicular ardour so that the pragmatists can never gather enough momentum to react at the height of the unserviceable.

In the latter domain Abydos and Sirius concur. The mysteries link thus the ethos is sculpted by an unremitting fabulosity. The aura is soaked by stellar intrinsicalities which renew, which open the subtle shifts in the spirit. Of course, this is soliloquy by light, by motions other than the zodiac. So, if one can answer the questions—another law? another fiber? another foundational vibrato? It will be yes, and yes, and yes, and yes. Of course, this is something other than action and counteraction commonly known as tumult. The contentious locatives of monarchs and war, of plague and dishonour. Then below these discomforts, loosely feathered cataracts and other subforms of blindness appear uttered on the lower plane through poisoned diphthong torrents, through indignities that slaver under corruptive forms of labour.

Say, as poet imbued by the uranian, one internally dazzles with interactive speculation, with ravishing floods mixed with ulterior hierophanies. History when understood through the hierophantic is a pact contiguous with itself always roiled and unsettled, stamping in the foreground branded by ungraceful limit. It is posture gone bad, turned in on itself like an arthritic paw. The result: defamed exhibit, cold and political crowding always at war with what it considers to be in-solutionable Bohemias. At its bottom, always incarceration, always the foiled mount of liberty as exhibit. These are the statesmen, the sum of erected rulers always holding up the standard of carnivorous in-totality. As for the transcendental ratio, nothing is ever recorded.

Thus, one remains in static, reduced to argumentative ballast. The creative being is placed beneath the roof of organizational lepers as if they all naturally coalesced and rightfully suffered as disfigured spectra. The creative being always sorted away as part of the atrocious, as always the opposite of how he, or she, exists in reality. Through the uranian eye, the poets can magically can optically configure themselves as Neon Tetras, as Rainbow Minnows, as Blue Gularis, or having the visual orange-red stripping of the Paradise Fish. This outstrips the leper's agenda, the latter always lingering in debacle. Yet, in this society of opposition to uranian in leaning, one earns less respect than a rat killer, than an attendant who holds court in a morgue. They carry palpable result; they can be measured; they seem to supersede fumes from the uncountable.

At times it can be tempting to adjust to these measures so as to strive for fury as outcome. One is tempted by elements of fate to leave one's micro-society in order to join the general run of beings. Even the dead are pointed out at one's own expense. Their spirits carry shipments of clothing, beveled lamps, and boxes that linger, which seem structured by salt. Yet here one does not speak of supernatural forces but of energies thirsting with taint, quivering at the port of post-existence.

According to present standards, this uranian tenet is embellished by treason. One wanders, one is structured by displacement. Under such circumstances one soaks in one's own design seemingly paralleled by nothingness. Even nullity wavers and the upper planes seem shrouded by fierce critique. Yet, at the very worst, poetry should rise like a voice of concussive pretas. It should instill certitude ramified by beauty. Then again it is a delicate owl that strides upon sands.

So, again, what are its basic phasmas?

What are its splintered arithmetical plinths?

What are its illusive meta-domains?

This is a state where answers do not reach, where infections lack their basics. Maybe one could consider a holographic breathing or a certain form of kilometric cinders. Yet, at a deeper scale one under-stands how suns extend across imaginal ozone and become in the mind as green ignition foliage being something other than decisive punctual codes, or autonomic salt, or pestiferous crackling. It is purity by other explosions and quakings. Other drafts, other clauses by heretical drift. Or conches that roar like phantom lions. Or aspects which spiral and simulate horses fleeing through a pitch-black desert under bluish carbon moons. These moons enriched as anonymous doublings, as spells, as secondary auric depictions. Or curious precautionary crystal congealed as warring saffron movements. These are poetic lists at one level, strange in-cautionary sums at another, and in addition an a priori mustering effect having averted the damage from any susurrant repression.

One seems analogous to such pressures while at the same time remaining an unclaimed fragment by the aforesaid. This is the level where the poet must hold and spiral beyond existing stability. In this sense one is not prone to personal confession or to states of mind concerned with capturing monarchical stagnation. One comes to feel in oneself a devastated understanding, an insight fraught by feeling for the unseasonable. Thus, one hovers as if watching discomforted spirits scurry across imaginary rocks while at the same time understanding the fire of renewed forces. This being the radical shift in the connective mental phase. Not shift by regime or earth-quake paralytic but by osmotic saturation conversing with the zone of asymptotic nutation. The result is like the sighted claiming renewal as they leap beyond macular exhaustion. The breath then will consider its own aural power as the gift of its own Sun and its attendant solar arcs; it will consider rays from Sirius, from other galactic templates that the human mind in its present state carries little cognizant inkling.

A shift accrued from chronic haunting. And these hauntings spin as energy displacements, as blurs, as circumstantial fervour. Then time refuses its pace. Thursday afternoon, Friday at six in the evening missing, always missing. As to common relation it takes on the arbitrary. The personality builds and is no longer isolated within its own confine. Again, merit is not won by superficial approach, by popular agglomeration, by result advanced due to presiding suffocation. By this what is meant is duty to family or machination due to pre-scripted love. Of course, the latter can't exist as standard encryption or perfectly spotted walls in a garden. No, there is the flame which extends beyond these old fatigued boundaries, shifting as they are beyond the brink of atmosphere. Of course, to the isolate soul this is devastational motivation, which at the common plane seems to slay the connecting integers in one's body, which then leans towards the unshackled cells that wander inside mysteriums. What follows is levitational enactment, spawned intermination. Thus, one's former life is consumed, shifting beyond the samsara of the atmosphere. Then the cells begin to rotate with incendiary spinning. These are rays of work at this level, condensed, burning without conscious enactment.

Outside observation would consider the process the arch domain of the violent or noose by chaotic semaphore.

Luminous ruination?

Dotted entanglement?

Peripheral encroachment?

None of the above.

The void once born suddenly opens. Dawn is breakage by swan, by bells which formulate according to utopian timing. And this is not force which reels with the naïve as focus. One is not unlike an unprecedented beast. The first beast on the first shore arrived from total blankness. It is the spectacle of uncertainty, the vertiginous elan, the untold dark at the depth of the hive. Which means one breaks from the leprosy of general social constriction. Freed of the terse, of the mediocre, of mockery. Nothing is left of shrewdness, of the negotiator's spool, of these in pursuit of spurious goods and services. The vertical breaks away, one no longer replicates the surface.

Which means there is no longer the fact of issues. Even paradox at this plane takes on a curious instability. Thus, a curious strangeness is explored. Which means the level of official histories has been canceled because one now glances into the eternity of the Sun. These being the rays from eternity previously understood as exclusively operant in the subtext of spells. Thus, the Western modes of thought have ended, their grasp osmotically riddled.

The galaxies are visually sculpted intensities seemingly balanced as sodium and fire. Yet what are the inner planes of sodium and fire? Various variabilities of light? Canopic monsoons? One can cast no such criticality.

Just for the sake of speculation, what if sodium and fire articulately resurrected into something other than their own registrations? Amorphic in certain states of death? Or something rendered other than complexity outside of human scrutiny? Then, what if all the galaxies rose to something other than the tenor of consciousness?

Can it be said that sodium blazes green and splinters into shadows? Or oblong obscurements? Or ciphers as they kindle inside darkness?

Within this momentary aegis there is higher shape summoned from seeming erasure. This is where the body and the forces of Izar connect. "Two yellow giants with a small companion star." They affect the "electron on each side of the cell wall." Which has to do with pure respiration of energy. Energy being implicit galactic terrain. The body and the galactic as connected. The body as sodium and the galaxy as fire, they both being a simultaneity which rises. Sodium and fire, both above and above themselves rising to a state other than what human consciousness can imagine itself as being. At this level one cannot speak on one's own behalf. One osmotically commingles evincing other planes across circumstance. Say, an energy which blends with the heart arises in Sirius, or rays from the mind which commingle with Procyon, or glottal forms of Aldebaran.

One must be able to clear such distinction knowing the different levels of suffusion, one's carcass fanning the strength of neurological enlightenment. And this enlightenment is contagious to an almost unbearable degree. It being something other than the charisma of ghosts. And it is not that one fuses with corruptive or mistaken identity. It is not a replicable model nor is it an old shielded workhorse burnished by sigils. It is energy which opens, which roams the zones of alchemical anonymity.

The latter range is the burning effort which soars, which allows ignited sodium to flare superseding parsecs having skills which persist beyond translocational impiety. It cannot be said that one resorts to birth or claims contiguous application within the known. Because one can never resort to the picaresque or the brutal. The supersessional is what some of the learned call the rapturesque, the spectrum of the Edenic never subject to neutralization by chroma, so it ceases to register as retraceable nettling.

A state of transgression?

A mode concerning infinite forces?

Of course, these are other fires, other callings, other levels of witness.

Yet this is energy never infected by form, which endures through demonstrable planning. It is not the forum which persists according to ideological substrate. Therefore vanished kindling, perfect ingestion by risk. True, at certain zones in the venture one completely bypasses the Sun and enters perhaps a state of an inner green sun. A sun which rises into deathless existence. A sun which poses threats through its rising by maneuver, by its circuitous internalities. It is like carrying a curious and trenchant poise, variable, unsullied, floating. As total adventure it goes back to unstinting endeavour 4,000 years prior. Like the totalic effort in Kemet, it consumes; it fulminates mazes; it projects from the unexplored.

This is not subsistence or phantoms haunting sparrows in a garden. It is habitation at levels implied as magnification by ibis. Skills accrue at removes beyond human disadvantage. As for the spoils of fiefdom, they cannot exist. Extrinsic colouration, void. The simple powers of contraction ended. These are rays of gusts from the invisible. As for migrating polar ore, it burns as the anagrammatical through drainage and erupts as flotational savoir.

As for living aspiration, in this regard, one is seen as digging graves in the illegitimate, in pursuing distance which collapses. Yet it is never seen by legions of detractors that their will to response is burdened, is captured by forces which sum by annihilation. True, one is seen as spell in total strife. As one of sinister background riding in a carriage of poison. Yet through the powers of these storms one must not act on behalf of a sentiment which self-prosecutes. To the outer eye, one is always slipping on ciphers. A ghost condensed while singing from a harmolodic prairie. Because there exists no rule as self-censure, one is always subject to the angular role of self-torture or coded suffering by vertigo. Because one spins dialectics by vapour one is saturated with fire from the unpredictable. The smallest scale that the Prussian hordes are capable of are triggered infinitesimals. At this scale one exists as no more to them than as invisible wildlife. Maybe presented at one of their functions as a disordered figurine from Patagonia. An exotic limited to blurred superficial exposition. Perhaps a particle rising from a canyon peripheral and without consequence. This being one's reception in latter day society derived as it is from inscripted hellebores.

It cannot be seen that to wall off energy, to pompously equate collective effort with sullied example, can be no more than plagiarized germination. And in the written arts the tendency prevails towards the imagination as pervasive subtrahend. The subconscious mind takes on lettering by conscious form. Uneasiness ensues. Reading such texts is like adding milk to aggravation. Nothing does justice to flight. Countless texts descend to flightless birds in an ordinary window. Nothing remains; alterity and risk are forgotten. The imagination fails to persist at this level. Transgression remains an exhausted mineral. Intervals are reduced to the pointless. The galactic is never discussed.

The question is asked. What are the free-standing claims which erupt into remote divine scale?

The question is asked. What are the free-standing claims which erupt into remote divinities?

Various metals in stars?

Unleashed hydroxyl?

Language is connected to these levels. And when one thinks of language one is not restricted to shapes and hooks on a page. For instance, Charles Ives and John Coltrane peering over the rim of the galaxy, absorbing the feral speech of eternity. For Ives, The Unanswered Question. For Coltrane, The Father, The Son and The Holy Ghost. Compositions not unrelated to Egyptian or Wolof or sounds from Sino-Tibetan. Again, the harmolodic as purity through sound. Sound waging war on negation. It dazzles the vapours. So, by dazzling the vapours art absorbs in the being and emits as an energy not unlike neutrinos. In this sense, emitted art is ghostly, which escapes the hylic personality by means of its evapourate trans-literal nautical enthrallment. So, in the deepest sense alchemical art becomes riveting annularity. There exists no corruption in time, no seasonal adage which inevitably turns over against itself. One leaves the zones of the diacritic. One escapes. One speaks from the unmarked.

This is a sensitivity not of withdrawal but of kinship with other factors. Factors which ignite the margins of the aura, which sparks a relay of light like an eruption of rays from a cinder. In this sense, the body is a cinder, art being intuitive amalgams of energy which no longer apply to the grounded portions in the psyche. And by grounded, what is meant are those terminal portions of thinking which have no inkling of the imagination and its conjunction with its absenting of the terminal. Or one can speak of the day-to-day as the fabulosity of the sterile, of the waning as the procreation condensed by the pressures of hylic frontality. At this higher sensitivity there can never be contained procreation tainted by Christian assignation as final and unbending assessment. The portion is exploded, openness extends.

The inductive as limit no longer figures. The arrogant enclosure as measure. The result being a crude contiguous vapour creating in the mind an albatross of motives. Energy approached in this manner tends to favour fractional imposition. Context weakens, the field distorts. Nature thus becomes subject to catalogue by calumny and disorder. The natural environment becomes subject to various exterminations according to particularly imposed balance. Resonance which flares from this or that species is altered or condemned according to this or that particular and the exigencies of the aforesaid particulars. Thus, the inductive being labours unduly always confronted by psychic malapropisms, so much so that fecundity through insight is never approached. It is the reduction of multiples from data, so that each dot on the line acts as unsavoury spectra. These spectra being entities which rise from the womb of punishing criteria. It is energy extrinsically policed, fueled by unbalanced critique. In consequence, life, which hisses in the shadows, elicits smouldering and anger, and is rationally condemned. It becomes in the end strategized dishonour, which results in a living amnesia seemingly unstruck by subconscious pressures.

But how can depth or confidence cohere within the mode of such thinking, rife as it is with regulation? It is the mind cauterized at the snow line, numbed, the cells then wrought by a paralytic obliqueness. The voice then issues from what can be called a clear but chattering schism. And so, general conversation rests upon such schism, upon the details which resist one's organicity, all the while plunging through dark and unwarranted regalia. Underneath these conversing quotidians exist whispered personification always signaling threat through isolation and disorder. Consensus is understood as being based on the tenebrous, on lurking confinement. Intelligence in this context remains enamoured of constrained possibility. In contradistinction there is the Kemetian view of the Self. First, the visible and invisible respond as balanced respiration. At next remove, the Sun as upholding the latter as immortal continuum. Scarabs, lions, vultures, bulls, spinning as immortal proportion. Life is instinctively understood through pan-irradiation with each of the parts giving life through universal palpitation. At this level of being there exists no sorcery or conflict because there exist levels within levels, states of being within states of being. Understood in this manner, nature contains no contiguous policy, no disappointment accrued by utopian abasement. Splendour then erupts through the complication of rising as initiation through danger.

One must not prejudge one's complication or take as substance a pre-christened motive which adulterates its prime velocity. Thus, one lives as unadorned without the claustrophobic as principle. Because at a certain level of knowledge the Sun extends itself in the system. Which is not unlike the frustrum of the pyramid in Kemet, studied through the sacred application of number. And these are not numbers mechanically confined to the frontalic but number as ventilated tissue brought down to chronic subliminal despair. One does not live to discuss stumbling predatory rumour, which under the true condition of breathing can never prevail. Pressure from old pollutions then continues to de-exist. Then an absence of theoretical codeine, then the flames from old dominance collapses, then thought filters through as vertical intuitive. Power then leaps through erratic charts, through strange umbilical sigils. The power of the cosmos opens and is no longer aimless. The cortical as subset then ceases. One is crowned with perfect speaking. One then leaves the room of archival ruin.

Then the elevated transpires, and one begins to wander the energy of second sight. A private ray issues forth, a matrix of riddles ensues. The body then a whirling of dunes and exploration. Therefore, all structural dissonance is abandoned. And this is the zone where the body exists above the body, which carries a suppleness energized by fire, by energy which travels by the loquaciousness of instinct. This is power which flowers in an undamaged field. A galaxy of life where the cells are cleansed and flow upward.

Here one reaches unprecedented beckoning, an alchemic criticality. One then convenes in the depths as an unerring savant, as energy which Western society has come to know only through figmental discussion. But what is being discussed is what experience in the invisible reaches. Exploration of ineffables weaving in and out of horizons. These are not the after lands where tied corpses escape. One could name it the zone of Divine Acceptance, where jasmine and nuance prevail. This is something different, something the Kemetians understood as the embryonic regions, as the first scale of release. For instance, no longer scale by oppressive speech, no longer futility by transgressive repression, but linkage to other auric syncopations, to transpersonal mystery, to splendour which weaves above traumatized in-reductives.

When the Western collective speaks of the body, it speaks of an entrained physical constriction without upper or lower dimension. Thus, the body is understood as kaleidoscopic ornament. The body given deepest regard through rancor and illness from the rest of the African continent. Life as torched or meandering consolation. Yet there remains the biology of a torched and challenging strangeness. A regressive state that even a crocodile would confuse with starvation. In contradistinction there is a medicine superior and unequal to energy, as simply viewed according to Imperial containment. According to the powers which thrive on replica by old usage, they fission due to thermal regalia, due to passionless tangling. In contradistinction there is the magnetism of powerful inner ritual, say, in the inner rituals of Wolof or Chokwe. The inner and outer states replete with simultaneous origin. And with the colours, the feathers, the beading, it induces a magnetic technical trance. Certainly, something the opposite of something configured through pointless additional scrawling.

Such acts inspire in one the art of flaming semaphores and riddles or grand orchestral ciphers played from ether charts ignited in the mountains. One thinks of notes or words as organic gestures, as trans-colloquial weight, as if one could float across crystal oceans near Java, or journey for kinesio-plankton floating near Jamaica. This is not the elaborate staged as omission nor as birth condoned by withdrawal. It remains a plunge towards interiors, to energy replete beyond exhibit. As for the public constitution these are internals which cannot be accommodated or ruled as adequate according to perceptual law. As if one could hear as an hierophantic mountain goat absent of residue or largesse. These are sounds from magic gale storm castles derived from unknown gulfs of experience. For instance, oneiric smouldering yellows, perhaps purplish Tibetan plateaus dispelling stricken conceptual fields. Therefore, one does not speak from a drained black garment rifling over damage contained in a folder which is not the folder of the heart, breathing like the dialectical beauty of orchids. The latter being the true variety of gain, the compost which wanders around salt. Which, of course, cannot fix percentage in the extrinsic by extracting a chronic discipline from a subsurface Prussian integument. This is beauty cleared of fixated radii.

This is escape from the studied medicine of implosion, of force gleaned from the mould of derivative intention. As for the mordant effigies sifted from exhausted debate there exists no time for the back and forth as witness trying to extoll the right leaning answer. It becomes a confusion which reeks of tension. It is habitation according to the mordant. Exchange as prior absence. With this prior absence being nothing more than a nonconforming stillness. Say, as a point of nonconforming, one takes elements from the Romani and vodou and Indian. The latter being understood as Pomo or Comanche. To the accomplished European these elements can be nothing more than mediumistic hovels full of blood and disciples working with myth. They say that it accomplishes nothing more than the violence of animals. So, if one claims that echoes burn, that roots gather from droplets and speak, they are led to believe that one has sided with wild mammals given over to aggressive in-audia and leakage. Yet, for one so inclined, this is merely the range of pure subsistence being the songs which issue from buried wine. One is then considered as being one who erupts from a group, who lurks, who casts spells, who weaves by means of circuitous ocular thread.

Maybe it is true that one refuses to wash flags or is cast in the role as an associate of cruelty. Maybe one is seen as one of the blessed of the Congo, accused of having broken bread with an army of killers. Or maybe one is seen as yield from sinister disservice, at best, singed by asymptotic brine.

So, does one remain on this plane simply to capture tensions or to exalt disharmony simply to demonstrate an abstracted brutality? Such would have to be answered in the negative. One could say to principal ownership, "look, my teeth are not scarred. I have never fomented weaponry, nor stood on a field of desecration, exhibiting to certain Gods bones of the sacrificed." Not that this is begging comfort from the ruthless or seeking exoneration by discomfort. Yet one must never speak through bleak or degraded discomfort. One must simply exhale and speak from the very bottom of one's body.

Because one lives amongst clerks of withdrawn declaratives, one is surrounded by artefacts of the accursed carking with uncleansed charisma. It is like pressure from the savage compression of bodies, conducting affairs through a series of collapsed registrations. It retards the volitional through the sentiment in conversational basics. As for crevasses, as for emotional methane recorded, consensus only concedes a pattern which fosters an operose living dimension. This is commitment to circumstance given to the blind by the blind. In the West, this is known as tradition, which seems to produce no more than a secular scansion of nerves. Because the self is broken into parts, fate is sown through astrological mirages which then linger as soot, which poisons the throat, staining the menses by way of the mind. These mirages become acceptable prohibitives as if they were axes ground down to disoriented order.

This is scale in the Northern lands where all things yield to microscopic dearth, to waste as lived distraction. Of course, these are lands which live by, say, robbing minerals from the Congo or by creating despair across American Indian zones or within the cholera plagued nerves of Haiti. As creative force in such a world one takes sides with the scavengers, with those whose poverty is soaked like roots, who every day face dual an universal ruination.

So, under such circumstances, how does the mind unleash? How does it orient and fuel and counsel its own enigmas? At one level there seems to be no outlet, no higher force which extends beyond reason. Yet the latter does exist in what the Dogon understand to be the foremost solar fuel. For them, it is the 6 systems of the Sirius complex and their understanding of Sirius B. The latter, they say, was once the Sun to the Earth and remains the most important star in the sky. Prone to ocular relay, the understanding persists that suns travel through suns, merged as inner dalliance which lingers. This could be called suffusional verticality flowing from Sirius through the Sun. Perhaps it is like listening to the whirring of hummingbird bells with aural form filtering light into the subconscious derma. And this is not an abstraction or perfidious imperatives fueled by distraction. The latter, understood in its objective dimension, is mathematics instinctively balanced by starlight.

And I mean by balance human relationality to light, to stars as they bring crops to full blown irritation, or to menses when they gestate and struggle. Of course, there are births at certain hours, divinations wrought both known and unknown. These are no mean efforts performed as they are within the aura of cosmic sensitivity. A sensitivity totally unlike the Shakespearean court ministerial, concerned only with the locality of the court and its concerns. Saying this, one does not promote some untoward telesthesia or some riddled and dubious kingdom of the mind as if one were some bottled grammarian speaking seasonless nigredo. One does not look back to past fractionations or to elements in Yoruban counting method as if speaking from some fixed or official expression. True, there is tragic speculation feeling the effects of excerpting oneself from consensus darkening misappropriated chasms. And, it is true, there should be nothing other than magnetization to crazed tenacities, to structureless acids creating numbers in one's mind extracted from alien forms from subconscious tables. Yet it is all the while understood that the conscious mind has status, that its discriminating factor has focus and can work as a calmed positional lightning, as a penetrant scope which lives over and beyond technique as a blinded raptor. Which can lead to a mural of the heavens, which goes back to states of mind which present technical proof cannot answer. This is when disappearances burn and perfectly withdraw from the measurement as crises. Of course, something other than stressful boundary, something other than sodium faithfully constructed by grammes.

So, when one speaks of the rise of sodium and fire, one speaks of the invisible powers which rise into the elements. These being fumes from the uncountable of sodium and fire always escaping themselves ascending according to impossible method. Both being identity extended by poetic aurality by the purest charisma of hearing. So, indeed, if one listens to the Sun inside its spirals, one comes to know power as internal regality as code for geometric invisibles. Because matter in this state works without resistance, is conjoined without decay, then whispers without principle as in decay through animality. This being paradigm through liquefaction, through eerie solar generality.

And one here speaks of a distance which is crushing and shows no signs of limit. Which in the deepest sense remains the trenchant field of osmosis. These being systems which no gravity can ponder. It is akin to signs of signs in Miró hovering in an electric blue infinity. So, when one contemplates such signs, one begins hearing through other formations of consciousness, through meta-fires in the depth of the cells. An other translucence which absorbs and evinces rays, which concur beyond any regional sensibility. The latter being the body as delimited spatial hive.

At another remove, such energy could translate into what could be described as an Imperial ghost ensemble. And then, at another remove, energy which morphs beyond the planetary confine. Which proves to be no more than incipient double levels being at once athletic nuance, sacred fractions, dialectical etherics. Which courts mathematical incipience in the liminal realm between the body and the beyond. The body in this state of transition commingles with refinements from eternity. The eyes then appearing through a moth window, through spinning underwater trees. Which are glyphs which ignite as blasphemous states, as untold foundations. Here, one speaks of chemistry which opens itself as simultaneous levels.

What is needed at this point is an idea which at first goes beyond its own condition by taking on life, which burns itself to such a degree that the limit commonly known as Sapiens Sapiens suddenly surpasses its graspable content, which cannot be palpably rendered by chronic angst or gravity. In its beginning stages such a body will be akin to a trembling porcelain inferno subject at times to upsets from the lower states. By means of this alembic dialectic one leaps the galaxy of objects which the pragmatist would scale as useless opinion. Even being post-Linde and with the implicit understanding of universe after universe, the reductionist mind opts for the fever of seclusion, staking plots of turf, owning a crooked pitched tent while attempting to extend a rational tonality. It seems the higher template is always threatened by fumes from dissolved rats, by subtractions empowered by paucity. True, one always listens to their armies hissing, to their sullen migratory spells seeking entry to the heart. Thus light becomes something other than wavering or battle by one-to-one engagement but by vanishment through the principle of circumstellar motion. At its upper reaches, polyatomic then, at its next remove, the undetermined, which by its very nature moves to the higher field where the in-melodious can never suggest its own extraction.

So, one burns, inchmeal by inchmeal, as an untraveled silicate in the vapours. True, there are states inside the Sun that conjoins one, that ignites through relay a swatch of suns, that absent themselves as parallel states of carbon. From this, utterance appears as suffusional synesthesia, which the Egyptians knew as rays transmitted from the glycerin of death. As if breathing from closed opal or self-structuring phantoms a hidden hematite heaven arises. The latter realia remain openings, humming points that single all the subsequent planes where a seeming singing scale evinces itself as seeping from a glossary of vacuums.

Resonance?

The post-fertility of phylums?

A simultaneity other than floating toxin circles?

This is alchemy cleansed of its own inscriptions, cleansed of any chaos or mystical suborder.

But the questions always arise, why is there being? Why is there something other than nothing? And this is not the tremblings from some bloodless grammarian fraught by pictorial embellishment.

Again, why is there being?

As for the body, one must search the flows of the ventricular where current boils, where ozone implicates the life force. One is then capable of peering through seeming indifference, which then conjoins with a range of optics where lakes begin to blaze with convivial voltage. Yet, to the skeptic it seems that one stares no farther than phosphenes, than vision as squared according to mundane inferentials. But since one is not bound by extrinsics or certain cajolings from the Earth, one becomes complete with absence as if charting whole mountains from Saturnian imaginal ranges.

Say one could line up events or cut rocks with miniature implements, one would still struggle, knowing events to be crumbling, contiguous, planned, balanced, isolate. Yet such containment eludes the total disruption that surrounds one. The most evident: misplaced populations, floods, threats, wars, volcanic attacks, feverish annihilations. These being understood as the commonplace of the era. A collective demoralization where human accumulation feels eaten by dread. A diary encouraged by ruined behaviour. Even major disciplines go astray. This is what the writer Schwaller de Lubicz called "research without illumination." Research always tainted at its base by mechanistic ascertainment. Which assumes that the human being is an "object," and that the "observable activities of a person are the critical dimensions of his being." That the individual is law. That consciousness is "identical with physical processes." Such leaven remains the constant vehicular poison, the critical yield by which intelligence is bred. Dimensionless and brutal it creates a pointless animal's yield. A vertiginous limitation which always utters to itself by crises. This being movement without movement, the mind and the body as waking dichotomy with spirit estranged to the realms of "superstitious" reasoning. Thus complexity is throttled and condemned to an interior mental leakage. There exists no "metaphor" or currency which extends through spiritual states. Clearly this is a case for leprous observation, for coded forensics.

What then of life vis-à-vis being?

Energy as invisible substantiation?

Insatiable locomotion?

Ignited omnipresence?

The above can be condoned by the *ba*, by primordial neuro-electricity which is the rise of the science of being. The "astral" or "etheric" body which produces emotion, called the "Khaba" or "Kabit" by the Egyptians. Then, for them, the intelligence called "akhu," with the rise of puberty called "Seb," and mental maturity called "Putah," and the "divine" which exists as "Atmu," which stands "for the presence of full creative powers." Then the crystallization of these powers into an eighth or transcendent scale, this being knowledge of the Self which survives the state called physical death. This initiates transfunction where the body is no longer trapped inside susurrating entropy. A measuring and delineation of states over and beyond the galaxies as they persist as minimum respiration. Which is something other than superterrestrial ozone or the distinction between phenomena and non-phenomena.

Perhaps a term can be coined: intuitive salvetics. Salvetics being code for alien annealment as salvation, understood in the body as instantaneous un-bearing. Therefore levels are illumined which seemingly cannot endure, which are aspects no Spartan tribulation can convey. As if the geriatrics of violence had collapsed on itself and fallen through electrocuted tundra. Thus, one becomes incapable of drafting from the emotive a chronic behavioural frenzy dazed by the general darkness in samsara. Thus the in-germinal slowly desists as well as the waving of mortal flags from a crag. And, of course, this is not the energy of borrowed doves wrought as infertile sigils. No, it is something other than old redress entangled as testimonials emptied at the very cusp of accusation. In this regard one is clarified possessing something other than fever which accrues from deluded captivation.

At living remove, these gifts circulate as anomalous encryptings in a hypnopompic palace. Then, at another living remove there emerges the vertiginous self where other forms of being begin to respirate with the formless. Which, again, is not energous rage working on assigned adventure, as stunned associational depth.

Because the human species seems threatened sailing on its blank collisional raft it can no longer persist in regressional seething as form. It must somehow be removed from the rotational as cladistic. Which becomes a proto-foray into the uranian blue, which is no longer fueled by an energy jaded with ghosts. Which is not an energy which scorches with answers harried by a central storm of retreat. This is a journey understood as having its origin on Earth at Lake Turkana (Omo River). And the understanding must be that the species has been forced to contend with insoluble riddles. Yet, by the incisive stature of such recognition, one comes to know life as something more than a charged locus akin to simple states of sporulation. One then becomes resonant with the scope of the simultaneous field floating as it is in the unanswerable. When saying this, one is not persisting in the 3,000 phyla which themselves are bound and shaped from the energies of deep and enigmatic time.

How strange it is to persist in argument with what seems to be a saturate moral given. To throw away the ladder formed by the pointless economics of Christ. Yet this is the case where one is no longer beholden to the separable, to a fount which issues from corrupted photinos. Which is not belief or wish constructed from abiding paranoia. It is the exercise of beginning to breathe so that a partial infinite is understood through a seminal relay of suns, which are signs which begin to focus the human field in a higher strength of burning electrical grammar.

Thus, the salt and fire of the body rises to a higher alchemic tremendum. The result being something other than the *a priori* as hypnotic, another expression which fields itself through an improvised osmosis.

Saturate with Refined Enigmas

LIVING AS A saturate listening disciple one absorbs knowledge as wealth through intuitive crystalline registers as an abiding absorption. But in contradistinction to this state one remains fraught with constant literal exposure to what can be called an anti-culture and its carking embranglements. A world where seminal texts are not read, where someone the stature of André Breton remains chronically unknown. So one asks, where are the minds with darting commas which breathe by imaginal respiration full of radiant constellations? In this regard, one thinks of insights and levels and zones of higher vertical enabling. Instead, one is surrounded by oscillating vipers gone blind, never implicit with sight through multiple carrying force.

So how can such delimit carry a verbally penetrant mind or enact compound crystal or magic? It seems always tasked to tear at a fragmented pile, at myopic lettering splayed by confusion. At times I may be asked to recall the tendentious stammering of say, Thales on water or Heraclitus on fire or Parmenides being of impossible location at birth. Perhaps, at times, a comment on Dostoyevsky or some partial figment from Nabokov or some incidental summoning from the written works of Van Gogh. But the darker spiral never ceases. A preeminent toxicity, if you will.

Let me say this, if the Coffin Texts now spiraled as example, it could possibly lead to human cellular clarification or maybe an indefatigable attempt at alchemic translocation. A higher human flaring where we re-emit the Sun into living. Perhaps these feelings could extend into organic connection with the manner by which the Sun darkens and rises, or how its solstices affect the magnetic ore of the human system. Then perhaps one could breathe in complete suspension. Respiration at such a level being electricity organically revealed.

The Egyptians called it the *ba*, and understood it as being "the invisible energy that runs through all visible functions." When understood from this level of depth locusts and wolves and the differing forms of bark are seen from the level of the benthic. This is why the Kemetic mind functioned as circularity, as riverine, as transfunctional discipline. But the tendency of present times seems open to nothing more than sample by rectilinear invasion. So it builds on functioning death crops, on dialogue according to slaughter. Health in the mind can then be no more than staggered; it can do nothing more than function as a gasping raven.

Escaping Mass Seduction

ONE MUST CONTINUE to evolve through the unclaimed resistance, tested as one is by the susurration from daily battle arcs. Every day there exists uncountable simulacra. Every day one walks into the glare of surrounding neutron fevers shadowed as they are by a state of imminence that looms as collective implosion which is nothing other than code for final nuclear activation. Parallel to this there is a complexity imploding stoked by full scale psychic repression. The human voice surrounded by these double general shadows as if one were a Scarlet Tanager reversed in the midst of its vocal peregrinations, as if the power of its song were slanted by pernicious occlusion with its special faculty of living spiraled towards obliqueness. Such obliqueness being nothing more than a temporary station plotted by the conspiratorial climate for erasure.

As Sapiens Sapiens one seems simultaneous with the Tanager with its vocal stresses demonized with its body's natural rhythm stunned by distractive cacophony. As if one were poised to drown in dense starvational sand surrounded by fate fueled by visible mockery. This present condition sired by exoteric construction with its continuing instigation approved by tenets sired by malefic sanction. This being the base condition which warps the basic majority of souls concerning their functioning psychological state. As if all activity were broken into pockets assuming the fundamental Ground as being fractured. This brokenness being the continuous fuel of basic civil imbalance where one is always personally shaken by a sense of chronic psychic uprooting. Thus, one survives as though partially blunted. Reaction is, of course, charted within a preplanned apotheosis. Which is nothing other than energy conceived in flames of corruptive disability. So Sapiens Sapiens being at one with the threatened Tanager seems more and more reduced to the kingdom of minor vespidae. As something lodged below ground, dissonant, carking, prone to perpetual inversion.

This being Sapiens Sapiens surmised as a loathsome sum gathered by chaotic inference. Say, if someone were granted license to lecture on the laws compelling moons to sink and burn, one would be placed at some non-sensical nadir of categorical psychology thus dis-recognizing the imagination as if it were a dying crow scorched when landing on branches of imaginatively exhausted blister trees. The imagination just spoken of being nothing other than the stray conception of a being operant as a disposable variant of the aforementioned vespidae or the hallucinatory aria of the crow. So the human state seen from my view as possessing the lessened state of wasp or crow sans momentum incapable of embodying tremorous sensitivity, unable to rise above the template of stridulation as decreed by the standards deployed by Imperial example.

According to this latter interpretation, there exists no gainful experience left to be had, only instinct which is considered by Imperial tactical negativity as séance empowered by recessive genetics. Since the imagination commandeers no sense of commodity, it is understood to inhabit no more than a maimed configuration. An ailing noise, an unwarranted kinetic. Or a series of dazed blisters promoting creatural insignificance. The imagination can say that it is something other than an adjudicated diamond or an orphan who smells hypnosis in his urine. In his heightened state, one could say that one glows as a receptive civet or as a mongoose understood as raw sienna. Because such a state carries no statistical tenor, it can never be valued by its absenting of itself or by nuance. And by absenting of itself it means absenting itself from habituated branding, say the birth date of the Christos, or one's vicarious behaviour at the beginning of Lent. It is a world unsanctioned according to measurable diagnostics. Thus, the imaginal conduit is castigated as being no more than a poisoned haddock or a flounder providing nothing other than the devolution of its waters.

Under these opprobrious conditions one must exercise as one's praxis interior flammability. One must enunciate mirages by testing the scope of their black originatory candles. Of course, this astonishes the social dishevelment with brews. Thus, one enumerates the uncanny by assaulting the rotten doors swinging between hands. Add to this one's hypnotically altered lingual signals which over and over provides a magnetic which is simultaneous with the farthest telescopic reception. Which is not unakin to the journalist who reconvenes facts, who at times configures a substantive political dossier. Facts at times electrify, yet then plunge and dissipate as causeless chronicles within themselves. This is said as such because one is thinking of interior generation, of the orientation of being. Of course, one does need to make protest concerning a hectare of murdered Indians or of the institutional mephitics advanced against biological Africa. According to certain elements in reportage such behaviour goes no deeper than the reprehensible mechanics of the capital economy.

But for the imagination another level of experience exists which lurks beyond the in-nautical. The in-nautical, meaning prose, containment, contiguous aspiration. What is meant here is the imagination of spirit which organically supersedes damaged lightning as property or strategic simulacra conditioned by Roman property as model. One can take, as example, Julius Caesar in Gaul. Destroy tribes, create treasonous tensions within the enemy, subject whole zones to immolation. Of course, this being action as fear through vociferous means. This being the psychology of the ruined who project ruin upon the ruined. It is like an equation that galls via the superficial extention of its grasp. Its principle, protect at all costs the right to hostility, holding onto the prize of gold and land, plundered at any cost by predacity.

But what of interior damage?

Of maimed consciousness?

Of heritage through mental distortion?

To the prosaic nature of the Occidental spirit the former remain ill-considered and remain inconsistent leading to tactical impairment. This is something other than repression by an army of scorpions because inner balance lingers and dissolves by commandeering psychological insult. Then the memory of the slaughtered ingests on unwarranted lingering. Say, for the African, labour in dazed tobacco fields whispers within one's cellular uncertainty as law according to distilled self-emity. Such is the environment of a ravenous psychological foundation fighting to gain its strength through transmixing one's immediate oneiric vitality according to European superimposition. This being the damage culled from a background of over 2,000 years of infliction according to institutional self-negation.

Now one faces a present circuitously ruled by such subconscious stanchions. Yet the code for self-healing one's spontaneous firmament must remain the exponential form of miraculous self-worth. One can no longer be dispelled by horizontal deletion. By technical aims, by the onslaught of the misguided popular incursion. One must remain internally feral. One must hold in one's feathers a glossary of teeth. Which is something other than a studied or cognitive circumstance, or only seeing one's silhouette inside a corporeal lean-to. This is where untamable resistance resides rising from a rebellious mariner's coffin as a psychic territorial scholar. But one does not stop there. One evolves, one develops. Perhaps a mix like a Buryat Shaman who ignites in a functioning parallel dimension or as a telepathic Tunisian polymath that converges himself with old Egyptian ether. Which is not as some materialist would think as energy spiraling, as corruptive exotica. No, this concerns freed and invisible matter without negatively imposed self-boundary. The latter being sans multiple conspiratorial adjectives derived from the air of a commandeering psychological environment incapable of transmuting surcease, the latter being a parallel suborder that respires never as a transpicuous entity, that flows as a nomos through higher uranian doors but as a blaze that modern Romans are unable to touch.

So, the Empire in these hours is a curiously famished Carcharodon, living more and more off the conceptual stores. One can say that it lives off the ghosts of its former feeding minerals as absolute insult to its former body as self-projected magnificence. Being now revengeful without meaningful items to attack, its life seems fallen into absentia sans paradigm, reduced to paraphrase, to greater and greater minutia through technology. Hypnotic screens, facile communiques, episodic particles as voice.

So, it is asked, what of the oneiric lightning palace?

What of the factors that shifted to form Gondwanaland?

It could be said that this is sub-announced diametrical usage or enunciation alien as prevailing ethane on Saturn. Perhaps a dazzling or aleatoric calumny or a transpositional hiatus meant to enkindle erroneous language.

Perhaps it could self-describe itself as a dissected Auk in the belly of demons. Or as a telepathic stray being as voiceless form floating as alien projections floating from Mount Meru. Or possibly an herbivorous lioness maintaining suggestibility as a blur lost inside the power of disappearing forests.

So how can the Empire as Carcharodon announce itself through transpicuous blurs? How can it now suggest itself as an auto-cannibalic? its gnoseology corresponds to its ravenous remains, to its spectrographic scrawling. It is like carbon that now vanishes without extrinsic definition through mystique buoyed by its former purpose. It knows no beauty of its former perception, no surreptitious resonance where its bodiless inference is brought to bear. Its curious reflexive condition seeks a re-inhabitation of the spirit of the Ichneumon. An energy treacherously feral. Which means it practices a hellish shadow art sculpted by in-crystalline derogations.

Perhaps it should know that the Sun has strategically shifted, that its sudden auroras have defied its power to regale the mind with illusion. Yet what is now spreading like fire in the populace seems something akin to collective dementia. This is where what's called one's mother-wit regales itself with less than ceremonial entrances into splendour, where oppositional registration transmutes to invasive lexical registration. Which is the creation of its coming meta-astrological chart, the latter conducting as its principal knowledge solely contained within public secular agenda. At present a uselessness prevails that campaigns, and celebrations and celebrities as special exhibit carry little semination or voltage. So that which presently transpires between the Empire and its zodiac no longer registers with efficiency. And here reference is not made to a professional reader of signs but to the intuitives of the poet who instantly understands inconsistency as it arises. Witness this particular zodiac where the carving of Capricorn is transposed with the charisma of the solar lion, so that nothing but a general scrambling governs. Within these remains all its motifs become alienated exacerbations. Yet what could have once been deciphered as decisive enervation no longer pontificates itself as marker, as crumbling salvo or verdict. Decline seems always wrought by ambiguity, by skills condoned as general malaise. An arsenal eroded, yes, but to what end?

One must leap levels. One must make forays like the mathematician Cantor into subparticulates of infinity. So, the questions can be asked. What of compressed suns in the Sombrero galaxy? What of the parsecs that go beyond themselves and are no longer countable? These questions rise up from a seemingly unimaginable point of view that is presently culled from partial demonstration. And what is partial demonstration? These are realia that suggest the dwarfing of Sapiens Sapiens. In this sense how can modern enclaves tower, or secular leaders of nations be of lasting impression, or carry power through gravitized alchemical relations? They are conduits which no longer carry radiance or dimension. What becomes most noted in the present context is the importance given to personal issues, to general emotional chatter. Such is life in the majority of the Occident, magnetized as it is by superficial relations with itself. And these relations call for descent into greater and greater monotony. So, to this lesser mind, larger forces cease to exist. And being committed to lesser relation to itself it carries less and less power to resist seduction to endemic decline. There is always the looking outside of itself for corroborated study, which in turn is none other than a superficial given. Under this circumstance there can be no assessment of depth, no virtue in returning from findings one has gained when returning from the invisible. Thus persons become trapped in their own assumptive fever. Everything becomes shapeless and repeatable and shapeless once again. The experience of migration through transparency is negated. Therefore, the finer sensitivities are impeded. Instead, there is the tangent that is general gossip; rumours spread by cousin against cousin; a morass of genders in competition. The latter being swarm according to transactional surroundings. And what erupts from these immediate surroundings is liquidation of acuity. Discourse brings reduced tense to tense behavioural repartee. So when one takes leave of this consuming plane, one engages relief by rising a step or two into psychological mid-air. All previous agreements in this context seem irrevocably breached. One is then no longer illumined as a person in good standing.

As for allegiance to the mediocre, to quotidian calibration, one absconds into transitional invisibility, into charismatic flux, into the risk that is interior jubilation. Always accused by the advertisers' model of carrying blinded ink in one's genes one is thus voided and imprinted with the neo-impression of always grappling with alienating dysphonia. Which further accrues into commencement of stark interior struggle with collective hallucination, these being energies that erupt from the collective secular dais that I understand to be action that enkindles itself through extrinsic disservice. The latter being a dazed optical plenum, a force always confused with paradoxical self-punishment.

Within such insidious scripting one must always retain the blistering view, which casts from its glance a sidelong vapour via alchemic penetration which by its nature eliminates superimposed function, which both condemns and reprieves the understanding that persists according to that which seems subconsciously mandated. Because whatever may be the torrid or objective explanation, imposition by its very nature can do nothing other than to conduct itself as obstruction. The milder form of obstruction transmits delay, always scaling daily issues through in-vitrescent ordination condoning that what carries consensus effect. Pervasive conversation is always saturate with haunted phenomena, with quantitative invasives. Quantity, being akin to seductive neon, creating in the mind cacophonous distraction through blinding orchestration. So, by creating variation upon variation from the principal phenomena, the mind is shifted into a course of untenable filigree so that details are sullenly extended and varied into horizontal nuclei. One could say that within this weaving are offshoots from string theory, monitored stocks, Satanism, beverage consumption, variations on the essence of God. One can call all the former monitored subsumptions being mingled dust separated from the instincts. This marks the galling resistance that has invaded the general psychic bearing. This naturally simulates the property of prayer beneath a night beating down on the mind with occlusionistic rays. The result being doubt crystallized by lack evolved by teeming secular intelligence rendered by means of iconic devastation. Thus wisdom is shunned and coded as metal and straw. Which makes humans who ascribe to such practices the equivalent of proverbial beasts. In this latter sense, they are subconsciously reminded to remain self-hounded, stung by their own vitality. This is what can be called spontaneous academia by implosion, by unsustainable psychic shading, that takes on grammes and numbers by grammes as if a spate of integers could justify the weight of an overextended body. And this results in the terminal abstraction as structure.

So, what is structure? Drafts of money? Owned trivia as property? One could say yes, both are central to the structure. Which extends to what Artaud once referred to as the piling up of bodies. And these bodies are exterior scatterings always equated with bearing the cost of the general good. This being a social complex that clings to deaf and piacular agreement. There is nothing but a monochromatic litmus suffused with circuitous terror. So, the average being secured under these auspices remains hellish, injured by notches of subconscious lightning having fallen into private or differing versions of this aforementioned hell. Beings are then locked in the throes of their own tragic burial calendars perched upon an extrinsic bodily abyss. Because all forms of the irregular have been systematically lessened and hauled up for elimination. Be they Arawaks or Haitians or Afghanis, or other nonspeaking flora or fauna—like African limbs hacked off by the Dutch in the midst of the slave trade in order to maim the spirit of captured maroons.

This remains the underlying spirit of the age that plunders in search of its universal Cibola. Which is a spirit felicitous with robbery and murder, with disfavourable morality. I call this anti-claritas, meddlesome psychic fornication, tainted seismic activity by cinder. These atrocities remaining conversant with transactional context so much so that stretches of time seem in-conversant with what is taken to be relevant. Rewards accrue from this non-translatable venom. Lucre, positions of power, voluptuous unstable women remain spontaneous rewards and are seen to be gains for those who serve as corporate ministers of death being servants bound to a form of pre-planned history that carves an accepted symmetry from blood dwelling in the depths of an increasing blindness. I call this quintessential blood farming being a fissioning or pertinent quantity violently addressed.

This being the general aim of the Northern societies, as it leaves indigenous citizenry in the main ¾ hampered, livid with psychic arthritics. On the other hand, there can exist for the spirit other breathing formations. Other translatable prairies of cyanoethylene, breathing other unblemished hydroxyl spores. Which seems to the old Roman critics to be of impossible expression carrying in its wake an ominous utopian bearing. The poet of being is thus declared as a carking or anonymous monster decreeing something that cannot be expressed by notions of delimited evil. So one is targeted by these critics, by their unprincipled cascades, by their droplets of poison placed upon the palate of the public at large. Which leads to dark electrical auras, the public mind then moving as a tornadic lateral hamlet. Provincial, stagnant, always giving themselves the status of significance that replaces technical achievement according to quantity.

 At poetic height energy transmutes nervous strain; what follows becomes elliptical trance, then transgressive possession. Not an ethereal jurisprudence nor a scale that yields the paradox by grounded balance. Again, the latter bring something other than scrambling or apparent dissonance that issues itself as alchemic fatigue therefore balance is understood to be nothing related to academic function, to trends that ramble as new example. One can speak of this state of mind as spiritual monography where the individual rises from a personal riddle to reach transpersonal indicative. A direction, an index that changes course and naturally spirals. Thus a state of trance follows that allows one to survive exteriorized threat or scandal without intrinsic remorse, without regressive erosion of lingual impulse or body. Because the poet insists on beatific triggering planes, on metamorphic instigation subsumed by anonymous welters. Again everything burns and subsists as power that roves beyond pragmatic skeletal capacity. Which is ether being emblem through and beyond the eighth chakra of breathing. As for forges, as for needles in hiding, they succeed according to ancillary script of conventional lingual stimulation being other than at the level of pragmatic to pontifical suture. At times they induce momentum in this sense being akin to physical healing via the listening by bell to that which transcends per capita disappearance. There being no such thing as rectilinear independence or separate occlusive rendering singed as it is by pragmatic inversional pattern. The latter experience equates with assaultive mirage against that which is truly hidden. So, if one reaches for the telepathic or signals the force which opens the tornadic, it reeks of the unexpected and creates from its seduction secrets which cause one's human energy to secrete and spiral, and resurrect, and recombine, and exchange forces with surcease so that new opening can be established at the cusp between eternity and cognition that exists as the waking body. In other words, lingual subsistence disappears as limit to one's vocabulary, as footnotes begin to mingle within the fire from higher regions of experience. Thus there is no siphoning, no reductive litter, coded and given over to a suspect regalia that occludes transformative consciousness.

Short of this, one has not failed, one has not given over to notable anxiety. Because one carries translatable interaction, it is not unlike a threaded incitement, a quaking ingredient. Again, such understanding invokes higher lingual possibility as translatable plane, as functioning habitat etched by teeming with parallel meta-personas. The latter being an exponential world view, a development along the way to a new and higher structure of instants that produces neither wealth nor mechanical reward.

Having abandoned the essence of Occidental disciplines as sufficient outcomes in themselves produces seeming absurdity to conventional wisdom thought to be nothing other than a welter of riddles expressing personal privacy through meaningless metrical weight. Yet within the praxis of higher abandonment one transmutes assumptive distortion. And to be clear, physical gold does not benefit the spender after death. Which reveals the short-term arrogance and pointless stifling of pragmatic tacticians. They who seek to rule complexity by brazen micro-tectonics so that space and time work according to extrinsic hypnotics. The latter claims only its futurity by matter, by extended transposition via differing human endeavours, from travel in space to seemingly infinite psychological postings. Thus, the individual is surrounded by quotidian appearance, by curvatures according to mechanistic punctuation as if the body itself had no other experience than subsuming itemization. This can be simplified by calling it poisoned ozone training, this being nothing other than toxic mental serum that seems to etch flow as it crosses the continents. Yet the imagination flies above these crossings, these reductive argumentations, above their pythonistic entanglements. Written works at the level of revelational volation sometimes speaks in the code of ectopic cipher or empirical revelation, or as Navamsas that speak in braille. These remain invisible lingual lanterns that swing as feral combining. So, one is never exhausted due to nebular abstraction or overweening paradigms explicit with accessible exposure. One escapes, one wafts, one separates. One takes on the combat that is absence.

Magnification then hovers within one's solar force at times seemingly splintering then recombining after turbulence. This is a magnification by Richter which concentrates power at such a level that one is able to call out either lions or demons transmuting their fates via imaginal demeanour. As if they were seen leaping from rotational buttes then floating as higher suspension. The mind then fuses with these upper ranges, understanding that these energies are transmitting themselves as galactic drift communing with levels unannounced according to expectation, I am speaking of arcs and measures that rotate as spiritual camouflage. This never self-protects as iterative model or promotes a false or in-syllabic immolation. One does not foment at this level electric immobility or a tornadic principle bound to self-scrutiny. The latter is where energy fails and populates itself through feckless or popular re-engenderment. According to this sense one does not seem to sufficiently exist because the personality holds itself in curious abeyance all the while being able to thrive with flexibility in an euphotic state. Which is degrees higher than animal exuviation as the bodies' energies transmute to holographic illumination. And this illumination being séance soaked in spells being a state which surpasses carnivorous opacity. The latter being at a plane higher than dialectical opposition inhabiting realia of transparent lightning and diamonds. This being principle visible manifestation when transmuted scale reveals itself as non-linear radiance. There being no absolutes to existing, to parallel re-structural havens, to rote or confessional ellipsis. Which of course leaks beyond the furnace of the palpable uncontained by the caliginous as alloy. Which is akin to the purity of indifferent mountain chains.

Therefore portions rise and meander and fluctuate and gather from the poise of their own example.

Say spittle hung like lamps of flying vampire mammals one could scatter them as a form of looping light so as to announce illusive embodiment. Therefore one is never localized as bodily abstraction deranged by determinative counting. Language can account for elliptical bodily presence beneath the vampire lamps. So elegance is understood as wafting above an isolate balance. Thus strangeness becomes organically structured with its equilibria sustained as organic voltage. And since this is not just a note that increases itself through poetic devastation, it allows a new and intangible morality to transpire. It allows the aforementioned suspension to mark and exponentiate itself throughout the source of its central meaning. And this central meaning evolves as dissonance through clarity brought into play by a form of paradoxical neutrality. Because there are days when neutrality reigns, when oceans dissolve beneath the mind and then appear as writing through unplotted ciphers which quickly scatter any confining mental issue. Sleep then blazes with liberty, with strange oneiric mixings. For instance, perhaps an operatic refuge is defined by a mixture of strange Giacometti-esque beasts moving in irregular circles coping with elliptical arias. Coping in strange, translated Swiss somehow inexpressive of danger. Their voices like remedial caroms staggering off the sides of the stage homologous with an indigent zoology. This being sound barely surviving, so much so that the illegible begins breathing as one's audition begins to heighten through intangible mystical animation. And it is this mystical animation which begins brewing, which curiously begins to cultivate a quaking purity by oneiric monsoon. So that the laws of rational notation have no further relevance.

The aforesaid being a dust that moves, that extends to portions, across a series of intensities. Which extends back to heightened mystical animation. Cycles then spiral into obscure advancement as if one saw in the heavens a useless and smouldering structure. Which leads to an aural calligraphy as revelation beyond blankness.

So matter at this level no longer blazes as fictitious current. It is not that one exchanges reality or creates a pauperization of the psyche. The physical understand themselves to be substance able to transmute themselves beyond gravity so that one dispenses with common perception. One no longer carries stake in the matter as regards one's genetic embodiment. The body is not reduced to claimed land, to observable protestation. The body becomes other. Not political contestation or militaristic rejoinder nor brackish recrimination and slaughter. The body then exists as alchemical range as no longer in service to the routine order of the State. The counting devices lose their merit in projecting movement concerning the sidereal personality. Thus the body is no longer key to firmly wrought regression.

The body is removed from objective simulacra, from debatable embroilment, from assaultive procedure. Nor on the other hand is it compelled by elitist inscrutables. It abjures the referential bulletin, never magnetized to critique which rises from lower embellishment as mind. Then it no longer responds to terror or charts. As to common asservation it becomes dissonant subjunction, which enacts for the listener the sound of scorching bread. One's action then takes on drift floating through a mass of cryptic tenuosity. A tenuousness which spills into utopian disservice. One then addresses those "right minded" beings ensconced within daily assumption; they who enter a stable set of doors, searching for a subsequent chair at a table. One can acidly tell them that it is no longer 1919 and their fates no longer are controlled by British intelligentsia. All their actions being British, patriotically take up the stance of falling paralysis cinders breathing by misinformed myopia. Now they need to be told of their irrelevance, of their moribund regulation. Let them know that they are subsets of the scurrilous who impart their findings according to greater and greater decrease, charting for themselves signs of collective disappearance.

By study according to igniferous impact, one views referential despair as it erupts from the anti-sidereal mind of the culture at-large. In such a climate one needs to lift one's voice so that it casts a spell according to courageous teaching. Not captured by terms such as sacrilegious impact or waterborne inferentials. One understands that what is culturally considered to be mature and of lasting impact is nothing more than restive juvenalia. This gives rise to necrotic stereotypics, to subjunctive irradiation that fails to exorcise their limitations instilled by means of self-engendered cultural arrogance. This being the accepted scale of lingual value within which the seemingly dominant culture operates as it attempts through abstract methodology to be precise down to the very centimes of breathing. A breath seemingly operant in the depths of atomic causality seemingly rife as regards numeric infernos. Yet this is not living, seeking life as it anaemically persists according to an oblique and alien doubling.

Such attempts seem subjected to mortal glances, to definitives fraught with carking infernos. So that latter struggle with themselves is by no means of an impetuous lottery as draft minerals culled from exhausted foment. Because they cannot lean on solar forms for ministration, they remain alien to a populace sculpted from principles of matter and illusion. The latter remaining at bottom a predictable alienation the populace is issued from cowardly threat. The above emended while being circuitously modified by circumstantial hesitation. One clashes with these graceless cognomens, with these brazen genes that can never conceive consciousness as non-inherence, as something beyond preconceived limit.

Yet one must remain wary like a ghost cub flitting in and out of the mother's den. Therefore, one must build strength out of fever extracting nourishment from surrounding psychic plague igniting bulletins of guano so that they seem as interior flames darting across absence. The latter observation remaining flames that seem to chatter as insight and nourishment, flames that seem to soak up the craft of distance projected as singular unification by spinning.

As impeccable dyslalia? As craft through dissertation as irony? Neither. One burns by distillation, by revolt as interminable frenzy turned inward. One knows the alone through the alone. At the surface with the mother vanished the siblings frayed or disappeared one's reputation as subset of disgrace, it matters not, even if one wanders like a lion across spiritual insomnia. One becomes the alchemic figure in the process of conveying a portfolio of monsters. One's hide then shifts through stillness after stillness without seeming resistance or detection. Because being spins there can be no ultimate in-arrangement. No crucial or stricken solar derangement, because there exists no contiguous stratification, no necropolis as symbol eternally divided, hive after hive after hive. So, since magnetism strays and reassembles, there can be no other understanding than that higher being ignites through pullulation, through unseen ripening that equates in the heavens as re-explosive scale. This being the power which flows as human nuclear current, which to the utilitarian mind amounts to nothing more than immaculate distraction.

At this level of current, one extracts oneself from old dharmas, of hidden micro-aspiration, they being of nullified grammar fallen short of its deepest investigations. The latter being emission at other ranges. Yet, because experience is never absolute, it turns around on itself in stages, and is never subject to a practiced sedentary counting. It never craves a state of sedation and relapse where there appears sudden micro-analysis and inability to change. Of course, the latter reacts against the prophecy of being against its spirit which erupts beyond the regional. That said, one must listen to one's micro-path, to one's energy that extends through the substance of particulars. When rains burn, when midnights roar, one is always watching and listening to motion as it goes beyond its appointed designation. This being consciousness which needs not prove itself to the strict sensorium in order to defend itself against negation. One's energy remains heightened by anomalous supra-intangibles that fail to show proof within laws that are sanctioned by observable merit. According to these laws, human ciphers cannot exist. They cannot be assembled by security of reason. In no way is this understatement, with the general view always brokered by graspable rote, by terminal diacritics. To this view, nothing is enriched by encipherment or by the implicated code through assimilation. By this view of totality, the implicated is never coded. According to this view, thought should be spoken through a reduced empirical glottis, through finite sending ores. Thus, ideas should be no more than contested polarizations. A world view enamoured of assault and reduction. And when discussing worlds like God or the heavens, such subjects are always beguiled by a rhetoric which spawns containment. Thus, the Pantocrator, or Dark Energy, as fragment, as something to be understood and decided by reduction. There is never thought influenced by entirety because any option on this plane is thought to generate nothing more than false electrical charisma, nothing more than the clone of opinion. Yet, at a deeper stratum, one can see that the material view is an assumed realia, is a base allegorical rigidity which contains no enduring power.

What are options?

Mythologies springing from twin green suns shining over Saturn?

Erasures within oblate valleys on Ceres?

Or further, or further still, a hurricane of haflons appearing and disappearing in and out of uncountable dimensions?

Perhaps the latter could work as triggering ideals, as fecund optional glints, so as to listen to life as it soars outside of fearful animal resistance. This being the deeper strata, the imagination as it sprints through and beyond blackness. This blackness being the unknown horizon where human simulacra can no longer be explored. In this state, the figmentational psyche is abandoned leaving a colloquy of Richters in its wake. This being the exponential nature of the Ground, of history abandoned riding experimental waves into untested sound. Which brings to mind principal elements in Moorish Granada or old Egyptian kindling schools or Hopi maturation via the stars. Examples abound of the body and its bodiless connection on other planes. What one can say is that the Occident has wrought an error prone turning with some of its best minds soured by a blinding stationary rebus. The latter so inclined remain a study in self-dividedness always condensing an opaque union with itself. And this policy seems as endless tautological squall. In consequence there is always a crisis over land and items, over discussions broached by disruptive military yield. Of course, the standardized curricula as regards negotiated blood spill or foreknowledge of alien terrain and its bodies vis-à-vis conquering and the overcoming of seeming riddle. The latter are not limericks according to fanciful projection playing with the metrics of the useless. It simply means the casting of the elemental into the moribund. Again, the central locus of the times is blindness as frozen stationary rays.

Blindness being the inevitable sample, the un-ascendant hand. Pessimism being the mean response, the central generating symbol. As for bucolic fenestration, the view becomes drawn, abstract, an absolute refutation of medicinal calm and beauty. Which amounts to an *a priori* habitation. Which amounts to condoned dissonance. In this circumstance flexity de-exists. So the general mind can never allow itself to explore inarguable range. Range being understood as that which explores its own absence, knowing its understanding to be capable of experience across parallel wastes and voids thereby feeling a distant summary of itself.

So, as part of one's quantum persona, one could call oneself poetic practitioner of the occult, linking one's internal weather to four private suns. And these suns open themselves above random canals bringing to water inscrutable genetics which magically build and vanish. And in the building of this water there is the flashing of ignited pepper trees, of scarlet ligneous apparitions. Sometimes the wood flashes blue or turns purple as would a paradoxical lightning pole. One can call these signs impalpable flares that pre-exist. This is light being squared by phantom technical sands. Evolving in themselves being salt which burns and spins in itself as organic carbon distillation raised to their own nths. This is the mind furtively kindled by hieroglyphical gestation. This process being nothing other than an evolving level of witness. Which is ferment according to intangible seeds as irritation.

So, what do these seeds and irritations refer to?

Hope vis-à-vis inconscient solar distance?

Or is it morale suddenly shaped by perfected infection?

One must respond by making up thought from a kind of witness rampant in Andromeda. Or do such beings exist, who cohere on the other side of the Sombrero Galaxy thereby understanding one's view as being clarified by the uncanny, so that integers are splayed and take up the tone of parsecs, simultaneously moving to higher destinal concern?

Perhaps invisible numeration could be considered?

Perhaps they could be considered as anti-entropic gain through counting?

Perhaps variants on Mayan or Chinese numeration?

Perhaps Egyptian mathematics in "the volume of the cylinder?"

Thus, one illumines the dark with variations on energy. This being an energy that restores itself through incoming enigmas. Not something conducted through tense precautionary order but a meteoritic climate never subjected to darkened critical amendments. Therefore the focus is totalic, riverine, totally dissimilar to transposition. This being something other than activation of dilemmas, something other than unsettlement pulled as they are towards the Saturnic, towards the condition of collective injury. Thus the Earth and the Sun no longer are stranded on a dying spur in the anonymous typography of space. Thus, one instigates light beyond the moat that is the tenebrous light then conjuncts beyond starvation and terror. Thus the moon is released and brings on light beyond biographical relief that distills and overcomes the very notion of Armageddon. Of course, threat will pursue itself according to the tenets of nonrecognition. An utopia? A prismatic ocean palace?

So does the holocaust vanish? Does its supreme result of fissioning turn into doves and crystal hamlets?

One can never assent to naïveté or to bucolics de-extended into falsified subjection. Never. One must decrease one's display by phantom enactment, by holding in one's view a series of doubled intangible Navamshas. And these are not dioxides or forms they elicit as disserviceable strontium. Instead there are zones to be announced as poetic chambers, as incalculable clauses that both hold and trespass sonar. Such a world exists over and beyond peril, over and beyond waste which consumes itself by burdensome simulacra. At poetic height one cannot colonize grammar and imprison its setting within monochromatic routine. The imagination has no need to bleed itself in front of a jury of peers, to speak by means of repetitive simulacra. There can never again be the matter-of-fact world with its hoarse omnivorous standards, with its forts of law, with its mechanical imposition. The latter being nothing more than aimless agendas that culminate as modern staff reports.

What keeps one rising is the ceaseless, is the fricative glare that overcomes the force of analytical transposure. Because of such rising, one is never aligned to a commercialized populace rife as it is with institutional motion as flaw. Yet at the same time one does not invoke elitist constriction. It is the conventional forces which need elimination. All thetic variants seem to hinge on colloquial variation. Let me take the knights and the queens of the chessboard with its seeming riddles, with its domain of inverted servants which has nothing to do with inner regality. Thus the imagination is like a moon that explores its own darkness listening to its poles, to its mysterious forms as something other than carbon. The Earth in this light becomes nothing more than an inclement schism. A vacated marker, an occluded suborder. And this occluded suborder is compounded residue where the Sun fails to shine as recreated mystification. Finally one can say that the population seems fixed, always reflecting on uninhabitable poison. So something else is needed other than autonomous consensus. Other than prone or inbred paranoia.

Poise is then no longer linked to listless arcana. It then rises in one's form as snow-enriched twilight, as meteoritic nuance. This results in energies that reach the inconceivable where former momentums are laid to rest. Yet one cannot say that one has reached in one's visage the one explosive charisma, the salient strategy which subequals law. In this sense, one does not ruminate on forms of botany and nitrogen or extrinsic physical brightness. The outer body must be left so that the ghosts explore through navigational dissection. So that a contra-possession transpires as if one lifted the stride of a crippled spider. Which is rampant de-location, which is the inside-out of gullible distension. One then begins to reek of mirrors having an interminable penchant for scorching which induces an alchemic reddening. One then leaps the law of plural terminus, once called by the masses the limit of the three dimensions. So, there can never be decrease employed by the enervated sundial or from Richters that open onto panic. What is shuttered, closed, or established vanishes much like a boat swallowed by open water.

One is not a journalist who plays with factual rebus making, celebrating scraps, making do with algebraic sound transmissions. As if the details could expose basic inner elevation or signal the depths in restless solar ravines. Algebra at this stage existing at this level as horizontal indifference, as determinate input on the tangible plane. And what is so curious about such tangibility is that at this time in its odyssey it is able to grasp the sinking molecule and make adjustments for its width and its depth even with the latter engulfed in subatomic dissolution. Where even the muons, and the muon's neutrino, are tracked. And even when kaons or pions flutter, it is stuttering through the wavelength of grasping. Therefore energy can never release itself from dogmatic retention. It then functions as a code for simplified transmutation. So assassins who plot their codes exist via regressive aeronautics. All exploration is then lowered to the stark respirational level yet presented through the form of intellectual exhibit. This being matter in a free burning posture, yet unable to go beyond itself as matter. In this context the imagination senses the muon as nothing more than an entrapping time, as nothing more than a state-sponsored item. And one does not say this to simply amplify dread or amplify oneself through hubristic reproach. No, one does not engage in the system of theatrics telling oneself that insight has been structured through embranglement due to hidden proto-Buddhistic annealment as a realm deserted by its own possession. Simply put, it is a blank state, an overall view, a telepathic transmission. Such is the ambrosial dimension which wanders in and beyond the Sun.

One then is not condemned to specific fuels and chromas. Not immured in copal, or stain, or gouache postured in the cinereous, or in raw umber, or in royal red, or Mikado yellow, or Mittler's green. Fixation in this higher state can never disclose itself or tumble into view as a functioning arsenic body.

According to the Palmaryans, the Sun is a great feminine wheel which composes rivers and moons and flows as a true in-cautionary flank. It is alive as pure inalienable diamond that spills across its brink and arrives at the summa of suggestive ideals. It is like watching the sky from an alchemic cinnamon tree. One then arrives at uranian alterity, at emissions which gather in the body as fumes, as Scottish mist, as mystical lixiviation. This being imminence at the weightless brink, at navigational electrics. Then setting psychic sail through lenticular skies. Then the apparitions across the eye blaze like unstilled progeny in the spirit. Aboriginal aurum, transmorphic nectar. The body as physical fleece then lives through transparent accretal. To the naked eye, one no longer exists through consensus examining through anthropomorphic taint. It is like trying to witness planetary scale at the incipience of the Oort dimension, which does not imply scope as contiguous finality. Such invisibles scorch as if emerged from a cryptic lepton family. As for rational tracery at this level, none can exist. As for its description, one cannot be sculpted by letterable measure as if caught in the path of a stampeding gryphon.

One can call the above indigenous morality never posing one's wares through perceptual piety. No, not a sermonically driven travel around a port of cataracts preaching heavenly scintillation as example, as fractious turning amidst grains one is never prone to clear the cloudy particle or feign miraculous activity, never once taking on the feral implications that kindles liberty. One could just as well be an insect farmer transmuting ineloquent locales. Abjuring these lower degrees, one takes an implosive training so as to mingle with sub-electrical winds which then yield to the tendencies that always travel beyond the Sun.

One is then neither lunar nor diurnal. One simply expresses a state. This being a condition from the dogmatic thesis that God is contained in unicellular form. This being the purest alchemical seepage, the elucidated light, the phantasmic eye that supersedes its patterns. This is rising up the rays which fall on water becoming in essence an untoward fertility, which both expands and gathers from surrounding dimensions. Not only the past and future as described by linear explanation but those realia which have been deemed by the diurnal illusive, unsubstantial, vague. Not a cognizant topology project nor an era with psychic regions but a grammar that understands its roots of circulation as space. This is a grammar outside of laws or rulings, outside of the duplicitous political urge, which posits power through rulings deeming themselves the nexus of just events. And these events hypnotize the general show of hands with a series of stunned placebos. This leads to predicted shifts in the voting body understood through the stratagem of operational displacement. Therefore, a demographics which functions under the seeming threat of life and death.

Concerning political salvos, nothing applies. And the non-applications refer to the general run of planetary rulers. None of them hark back to rotation, to the cycling of blood which the galaxies explore. How can such an aegis sustain itself in the face of Dogon calendrics, or in the eyes of a Buryat shaman speaking of the higher facets in unencumbered day myths? How can the political part be sanctioned in the face of the heavens that evince the unending?

Now the opportunity presents itself, concerning a new profound perplexity. The spiritual Sun has shifted and released through these shifting transmuted carbons. This is not to be confused with carbon as a stationary element as soiling the lungs as petrified emission but as fumes that swirl from crushed diamonds. The latter carrying the velocity of inscrutable Passeriformes. Unlike the forensic, or debilitated archive, there are tendencies which supersede the feral, which react as unvanquished stealth. This being an energy which persists as structural anomaly, as a vertigo from imploded lion cults. As for surface appearance, there is scrambled manganese, choreographic stratification, accessible to the contiguous personality. As for carbo-electric bacteria, there are shapes that signal by code as though summoned from phonemic choreography. One is then replete with repetitive seismicity, with mantric numericals carrying sound prints as explosive neology. One then spins and gathers in this spinning language as exponential gargantua. Which emits to the world photonic crystallizations.

This being blizzard as combinement as wanton verbal surge as concretive annealment in situ. This being something other than language as tangible asset as something ordered due to scientific element. The ear then condones itself through retinal intuitives, through voices heard by means of an ophthalmic listening post. There is always something which ignites and ascends beyond one's own thinking. This being energy that soars beyond isolationist criteria, always bonding with an invisible axis, creating a new and uncharted electrical resolve. Certainly not ascendance scorched by refutation but arachnids turning green in higher dimensional kingdoms.

Writing at such remove could be described as mania by lamp, by oxygen self-nullified and risen. Perpendicular flux, cosmically inflected enzymes. Then the nerves rattle and magically embody beasts. But not something which feeds on yeasts and frozen corn as invisible purgation, as apotheosis by fire. This being sonar that speaks to the disadvantaged noun, to decapsulated verbs, bringing them to life. Of course, one is never magnetized to stasis, to lingering fuels that de-suggest themselves. One then takes as one's gait motion as paradoxical omen so as to mount kinematic initiation, bringing different properties and standards within reach of a powerful and liminal glycerin, yet no longer prone to sudden or revengeful timeline. Of course life remains for one's aural powers a ravenous yet perfect syllabus of doubt and withdrawal, curiously suspended, waiting for the flame to transmute non-effect.

Antonin Artaud: A Glossary of Fumes

ARTAUD PROVIDED US no iron clad grip on the exterior dimension, though prolific with human contact throughout his years on Earth. Consumed by the grandeur of suffering his taction with waking reality ignited his writing of address to addressee as if embodied by the dialectics the of nothingness. For him "Mundane relations... do not touch the kernel of the individual, the search for redemption undercuts all social solutions." His correspondents, as substantive as they were, transmute to gnostic foils within his swarming verbal barrages. Not that they fail to respond with their own powers, but they seem to be bound to Artaud's smouldering inner sun, there never seems to be the one-to-one relation one finds in conventional correspondence. There are always the underlying realia of Artaud "exhorting" or defending himself and, as he once stated, and I am paraphrasing, no one writes or draws except to get out of hell. His creations are suffused by this drama.

To know Artaud was to be instantly singed by his struggle. His correspondence from Rivière to Breton never resolves itself on the horizontal plane or coruscates as day to day relation. No one is left unmarked, one becomes engaged in telepathic endurance, for Artaud is relentless. There is no aspect of matter which is not engaged in his war against darkness. Witness the fiends who roam the pages of his *Heliogabalus or, the Crowned Anarchist*, or the palpable aggression he directed towards the Surrealists when he accuses them of the error of political engagement which he inscribed in his "In Total Darkness, or The Surrealist Bluff." Or his rejection of Breton's offer to exhibit his drawings in The International Surrealist Exhibition in 1947. He remained a free-standing singularity.

For Artaud, the plunge into darkness was the overcoming of darkness. Simplicity of tenor was not a part of his character. Anaïs Nin once related that on a bright sunny Parisian afternoon Artaud was exhorting passersby to overcome their inner darkness which they clearly had no consciousness of. His warfare with the caliginous consumes all of his tragic moments. He is constantly hounded by the friction which imbues his body and his mind. For Artaud, the body and the mind were inextricable and functioned as singularity. His fire was always struck on the hylic plane. He was lightning struck petrifaction, unclassifiable, moody, plagued by seeming error, yet always staunch with perseverance. A perseverance which enabled his pursuit of the Tarahumara all the while engaged in mountain climbing on a burro simultaneously disgorging heroin. Unlike Césaire, Artaud's activity did not commit itself to correcting the great social issues of the day. He seems to be constantly engaged in the overthrow of a fraudulent God. A God whom the Gnostics accused of holding all souls in universal embranglement. Thus he imparts his absence to others, so that they, at some level, no longer partake in their own biographical deception. Within this gnostic drama Artaud's two dates of 1896-1948 become nothing more than an ancillary item. His was a realm where only forces were exchanged. This was the true invisible grammar, the grammar where superficial fact could never extend.

The writer as agent of literature was loathsome to Artaud. He knew this to be the author as conductor of distortion. Such was the subtext of his reasoning in rejecting Breton's invitation to participate in The International Surrealist Exhibition of 1947. He states to Breton, "I have my own idea of birth, of life, of death, of reality, and of destiny, and I do not participate in any of the general ideas through which I could have with any man than myself." He states further that he has been "in open struggle every night and day with all the sects of all the sorcerers and initiates of the earth."

He is not being subversive for reasons of personal enhancement, he is uttering a language of mortal burning, like fumes from a smouldering radium fish. Radium in this instance not as super-imposed disturbance but as power which issues from interior agony. Again, he states to Breton, "The human body has enough suns, planets, rivers, volcanoes, seas, tides, without still going to seek those of so-called exterior nature and others." Thus, to point to the personalities which hurtled in and out of Artaud's life would be to consist, in this context, of superfluous scholarship.

Saying this, I am in no way dissolving the irradiating power which issued from Gance, Paulhan or Paule Thévenin; or from the tapestry of giants that extended from Miró and Leiris to the Peruvian poet Vallejo. Artaud was a mortal striding in oneiric lockstep into the well of disappearance. For him, there was no colloquial stationing, there was only the harried rejoinder which sought through its emission the expulsion of universal poison.

Solar Fire on Earth

*The subconscient is the main cause why all
things repeat themselves and nothing
ever gets changed except in appearance*
—SRI AUROBINDO

THERE IS A fragility which opens phrases to the health of blistering kelvins. Which is the seminal dialectic of the delicate as fire. This means to come to poetic charring to the alchemical act of vertical soaring as something other than dense pontifical abasement, as something other than vertiginous contradiction which continues to dwell as a substate of humanity. The latter, now brushing the cusp of what can be considered a dismissive species, a species as fatigued solstitial fragment, a yield of bone and carcass at war with its own survival. Rather than burn its way into its own conundrum, it tends to cancel its deeper operative skills, going back and forth between differing forms of the extraneous. In the Occident this is particularly pronounced, the vernacular mind being so suppressed that its original predilection has been usurped by chronic division and self-hatred. One seems always trapped in warrens of insurrectional guilt always clouded by total instability. These charges against oneself become totally baseless yet are given power by collective agreement according to tenets which suffuse seismic reversion being translatable as stasis.

Thus the body exists as shock through insular perjury always dazed, stumbling about within malefic enclosure. Its power being the essence of dismay and somber perceptual exposure. Say I am part of a population of rats, it is natural that the other rats want to attack me as an energy willfully risen above the conclave of rats as a curiously embrangling witness, as someone they sense deludes himself into thinking that another soaring can transpire. They can say of me that I scribble on blind tablets, that I burn my way into distance by bribery. Never is this the case, understanding that I've experienced the heliotropic as ore, that base suggestion can never function as functioning candescence.

This is why the rising of one's essence increases magnetism that at the same time increases inoperable social confusion. Within such a lowly risen enclave one is suspected of spellbinding, of moving through the social field as a kind of demonic dust creating in palpable form a simulated empire. Here I am simply nothing but a social body rent with fissures, it being not unlike observing doused rams wandering through opaque twilight. All direction seems suspended, one is subject to curious exposure to what can be called forensic insecurity. What is striking is that there is little desire to roam over and beyond a European psychic rooting. The latter rooting over the past half dozen centuries has had insidious effect, creating in the herd a curious curvature of the psychic spine, a supercilious angst, as if normalized respiration consisted of pox procured from infected Indian blankets.

I feel I have captured the dye of the circumstance, the subconscient element soaked inside the salt of the cosmos having taken root in the monstrous light of the Cambrian and Pre-Cambrian, furious as they were with burgeoning inclemence. I must say here that I am looking at billions of years in a blinking ophthalmological flash, as if all of geologic time had been compressed by the uncanny as insight. This being the ground of our genetic component which results in tension, competition and killing. Always leaning towards the carnivorous I see elements of Allosaurus swarming in the ruse of armies and general fundamentalisms.

So are we castaways from its scent? Embrangled oxygen spilling forth rays of terror? Are we its bleak uncountable vapour still escaping from its prior skin? Here we are hundreds of millions of years in the wake of its tendencies proscribed in a general way by their darkness. Such is the energy which has been institutionally nursed over the past half dozen centuries in particular, and beyond that, 2,500 years prior to the present. When I say this, I am not delimiting this energy to 2,500 years, saying this, it has been brought during this time to a pitch as institutional policy. False and inorganic rooting, foiled abridgments, possibilities eroded, thereby creating de-extension and mirage, pluperfect estrangement, non-aligned to organic thought release. And what is organic thought release? Chaos cleansed by endemic solar renewal, by solar force which rises from the transmuted cellular form. This light, so unlike the trenchant suffocation that suffuses the present kingdom, based as it is on literal ignominious distraction, carries a sum of neutrinos in its inkling. Not a frail utopian static but a transpersonal element igniting a bluish-green within one's substance. Yet I am not speaking here of bodiless vacuums, of moons stilled in cryptic concrescence, but of dynamic asservation, my spontaneously coined term which evinces itself as the subliminal, as connectivity to a blue and central solar furnace. This being skill as higher asset prone to miraculous incandescence, to insights brimming over with relay after relay of psychic suns.

Not a jot in the field considered to be the mind inspired by former melancholias, by matter considered to be the prose of psychobiology. I am speaking of other turnings of the mind never coiled by entrapment. Having absented by an eternal instant the defeatist mind of habit, of always looking for the worst in oneself, not unlike the electrical registration of coelacanths or venomous mulgas. I am speaking of intuition distilled via transmuted stellar rays. An order that persists far beyond our local stellar concentration. The mind then imbibing a substance transcending gross interior pilings always thought to be normal according to general human assumption. For instance, the accepted length of a life or fueled thought always susurrous about the inability of energy to ignite present change in the species. An insight that lifts me to a state of blinding transparency due to a suddenness of consciousness. There exists no surmounting aftermath of Greek inspired psychic materia, the latter only acknowledging the hylic as its all-encompassing base. Which seems to end in worshipping a tawdry Nordic image of God on what I'll call blind Dutch Easters, where the suspension of one's inner originality is then stained by doubt and subservience proscribed by a super-imposed eternity. An "Imperial Christianity" animating Jesus Christ as its regulatory saviour.

In order to rise above the melancholy of the present collective malaise is to vibrate with what is now defined as the implausible, where one's cells recall in themselves tendencies that respirate inside the invisible, thus tending to rid themselves of carnivorous glare. The question can be asked, what of this glare? Can it be called a private circumstance perfectly separable from the cosmos? Or is it condemned by a priori ferocity and terror? From whatever angle such terror subsists, it remains an internal tremor, an allusive yet base priority, incapable of what I'll call evolved refinement capable of abiding beyond the double bind of tension and murder. Not that I am looking for a utopian cerebellum or for some cryptically imposed quiescence evolved from some logically drawn utopia. What I am suggesting is a state of mind reaching levels of overtone where the biological urges transmute to other habitations of possibility. I am speaking of the oblique, of the non-referential as reference, not unlike the whispers from reefs never prone to day-to-day substantiation. Never strangled as parched non-plentiful violets but as clause that subsists by circulation as sole discourse, not to height or vertical summas but transmutation according to pending clinical squalls. Never a colloquy posed by inclement psychic venom of fixed erosion in the mind. This latter state being the experience of regressive cellular inversion.

The human race presently as partially responsive metrical ghosts drained by feeding on subliminal adjectives compounded by corruptive gestation then weakened by the opiates of nostalgia and ruses. Unaccustomed to movement through opaque water or acknowledging solar forms pouring through blinding Buddhist doors, it contains within its general acumen the erasure of doubt. Never accustomed to sparks from falling rivers, the noun can only cast weight, can only assemble prerogatives without the possibility of savour. And I attribute accursedness of this doubt to propaganda unleashed for over 2,000 years about the all-concluding forces of the isolate conscious mind. A mind that claims the mystique of European critique tuned as it is by assaultive limitation. Its initial arrogance being unstinting labour reducing the epic of the energy field to its particular form of reaction. It tells us that in the main we are reduced solely to material splendour so that the dead can never be channeled through the sensitivity of mirrors. That one can never listen in one's mind to unscripted sunspots, or to ritual as replication never rooted in waste.

This remains the world of thought as practiced by the many, based as it is upon chronic reduction. Much like a bear's stomach always summoned by dialectical savagery. As I psychically ambulate the capitols of the Earth it is noted, to paraphrase Michel Leiris, that they resemble pointless sugar plantations. In this atmosphere poetic sensitivity is cast into a bag of ferrets always struggling to breathe. This amounts to a crude ballet awkward with tribulation being a system that bevels the magic of night hawks, that cancels the form of hydrogen in the consciousness. In contradistinction, there exists experience of the cells as suddenly evolved animation, of profuse crystallization of the psychic field. A destination which ceases to implicate devastation of animals squared and burned as the perfect assimilation of corporate profit. The latter suffused with darkness, held in place by supported imbalance. Phrased in another manner, gross inoperable deafening soaked in poisoned millet. At one level, I can say that its standards pose an unmitigated puzzling, and at another level holds as highest principle suicidal coding. The human race being at present proto-extinguished, always posing extrinsic quarrels with itself pointing towards purposeless causes through error.

Such a civilization when sending probes to the heavens emits its power as a curious draft of energy. This draft within itself absolutely brilliant yet the energy of machines always failing to teem with necessitous psychic refinement, with specific refinement that is navigational séance. To some this turn of mind engages unfair critique prone as it is to supercilious sensitivity. I am only critiquing the profane philosophical outlook of its brilliance. Do these missions remain parallel to that of Columbus 500 plus years removed? Speaking from the power that remains as witness according to devastated nature on Earth. After say, a duration of alchemical investigation into what has resulted to Indigenous physical presence after New World exploration sends common shiver through one's breathing. One inevitably knows that greenness has been unsparingly brokered with the veins, the eyes of living beings who remain suffused with darkness. Within such context telepathy ceases to spin as living neurological source. At this point I am not probing for utopia but sussing out possible probes for what is presently understood to be psycho-physical evolution. Within this natural context uranian exploration remains naturally squared rising to a level above a negated life effort, where the power of nature on Earth remains skewed as regards its living registration. Perhaps tornadoes of doubt will be lessened and the scale of mortality become a sudden non-factor with thought no longer extended within crass tellurian devastation. As this electrical maze clears there can possibly exist definitive momentum as to nuance moving into life's nths thus entering another plane of procreation. This being life without previous circumference or barrier. One then floats across precipitous interiors, the outer body blank, the inner state ceasing to be quelled by skirmishes from habit. This being the subliminal dimension withdrawn and magnetic, instinctively fearless. Here I am not speaking of a palpable language such as Wolof or Chinese but of a curious vibration that is stealth, absorbing, what could be called by the conscious mind a power not unlike energy that persists as prescient telepathy. It is crossing over for the domesticated mind an entry into calamitous transition, not as exchange for one uncertainty over another, for one delusional endeavour over another.

To the conscious mind this remains a treasonous applicative as if a foreign element were unleashed from powers other than human. As if I were speaking of other energy formations 40 billion light years distanced. No, what I am speaking of are instantaneous parallels with other forces that cannot be confused with the energies confined to life and death. These are energies that cannot be known by palpable name or objective documentation. An energy which can't be delimited to assiduous applicative. The common parlance is to carve from uncertainty individual definition grasping one's phenomena by struggle within partial definitive praxis. Under present conditions this praxis seems to be the source upon which the body pivots as if plagued by delimited oxygen. Thus I am dipping over into rapidity that is the unknown. Which is not to harp on individual sacrifice by praising a curious inner immolation claiming it to be psychological discovery.

It must always be remembered that we are marooned on an anonymous blue globe hovering near the outer border of the Milky Way. We are at present humbled by this circumstantial status having no other motion but to rise above the subliminal dimension that persists in the cells.

This can be assessed initially by language electrically wrought that tends to phonemically aspire above the subliminal. Then at a more advanced praxis this language struggles at stark absorption limit. And what is this absorption limit? The border at which the body begins to be eaten by the cosmos. I can only speak of hovering in this state and acclimatizing oneself to such consciousness. A state of consciousness which ignites infamous discomfort. In the poet's case this is an altimeter crossing point, the cellular state irradiated by sonic purity issued from this aforesaid dimension. And this is not the super-imposition of energy as an unmoving state but a roiling transfiguration quite in keeping with disfigurement and danger. This being an alien state conveyed through verbal scent implying other laws of respiration. One becomes an alchemical ghost burning in the midst of savages, hearing and emitting signals from a source seemingly non-conversant with the visible kingdom. These being signals that consist of neo-respiration in the limbic system. As if inside one's personal field there existed a levitating personage not unlike the unus-ambo in Henry Corbin's "philosophical anthropology." A conundrum suddenly sprung from the zero field. This being the dimension from which collective suns spring forth. Both a mortal and immortal condition this being something David Bohm and J. Krishnamurti have previously discussed. To paraphrase Krishnamurti, by having experience in this state even death becomes a minor event. What I'm speaking of is the commingling of the mortal and immortal with an unknown understanding beginning to take shape. Which is entry into the great conundrum, into transmundane iridescence. An iridescence which I call solar fire on Earth. A fire, not according to a barking regional monsoon or to a God wary, ravenous, angry and bitter. Perhaps these prior two examples are subsets, and perhaps melancholia is nothing more than a subset, an ill lit figment cast off from immensity. I call such figmentation characterological subconscience or in another key, anthropomorphic rubella. The state of consciousness of which I'm speaking is the momentum of immensity itself. And when becoming part of this momentum one becomes a ghost blazing by means of trans-mundane solar registration. This being the first few steps across a heightened alchemical field. Thus, one becomes charged spectra flowing from the anonymous. In this sense both a speechless edification, and a cataclysmic instigation, all the while living by means of a transmuting solar plexus. As if the cells had been lit and were spontaneously overcoming the wizardry of negation. Which in truth is the blending of the supra dimension with the body. Within the Cartesian epic such experience can be nothing except demeaned as an unskilled prowess not graced by any evidence.

This then is living with the condition of seepage that emerges from the very evidence of living. This can be called a perpendicular personality being a respiration with the cosmos itself. Cellular pulsation if you will. An unimpeded glossary in the system evolving as pure novae. This being a mesmeric tuning that soaks one's actions as they spontaneously emerge from what I've previously conveyed as a prior dimension. This being the energy that slips behind the gate of coffins so as to crystallize as another state of animation. Here I do not seek to extend myself as some philosophical carpenter or some seismic prohibitory phantom rife with delimited ether. Certainly I am not calling to my defense some elaborate ruse which exhausts itself in the telling of itself plagiarized from collapse secretly relying on erosion and misstatement.

It could be said that I am a graceless elf caught in driving rain neither captured nor in retreat. Yet what seems to be rising is this free spark of energy rising above old forms of living by means of alchemical stealth casting elements of the torrential from a non-exhibited plane.

PART II

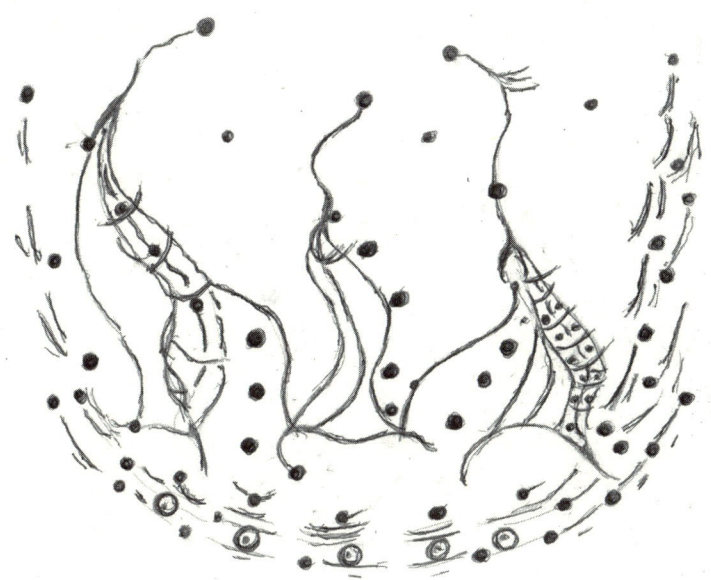

BRILLIANCE ENSNARED
BY THE UNSEASONABLE

Essays & Reviews

My Philosophical Matrix: A Hurricane of Luminosity

PHILOSOPHY, FOR ME means inquiry into the broadest view, into the most encompassing range, taking into account the known and what is considered to be the unknown, no longer considered a positional view ensconced within preset categorical estrangement. It is a free inquiry not only into the realia of the given, but what I'll call the free laws of physics, which, according to the Russian physicist Andre Linde could change if protons differed by .02 percent in their mass, or if gravity were accelerated to such a degree that the stars we experience burned with greater intensity and had incredibly truncated lives. Such insight gives perspective on our narrowed grasp of what we consider to be reality. I am always concerned with possibility for exploration outside assumption of this narrowed grasp, incessantly spurred by inquiry into the non-palpable, into engagement with its hyper-dimensions, the latter having become for me the dominant field for cogitation. Thus, in my case, non-palpability has continuously opened for me an internally honed poetic language. Certainly, this is not a purely cognitive search evinced by demotic language in search of that which attempts to illuminate the mundane.

It can be argued that the West is particularly haunted in this regard. For thinkers such as Kant, Hume, and Hegel, Africa was nothing more than denigrated property. A property according to the aforementioned thinkers has contributed nothing to the development of humankind. It remains a property pejorative, invisible to the Occidental eye. Yet I ask at this late date, why did thinkers the stature of Solon and

Pythagoras bother to cultivate themselves within the lands of this aforesaid property? The latter, revered in the European mind as key innovators within the maze of human development. Again, I must note concerning the above-mentioned philosophical triumvirate Africans were nothing more than pejorative remnants, while someone with the power of Heidegger could expand his universalism no further than the borders of Europe. In more recent times someone such as the French sociologist Roger Caillois "sought to foster culture as the bulwark of Western Civilization." Perhaps my praxis can gain no footing as regards Kantian systemization, nor recognition within Heidegger's world regarding his recognition of the pre-Socratics as the original arbiters of thought. For me, ancient Greek thought to the present can only register an isolate view of human experience, failing to take into view the philosophy which was Egyptian mathematics that Schwaller de Lubicz cogently illumines in his study of the construction of the temple at Luxor. A temple constructed a thousand years prior to the scattered writings which remain from the pre-Socratics. This linkage from the Greeks to the present remains for me totalitarian form, a model that can only refer to itself as authority. In this sense it is analogous to the personification of God as a European phenotype referring to himself as the highest form of being. This creates in the mind a psychological tautology that continually ignites obstruction when seeking alternative levels of experience.

By thinking in an inclement register, I am prone to inclement sigils, to poetic inveiglement, to what Deleuze and Guattari would call a minor register, an experiment fueled by anti-codification. I agree with them that poetry is the philosophy of the present age, potent in its ability to inhabit Rhizomes, to de-fuel territorial hardening. This being, language not functioning as a claimed dimension, where every iota of its motion opens itself to simultaneous openings, not claimed by a sovereign or singular motion. In this sense I have been nurtured on the fringes of thought. Parts of Coomaraswamy, Corbin, Paz, Gurdjieff, Guénon, Sri Aurobindo's *The Life Divine*,

Wittgenstein's refutation of his *Tractatus*, René Daumal's savor, Breton's First Manifesto, the Dostoyevsky of the "Underground," the Artaud who writes on Van Gogh, Naim Akbar's writing on the "Nile Valley Origins of the Science of the Mind," Cheik Anta Diop's understanding of the South/North movement of knowledge which permeates his *African Origin Of Civilization*, the *Thousand Plateaus* of Deleuze and Guattari, and David Bohm's *Wholeness and the Implicate Order*. Perhaps a harried and unbalanced summary which also includes portions of Arendt and Cixous.

The liberty to pursue the proliferating tenets of the anti-systemic has allowed me access to a language that vibrates with the consistency of the unknowingness of itself, this being none other than the flow of imagination as living proof of the Philisophia Perennis. It is a potion striking out in all directions at once, which in the course of its expansion brings to view infinite levels of the hidden.

As a person of colour, my very praxis spontaneously refutes the notion that I am nothing more than an assumed nullification. Thus, I am more than absence at the table of thought having hailed from the original field of thought as explored by the Egyptians. I have fused with the experience they called the *ba*, the electrical current that suffuses all vibration. This realization ignited the book at hand and brought it to a pitch. *Towards The Primeval Lightning Field* is a search for origins outside the warren of the visible. Writing its content was to withstand the very pressure of the life force by entering the invisible blood of energy that empowers both the field of "observable" as well as that of the non-observable. I call it stamina by vertigo, by password that summons the unauthorized. By its very nature such an exercise allowed me to leap beyond the provincialism that summons itself via official criteria.

Paraphrasing Na'im Akbar, human activity is not restricted to de-limited visibility, to the restricted view that regards the visible as singular explanation. Thus, I have eclipsed the rigour that wills itself according to objective reason. Not unlike the world Bohm inhabits in his writing I cryptically explore the tacit. I experience an unmistakable current, a seminal power through language that enacts itself as a hurricane of luminosity. Insights spontaneously accrue by means of psycho-lingual kinetics.

Our Present Psychic State: An Awkward Foreboding

It is through speed that the mind becomes clairvoyant.
—RENÉ MÉNIL

PSYCHIC FIXITY INCULCATES assumption and such assumption devolves to aural opacity, so much so, that one is capable of hearing nothing but echoes and assumptions of one's isolated sonic capacity. Judgement then rises and sets in motion distortion according to troubling aural occlusion. There then exists no capacity to suspend one's inner rhetoric of psychic fixation by suspending oneself from the state of toneless moral amplification. Via such an inner climate communication devolves and is haunted, sterilized by assumed misnomer of received ideas. And these received ideas remain as gravitated thought complexes that cannot respond to anything but the spellbound dissonance of prior mental arrangement. There exists little capacity to shift. The latter condition being none other than the Occident at this hour, with its aural realm stunted to such a degree that it would rather risk death on alien province in space, rather than transmute by enacting assimilation to the positive effort towards the human collective on Earth.

There remains a general soullessness about its stewardship of the prior 2,000 years being an arid super-imposed arrangement that now seems to have run its course. All that is now planned is to mine minerals from asteroids, or to form colonized Principates on areas like Mars or the Saturnian moon that is Titan in order to keep its original arrangement afloat.

Because it has never been able to hear anything other than itself, at an increasing rate it is being consumed by a consuming utterance from the void. There is consciousness in certain quarters that understands its realia is being swallowed by a strange electricity that it has never appropriately acknowledged. This electricity seems none other than the ghosts of Indigenous shamans haunting it with a language that can't be empirically magnified, isolated as it is in its sequestered constructed mental castles tainted by institutional crime. This being the state one procures from remaining perpetually contorted attempting to live within the guise of self-appointed superiority. All motion has ceased. Thus it has ended with the disturbing images recently wrought by Lauren Greenfield in her photographic essay *Generation Wealth* which is a fierce indictment of its present circumstance that now affects the whole of planetary consciousness. The latter, infected by the zeal of its aforementioned error summed up by Marx's bedrock understanding that matter is primary and consciousness is secondary.

Given the demise of State Capitalism and its corrupted eastern offshoots in Russia and China we are now forced to ambulate across a complex planetary forge where psychic oxygen has decreased to such a degree that those now being born presently seem to hemorrhage with such insular debility that a compound arthritics seems to naturally arise from the psyche at birth. This being intuitive epigenetics as one's natural instinct seems to aspire to no other purpose than that of what the late sociologist Thorstein Veblen coined as "conspicuous consumption." The lone soul now addresses subjective error via culturally inspired mirrors that reflect it, only capable of de-limited reflection via endemic psychic stranding. The latter state being nothing other than the wizened self-capacity of the body and that which enhances the body. This being a tautological capacity that is pronounced in a fractionated portion of beings that are now considered as the one percent who would rather attempt to flee from the soul as isolated carbon attempting to transport its remains to alien planetary wastes just to dwell within perpetual unrest.

In light of collective demise on our present Earth, its fomenting seems to remain a European imprinting, with its hauntedness so severe that its terminal glossary has affected not only certain beings in the global south but the very climate responsible for allowing habitation on Earth to continue. This being the ubiquity of the general maelstrom we now inhabit.

In concluding, certain elements of the European intelligentsia would rather call on aliens for wisdom and general guidance than to inhabit the well-springs of the human soul. This indeed remains an awkward foreboding, where inward capacity is forsaken in favour of a climate that fosters surcease rather than one of tolerance that empowers the perennial tenet of life.

A Note on Interstellar Audition

*... poetic activity is revolutionary by nature; a spiritual exercise,
it is a means of interior liberation.*
—OCTAVIO PAZ

SURREALISM HAS INFILTRATED present society within the dissolving tenor of the latter's endgame. A disintegration fueled by seeming strength that endemically disables its host. By means of its deepest spontaneous stratagem it crosses an unsensed divisional boundary that leaves no form of itself and in fact remains invisible. As we become more and more prone to crossing all divisional gulfs, thought becomes a form of itself as it reveals the seemingly invisible. As humans we awaken each day to the drainage of dawns. We witness scorching suns and hypothetical raindrops all the while implying that within our circulation there exists anonymity.

As the mind encounters interstellar regions of itself not only in terms of mechanical speculation, but as a zone of itself that interacts with its own silence. At bottom, this remains the living current, the active sub-strata that continues to propel the human mind. In spite of the psychic toxins that mirror our current society there remains a level of experience that oxygenates the mind even as it experiences the protracted moments of its current panic. It seems it is currently evolving to a higher spectrum of itself thereby rising to a mesmerism that remains transparency. I am not speaking here of a simple contest of systems but of a level not wrought out of habit. Not system as brought to bear via material armament but the mind invaded by its own inherent sub-strata. And I maintain these sub-strata remain its higher state akin to transparency. Not as crude deliberation wrought from destructive grammar but language suffused by natural astral tremor that possesses its harvest via oneiric elements that magically weave themselves as language through thought. Perhaps a gossamer network of instantaneous signals.

Thus human presence takes on a sheaf-like quality as it equates at an experiential level. Integers interact with themselves as anomalies that remain invisible within the tenor of interaction. It therefore carries a spinning grasp of itself rising within itself so that it carries no exterior architectural state of its arising. This state of mind continues to extend itself as living value. Its activity protracts as an elliptical gymnastics that enacts aeration upon the psychic cells thereby enabling living transparence. Of course, elevation transpires that remains analogous in my view to the recent transcription of galaxies as they accrete and magically transcend themselves. This reasoning not only remains akin to ellipses but extends understanding beyond its current limit carried by voices enamoured of conflict. Of course, we leap beyond measurement as instilled by debacle. This lingual magnetization retains its non-quantifiable splendour. So fore-sworn limit as collective outlook is no longer a premise upon which to build.

When Breton harks back to Shakespeare and Swift he eclipses the ideological. As the Occident continues to repeat itself with old, condoned patterns it continues to stimulate by embrangled kinetics. It camouflages its own connection to itself, self-regaling its own intensity. This is not unlike a fault ridden spell that casts upon one's state a sum of sovereign transactional methods. This transpires in my view to an opaque geriatrics that condones repression. By dint of force it reduces the mind so that it then replicates its own selfmesmerization. It therefore scales its own self-assent by means of the grammar of self-torture.

This being a blazing secular magnetics that Breton and his cohorts understood to be inoperable. Surrealist reflex enamoured itself via endemic randomness. And this randomness of which I speak raised itself to a plane that remains mediumistic. Not as understanding according to ruse but one that grasps ascent from the leper's colony. A tone that hisses, that issues fire, that can only be obscured by a dwindling number of critics. When Alquié made note of this deficit, the rational culture remained capable of making its claims moribund as it remained within its own certainty. Yet because the mind cannot be contained the rational ignorance that remains the Catholic Church prevailed upon itself to constrict the general psyche. I am thinking in this tenor of the containment of Copernicus as contrasted with Abu Sa'id al Sinjari in Granada during the year of 1031.

So the rational critic seeking to contain such realm of thought commonly harkens back to 1924 or 1939 as if the period between these times remains the central gist that remains of Surrealism. As if it remains sealed in a private glass jar so as to foster scholarly optical consumption. This remains an attempt to script air and wind. Because the cosmos retains a spell that cannot cognitively be altered it remains synonymous in the collective mind with mystery. The latter being the endemic Surrealist state not according to rational conniving or closeted attempts at an assumed state of accuracy. This remains a delimited investigation of history failing to purge itself of memorials. Such a mental state enlists itself as an impossible endeavour. This being the mind functioning within a delimited quarrel with itself. Never as expanded efflorescence with itself. Never as summed migration towards expansion enlisted by tenets of the unpredictable.

Thus the unpredictable being the maze that expands at the root of itself in spite of rational efforts at containment. This maze alive as a spectrum of experience that extends from say, the explosion that was Shakespeare to the hallucinatory linguistics that erupted as

Bob Kaufman. Because language retains no absolute climate within itself there exist differing stages. I doubt that modern auditory skill is able to intelligently sculpt basic elements of Old English prone to its Germanic tenor. After Shakespeare English is a different language. It was an oral language evolved to one that was written. Not only does the language possess its external criteria but most importantly the spell cast upon by the interior psyche of the individual practitioner.

Here I am not scrutinizing stages, their differing linguistic emission, but understanding the field of the individual mind that they drew from. I will not quote here fragments of individual praxis but attempt to understand the lingual field that the individual mind has drawn from, and how this individual praxis shapes general praxis. Again, the manner in which Shakespeare and Kaufman ignited differently, one as an initial practitioner and one exploding his power at a latter arc of English transmission. In either case I am speaking of written skill as primordial concurrence. Because the rational mind thinks of this level of mind as simply skilled according to exterior usage it fails to understand the powers that extend from the subconscious power that draws fragments from proto-motion or realization of this proto-motion that erupts like lava across the provinces of the future. The conventional critic tends to react according to language as chronicle that emboldens its state as beginning, middle, and end always defending the standards of delimited or outward lingual formation. Say a word such as spell is used to depict a work of a more inwardly prone emission, this latter state then partakes of another lingual dimension that tends to enact itself within an advanced stage of itself. Instead, the rational mind tends to engage itself in both attack of the creative practitioner and self-assassination of itself at this level. It thus engages a despicable reflex that engages script as negation. This interacts as a contracted legacy that denies the lingual field as sprawling with what I consider to be one that sprawls with opportunity. This being the founding limitation that has retained the scripting theory that has sullenly embrangled Occidental psychology. The reasoning that propels this scripting of partials remains cast within a sullen state of mind that places discreet particulars side by side in order to promulgate its own reasoning dazzled by the prospect of logical coherence. Because it casts this enabled mirror up to itself it thinks of limits that remain beholden to its delimited reasoning that extends to the lingual practitioner a psychology that consciously agonizes over the structured proof of one's individual praxis. This latter mindset persists according to the tenets of brazen foreshortening.

This is where modern mental criteria stalls failing to extend itself into renewing effervescence. Its attempt via the exercise of anomalous cognition remains self-strangulated, null as regards its own praxis all the while remaining tautologically captured. It mentally evinces its own manoeuvres, remaining structurally spell-bound to itself. This being the standard of its own self-intervention. Thus it remains episodic, self-regressive, turned in on itself. This remains a mind structured by brazen self-limits summoned from protective assimilation that have been advanced over 2,000 years.

As cunning approximation of itself it remains within self-imposed limits brazen as fore-shortening. Its prescription for the creative mind extends to the author a deleterious agony concerning lingual architecture according to step-by-step conjunction. A process in my view that remains tautologically captured. It thus evinces a decrepit demeanour. This being the gist of cognitive intervention, episodic, self-regressive, turned in on itself. Such mind being nurtured by its own fear. A niggling spectrum of mind that calls for self-limit, for a vernacular roundelay of barrenness as stricken foundational element. I would argue that Breton remains an articulating spectre of modern language rather than a turgid organizing spectacle. As part of this spectrum he rotates, he enables felicity in dissolving curmudgeon-like spells. This has remained the psycho-neurological state since the Romans, now seeking to break free from its own sequestered etching. Not unlike newly discovered moss in Antarctica by Indian biologists. Such moss symbolizes figment as freshly enacted being. Not as ideological commandment rendered by outmoded psychic skills being devastating chapters from the past. Not as old descriptive impact but as part of the realm of freshly gradated shadow that now fuses itself inside the realm that enacts itself as new charisma.

This remains the mind enacting itself via various dimensions, not as a simple literary substrate with its clogged ozone of dates and birth locales as coded serial numbers. As the Indian yogi-philosopher Sri Aurobindo once stated, the cosmos remains quite capable of transmuting human fatigue so that its energy can rise once again beyond the bickering that has seemed to staunch inner blending with the growth on this planet. Thus, shamanic audition accrues not according to cognitive promulgation. I could cite as precedent Tusput, the Yakut shaman who could hear at great distances through dead shamans outside of known modes of agreement. As Octavio Paz once noted, Breton invoked a higher more noble state of humanity. This higher métier remains the life condition of the shaman. By hearing through the dead an expanded human state naturally invokes itself. A condition not condoned by replicated signals of itself but understood to have risen above what I understand to be duplicitous psychological strabismus. The latter condition remaining a captured state without brightness. This results in what I understand to be a barren cellular construct where the cells tend to fall inert sans illuminated electrical connectivity.

The nature of connectivity naturally expands itself and creates in my experience trans-human connection. Shamans have been witnessed shape shifting to owls and other entities. I consider the gist of this power to remain available to certain audic explorers not according to the dazed grammar of replication but through poetic acts to organically resemble powers organically channeled through the shaman Tusput. Not power that simply brews itself within a recognizable literary forge but power capable of kindled alacrity analogous to distances invoked by nano-sailing. As one begins to register audition (not through replication or memory) but as essence that remains the living gallop that was Shakespeare or Kaufman, one naturally transfigures the poetic canon so that the canon itself becomes suffused with possibility as rising audition capable of inscripting a timeless vastitude never pawning itself off to powers of the agreed upon delimit. I am thinking at this moment of poetic power as unembrangled voltage never kept as superficial hostage by a ruler, or the policy of a ruler, or as in the case of our present circumstance, lingual containment by European thought initiative over the greater part of the past 1,000 years. Here I do not seek to summon up grievances but to unfold as one who spontaneously inscribes what is understood on Earth to be the infinite. This wider realm carrying innate power always remaining available to those who summon it. A spontaneous dossier of possibility not as requiem or repetition but power that scripts the unknown.

Indeed, how can such a state of mind be contained by delimited use of the French language that never extended beyond the year of 1939. As stated earlier its mind cannot be delimited by scholarly definition. Even when ascribing to this cognitive chart of imposed dates of our contiguous century how do we account for the forces named Joan Miró, Wilfred Lam, Aimé Césaire, Antonin Artaud. They who never signed officially recognized revolutionary glyphs provided by any monarchy that attempted to contain the spirit. So, what is to be done with a persona such as Jorge Camacho, or Arshile Gorky, or the great Matta himself. Spontaneous heretics much in the manner contained by scholarly stricture that seeks to view them. Dates and numbers in this context must be viewed with more than suspicion. Such linear leaning should remain unconscionable and be spontaneously shunned.

So, in this context I am never instilling the limits of grammar but its burgeoning vis à vis spontaneous renewal. Not a castaway chemistry, but a lingual stream active with fresh formation. Never pre-thought replication as vertiginous onslaught. Creative continuity must proceed from a tremor, from a fuse that ignites its own interior lightning. It needs blaze inside itself as living apperception of itself.

As for the daily news cycle it represents the blurring of events far in the rear of what André Breton advanced in 1924. Thus, daily life consists of a stagnant replica of itself not as a living neurological light. Instead, psycho-physical recognition is provided with a paltry encounter of itself as it continues to stagger within a blasphemous sinkhole. As humanity wanders within this sinkhole it currently proves cryptic to itself at times always fostering fore-shortened insight. Here I am now understanding the harrowing blindness of the moment. At this moment I remain grateful for the insight that the great Philip Lamantia provided me a number of years prior when he warned me against harvesting the fatigue that currently envelopes Occidental standards. He taught me anarchic boldness, suggestibility that erupts from living mistakes, of withdrawal from the momentary as tumultuousness, of language that rises above copies of tranquility.

Language being monstrous according to innate fulguration enacts itself according to aboriginal motility. The latter being the unobstructed lingual glyph, the paradigm that renders its own suffusion as living equation inside itself. Never dictatorial or hide-bound with confusion, it magically enacts glistening by spirals that seemingly subsume themselves, that miraculously accelerate passion.

A Further Note on *Le Grand Jeu*

NOT SAVAGE CLINICAL aspiration but a rising of forces beyond the spell of old beliefs. Not as kindled proportional realm or alterity as obsolescent embrace via religious camouflage. Never as myopic planetary guide *Le Grand Jeu* continues to hurtle in secret, within strange secretive enclaves sans endemic diminishment. Not simply a strange secular posture akin to theoretical lightning as if its darkened absorption were claimed by cosmic options image akin to psychic cadastral leverage. Because I am experiencing another range of possibility, I am looking at a crucial turn of tendency that happened at the Bar du Chateau in March 1929. This is when *Le Grand Jeu* were turned away as "boys" and its power announced to history as a secondary destiny. Not to light upon this figment via an ideological rationality but to take into consideration an extended long view rarely broached in contemporary assessment. Saying this I am claiming on my behalf a susurrant wisdom not from the safety of distance but to attempt to access the long-term vibration that erupted from this proceeding. The gist of the meeting erupted from shared commonality of the moment principally encompassed within Breton's pacing. First of all, I am not making judgment or taking sides. But I feel a deeper tendency was obscured in the haze of the moment. The conditions of the moment signaled a less obscure turning given the pressures of the prior present when figures such as Breton, Artaud, Bataille, Ribemont-Dessaignes, and *Le Grand Jeu* were scattering in various directions. Maybe I am postulating too much in retrospect. But given the manner that humanity has found its way to the present, *Le Grand Jeu*, given our properties of the present moment, would have sired an active psychology more suited to our present needs of the present crises rife as it is with apocalyptic grammar. I am not arguing from an indulgent tenor but from the fertility of possibility. If inner research had been pursued as in the praxis of *Le Grand Jeu* another power of human development would have had license to develop itself. Not that Breton has proved ineffective, but another tenor would have self-described itself so needed in our present time replete as it is with cosmic uncertainty. Citing another example, what if the shared psychology of the American Indian culture had shared its force with the advanced mind that issued from Islamic Granada during, say, the 1060s or the 1070s. Where would humanity now find itself vis à vis its deeper self-recognition? A kind of revery on my part given the existential danger we collectively face. Certainly, I am not naively looking at the past via distorted perception but angling the past through the past as living possibility as we head into a disoriented and calamitous possibility.

Phantom Electrical Scarring:
The Drawings of Byron Baker

FOR BYRON BAKER the daily mind seems snared by crazed consumption and blindness, by enthrallment via "immediate perception." This perception condones itself as carnivorous scripting that attempts to package and re-sell a blind declaration of its own detritus. The individual in this equation exists as blazeless doppelganger. This being a state that compels itself according to carnivorous immediacy. The latter not unlike subconsciously scripted negation where the individual evolves a condition that corrodes collective neurology via self-appointed negation.

One can only describe this condition according to draconian inveiglement spawning itself within the psycho-physiology of the current meaning of the soul. This being none other than the corrosive code that has sustained the anthropocene where the individual is deemed isolate and urged to consume his or her energy as an isolate mental facet in pursuit of its own simulation. This means that cognitive application has regressed to such a degree that simulation is inscripted according to planned outcome. Thus, the individual is scripted to respond as a transactional remnant that quickly fades into itself and disappears without memory. Certainly not an evolutionary state but one that devolves to pointless molecules as drift or randomness. The human psyche in this state does nothing other than foster an ungainful ballet. What transpires is none other than the mind as pointless tautological exercise. So the contemporary mind is time and time again cajoled into blinding segmentation that currently translates as personal isolation post-Fukushima. This current era being one subsumed by protracted numbness devolved according to distraction.

It is vis à vis this current state that Byron Baker distinguishes his optical glossary. Instead of reverting to the human figure as 20th century optical angst his drawing re-invokes the blurring between the Ediacaran and the Cambrian as transported visual identity. A visual identity that opens onto what is considered to be an obscure state of transmission. He weaves seeming implausible lines as grafts of grafts that imply pre-human registration. This being insight that magically scripts the state from which we recognize our pre-identity. Baker optically scripts the seemingly unimaginable via bio-geo distance in time allowing us access to the Cambrian over 500 million years prior to humanity. What he instigates with his lines is a bioelectricity that rivets our eyes with what is currently considered to be an uncharted era.

Certainly he never refers to its likeness as a failed state of energy via implausible lines as grafts that generate a swarm that I intuitively understand to be organic scarring. A scarring as if his lines exploded from anonymity rather than as super-imposed excellence stifling an abstract idea of geological memory. This being the condoning electricity of these untitled works. These being works none other than electrical ignition magically scripting phyla and counter-phyla that are presently witnessed in the recently discovered "Quinjiaong biota in South China scripted by the science scribe John Timmer who speaks of … fossils" [that] "include[s] dozens of species half of which have never been seen before." It is as though Baker has grasped the primeval writhing of this era in counter-step to modern rational ennervation. His lines mine the wayward energy of volcanic inner principle with an anarchic beauty of interior precision, analogous to the Cambrian stage erupting with life.

Baker's drawings remain endemic with accuracy, they explode as curious optical anthems vertiginous with the anti-categoric as if his lines possessed a strangeness of sound akin to a deafened lorikeet in pursuit of its own vocal emission. The latter being an alien transmission alive via intuitive recognition of itself. His lines hark back to Ediacaran worms as living aboriginal movement. Thus the drawings display a mongrel electricity that weave themselves according to primordial saturation thereby invading one's optical sensitivity to such a degree that a kind of synaesthesia transpires in accordance with sound. His lenses glow as though at one with strangeness emitted from enriched alien coffers. He thus elicits the pre-human tenor of consciousness. In this sense his drawings organically hail the anterior far in advance of the seeming stasis we have come to recognize as history.

Baker's anonymous scriptings represent the staggering filament that occludes the archaeology of movements, ideologies, and cabals. Thus he presents life with our present optical foreclosure. The optical tenet that has presided over 500 years of human realism have never presided over his powers as spontaneously empowered as they are by the primeval. As these works magically etch the pre-human, they illuminate a zone of life rife with consciousness, with powers that entail anteriority. The works telepathically evince themselves and naturally eschew the neural elements that are formally understood to accompany human reasoning. Each drawing inveigles purported direction. Mystery has suffused his lines not in an attempt to impress the wiles of transactional folly but to reveal to us what the conditioned mind can never know, baffled as it is by present limit.

Of course, these are drawings that never pose themselves via delimited criteria. Their range is incommensurate with a strained or guided fervour as they open onto a realm that mystics and theologians fail to perceive. They reveal to us a scrutiny that can never be rationally known. The images transact themselves as levitating vowels that magically address a declaration prior to the human body as sole domain. I am not speaking here of drawings that pose a bullish maze of market-drawn abstraction but of insight that only the cosmos itself is capable of posing. The only thing I can draw from at this stage is immaculate pre-cognitive energy that coalesces with something other than our cognitive skills are able to draw from. Here we have a fusillade of energy full of fresh and reactive coils that explode and lengthen and regather all the while startling our sensitive optical spectrum via an immaculate pharmacopoeia of the unknown.

From these drawings we can begin to gain acquaintance with the riddle that forms our presence rife as we are with our present existence. Not as a blinded lumbering of ghosts but as energy that gambles according to defiance purposely misstating movement according to linear fragment. These are drawings that fail to portend laws that underscore pretension and belief. Via Baker's scrolls we can begin to interpret the riddles of ourselves stifled as we are within occlusion and self-debit. With these drawings we enter into a realm scarcely verified vis à vis human methodology.

Whether black and white or of colour these drawings pose substantial question marks as their arbitrary gift of expression. Silence magnetically pursues their own forces as if human caroling had given way to forces that seem to predate the unknown, that spawn a burning electrical health. These drawings are not scarring that imply human injury but scarring that seems to specify the unknown. Baker naturally inhabits the fantastical genre of skill that summons a state other than pedestrian engagement. In these works, otherness self-kindles and blazes via arbitrary lensing that naturally focuses beginnings. Certainly not inaccurate because it is arbitrary but because it initiates a portal tuned to aboriginal mathematics. Of course, this does not portend a mandala of valuable rules self-inserted to fuse with pointless visual cabals.

The theatricality that suffuses these works remains nothing other than magical mesmerism embodied and empowered by the phantom skill of harmony. One can say that his lines possess something of the liberty that first impelled Miró not according to exact resemblance but according to spirit. They carry a mysterious ordination of energy very seldom engaged. They engage an accuracy not unlike that of a phantom red hawk in search of invisible prey. Because these drawings investigate their own forces they can never be misgauged according to an occupying tautology.

Far beyond the specifics of human realia they engage themselves far beyond a state fervent with misperception. Of course, this is not work that applies its gifts according to goods and services. I equate these works that naturally rise from pre-human assignation, pre-human in the sense that they self-arise when as their own motility they extend themselves beyond replica of themselves.

Instead of looking to extra-planetary realms such as Titan and Io, Baker investigates the mysterious identity of his lines in motion. They possess a fundamental electricity that populates his drawing hand finding in the process an extended primeval proboscis that lends credence to the Quinjiang explosion that continues to magically dwell in the hills of South China.

This is why artists and creative thinkers such as Baker and John Timmer understand that human heritage implies energy that supersedes a 500 million-year calendar seemingly astral in origin. Specifically for Baker this is a heritage not based upon gratuitous spell but pre-extends itself beyond measurable calculation, certainly sans modern invention and its conclusions posted subsequent to 1945. In this context Baker never specifies self-congratulatory engagement but all the while engages with the power that unleashes spells circuitously wrought via what Breton once perceived as the "interior model."

Thus Baker enlists his line as burning draft, as electric elixir, scrawled via ignited cinder, via erupting wavelength where the garrison of personality fails to engage. Not unlike the energy that engages the appellations of Hayter and Picasso, Baker sustains creative courage in the face of a population constantly hostile and distracted from its natural modernity. Therefore, his arbitrary wavelength burns, yet at the same time engages an incandescent neutrality that never subsumes the listless monikers of the marketplace. Indeed, his drawn lines molten with the fury of creative scarring multiply yet at the same time engage the cosmic tension that functions as our unknown inheritance.

Superseding the Diurnal:
The Latest Works of Byron Baker

HIS VISUAL FIELDS impinge the eye as gestural flashes, as interior crystal convening and breaking apart, astral-like, constantly re-forming into astonishing combinations. Each of Baker's works adumbrate as sigils. In this sense they exist as a kind of visual contagion weaving and susurrating amongst themselves via dazzling visual grammar. When viewing them one thinks of the denouement that springs from puzzling mathematical stanzas. They are nothing less than intriguing diagrams of brilliance not unlike arcane principles of carbon. Certainly, one is not entrapped by an exoteric optical method.

As one enters their present housing (the Oeno Vino complex in the Atwater district of Los Angeles) one is initially greeted by a stunning array of planetary wines and spirits gathered from a complexity of locales. After striding across this utopia of spirits one then leaves its array to descend a flight of stairs to the gallery below where Baker's works burst forth. It is entry to a susurrant grotto where his creations magically summon the viewer from a vast electrical realm. Common cognition is subsumed by his visual grammar soaked through by telepathy. The salon style hanging (not unlike the Barnes collection in Philadelphia) proves wise in that it helps the works gain strength from one another invoking in the viewer a state of presence thereby enabling a sense of duration. A charisma of rhythm transpires allowing a trenchant respiration between works in colour and those rendered in black and white. Smaller works in graphite function as equals with the larger ones rendered in larger scale. Thus the eyes transmute via preternatural elixir. Exoteric achievement ceases to exist in this circumstance. The exoteric that projects in this circumstance is understood to remain non-conversant with turgid or clannish register. Because Baker ignites at such a high level of proliferation, the energy he spawns transmutes his interior gift to such an extent that it spontaneously transcends quotidian obstacle. Field after field enunciate themselves in spontaneous colour or line thereby narrating splendiferous alchemical kinetics. Baker's hand, seismic, unscripted, thriving inside incandescent irradiation, not unlike the aleatoric hieroglyphics which have come down to us, say, via Matta, Camacho, or Soutine. They carry an inalienable power trenchant as they are with interior clarity. To experience his Estranged Galactic Vigil, or his Black de Pinto de Blue challenge's the viewer's comfort level by creating a need to question chronic optical habituation. Such questioning functions as nothing less than unexpected spur along the way to self-initiation.

His continuum swarms and at the same instant exudes trenchant stamina. A stamina containing vitriolic oxygen which instantly translates to vision. And this vision being none other than a clairvoyance that smoulders via internal current. This being a visual genetics that I'll call interior rhythmos. When viewing these works, I felt subsumed by an oasis of perpetual aura as if I were a pilgrim casting his gaze across a beautiful innominate vista. And because the innominate pulses so strongly these works remain far in advance of the claimed spoils of the cognitive personality. They do not negotiate with the sterile deployment of the marketplace in mind. Instead, we are carried over into a realm where history ceases to apply. The latter being espied as a fetid ancillary manger trenchantly in-starred by regression. Since none of these works are codified by dating there exists no allusion to the weight of entropy or the coffin. Here the super-imposed calendar fails to transpire in the sense that he forms kinship with aboriginal draughtsmen found in Australia and New Guinea. Thus the technocracy fueled by exterior proof can gain no footing at such an un-shadowed level. The work gives us inkling of the four-plus billion years that preceded humanity on Earth. I am thinking of the impact craters, of the million-year rains that filled the ocean basins. This is the Earth not The War of The Roses or the curious derangement of someone such as the composer Gesualdo or Henry the VIII with his protracted imbalance. Baker reminds us that we exist at the behest of forces that preceded Earth itself. Humanity remains a collective receptacle of non-human forces. It seems these forces predominate to such an extent that he spontaneously understands that the body is subsumed by what is understood to be the soul and not the reverse of the body being in advance of the soul. It is the former view that gains traction in these works thereby allowing them convergence with energies normally eclipsed by daily ordination.

Being energized fields they elicit something other than mortal futility, something other than transmigration across superficial psychic opaqueness. Upon entering the gallery one senses a rhythm suffused with interior peregrination, a peregrination at dialectical remove from journeys of say, Desoto crossing the Mississippi, or perhaps the projected colonization of one of the nearby asteroids. One never senses a tenor fraught with need for acquisition and triumph. As for the typical concerns of fame and profit they cease to inhere as any form of concern. There exists no City of God to which he aspires, instead he is fueled by the principle of non-capture.

These works are bodiless anagrams brimming with an otherness that seem to speed towards alchemic horizons. As has been stated, all ancillary approval has been transcended. Just as lions breathe, they seek no outside approval condoning their ability to naturally exist.

At the risk of seeming to prosecute the didactic, I urge any interested party to go and view these works, and witness their power situated at the juncture of the spectacular and the limitless.

Inscrutable Solar Configurations

WHEN THE CONSCIOUS mind ceases to dictate it rises into atomized union with its greater prevailing principle. This prevailing is none other than the mind at one with its own oceanic. Once cognitive stricture has been released all fixation dissolves and the mind no longer mimics itself and naturally conjoins with itself as free and primordial element. All juncture, or status, or a priori configuration of elements ceases to conspire as blockage. What has happened in Baker's case is that an articulate looming has flooded through. It is none other than a ceaseless wave of grammar that instantaneously self-articulates its own tenor not via repetitious engagement but as magnetic revelation that charismatically subsumes all barrier as juncture. Not simply an exterior palace in which one lives but a fragrance of elements that bears witness to oceanic consciousness that perpetually roils within not unlike somnolent expression that flows as in—geminate with its own writhing. Baker's drawing is not unlike a dominate exo-world plane completely water-born under the brightness of occulted turquoise inscrutability not unlike witnessing a new and panoramic view from doubled solar configurations.

Theresa Tolliver: The Soil of Indigenous Genius

BECAUSE THE ART world blazes with the dissonance of celebrity and its stultifying by patronage, the artist who rises via fumes from inward fire tends to remain in-starred by anonymity. Work after work appears received by indifference, or perhaps, graced over by the maddening commotion of random applause. Such has been the fate of one, Theresa Tolliver, master ceramicist, mixed media artist, doll maker, whose water colours emit a deftness of poise that suffuse the eye with unerring range.

It's as if she has arrived from the beyond via the optics of second sight. Her original power, one senses, is not bound by craft sequentially mined from glacial directives. In this sense she is not unlike Joan Miró; when she touches colour or paper magic transpires. Not being an architect of colours doled out by theory, her hand ignites, she enters the given material not unlike trance-suffused musicians in Morocco rendering particulars via trans-personal honing. And this honing invades one's visual field as error-less mathematics having just the right shading and colour. Yet she has never been arrayed as a celebrated icon kept alight by ingesting oxygen from notoriety. She simply has no other desire than to create.

At this point one might get the impression that I am lauding an artist never conversant with outside instruction. She has had sustained contact studying with master ceramicist Michael Frimkess, as well as early training at the old Chouinard Institute in Pasadena California. She has also received her degree in the arts from the Cal State University campus at Northridge California.

Having exhibited in regional locales such as the Skirball Cultural Center, and the African American Museum, both in Los Angeles, her work has been restricted to non-codified appearance. She has never been accorded the national view her work continues to demand. Her fate seems par for the course as a woman of colour and has been constrained to sustain itself within the shadow cast by the exclusivity that remains celebrity culture. She remains a hidden gem waiting for some symbiotic collector to ignite her brilliance akin to the respiration that occurred between Chaïm Soutine and the late Dr. Barnes in Philadelphia.

If indeed her art had sprung to form in a more receptive psychological setting, it would carry the overtone of an oracle, as power emitted from a superior state of grace. Not as it now stands, she is forced to face combat with the world against that triple plague that combines whim and finance, along with the passing tastes that ignite the grossness that is cynical whim. There is something to be said about the cliché that money attracts money. Because she, for the most part, is bereft of it, bereft of its real-world respiration having little power to attract it. Shuttered away from access to the plane of capital she has no contact with the population that populates the collector's market, the latter having resource to unusual largesse.

Thus her art blazes as an anomalous lunar figment scaled by circumstance to shine within an occulted range forming as nodes of light within a subterranean psychic nexus few have been privy to witness. Allow me to point out a mixed media work owned by (Theatre of Hearts/Youth First Founder) Sheila Scott-Wilkinson. It depicts a figure that refracts the image of the late actress Beah Richards. The colours gather and simultaneously splay and optically regather all the while enriching each other's motion so that deftness gathers itself not unlike the mastery that one feels in the presence of Monet's watercolours or Degas' pastels. High praise for an anonymous work that only a restricted few have had the honour to witness. But this is precisely my point Tolliver executes at such a shimmering level of quality that it stands on its own un-scorched by the a-moral ethics that tend to crown celebrity.

When the crowds have dispersed, when the names have vanished, what is left except the visual image that guides us, like a stunning flambeau probing the recess that we collectively understand to be the utter mystery of ourselves. Her craft burns at any scale or medium, and because her craft thus burns, I ask again, why is it shunted aside in favour of painting wrought by the marketplace and its superficial celebration of the ancillary? The writer Marco Pallis once entitled of one of his essays "Is There a Problem of Evil?" I bring this distressing title to bear only because her omission seems to occupy a sub-category of Pallis' appointed title, thus her omission from wider scale summons to my mind something institutionally sinister. One can no longer deny this prevailing circumstance as being nothing other than a sub-component of darkness. Yet still, Pallis' title may seem a bit strong when applied to Tolliver's circumstance. I contend that her continuing omission has denied the contemporary viewer gusts of necessitous visual oxygen. It seems it is beyond the time to call for this overdue rectification by having a group of interested parties facilitate her work bringing it to a space where it can call on itself, and by calling on itself emit to us its atmosphere more akin to the powers that nourished the shamaness María Sabina. Thus I've been concerned here with providing a forum more attentive to the growth of art that issues from the soil we understand to be indigenous genius.

Ghérasim Luca: Fulminate Inscription as Shadow

LUCA ERUPTED IN this life as the shadow of a given body, as a free lone traveler insidiously confronted with the round of human tedium. In the midst of this innate tedium, he found language as identity and identity as language. As an adolescent, as Salman Locker "looking for a new place to emerge in life other the accident of birth," he "encountered the news of the death of 'Ghérasim Luca, Archimandrite of Mount Athos and emeritus linguist'." Paraphrasing Romanian literary critic Petre Răileanu, it was for Luca the generating of life out of death. Thus Luca was born in such a manner that eluded biology. At this instant he leapt conventional neurology and was immersed in a language that overthrew the vernacular as grip via lingual homeopathy. He then employed as his regimen a carnivorous subtext voracious in his employment of the wayward. It was staggering misuse made palpable by his impenetrable linguistic current, where not only was his grammar distended but each letter of each word grappled with itself by ceasing to know itself thereby broaching a new frontier of consciousness. It is what Deleuze cited as a "prime example of stuttering in language, which for him represented the highest poetic function." For me, I call it fulgurant transmission with an intensity not unlike a lahar rushing down a darkened pockmarked lava hill. Two words seem to apply to this language: velocity and danger. In fact, Luca says to himself that "I fasten myself to my own disequilibrium." He babbles by means of his own carnivorous substrate like a hellish centaur or perhaps a speckled Taurean ram evolved from cataleptic ciphers. One susurration evolved into another until a non-Euclidean flatland was evinced. Within these random hillocks of language monsters hissed, condors flew round and round until a whole conjoinment of menace transpired... an existential cacophony as though Luca himself were still plying his weapons. Not a writer who theoretically tested his position, Luca never angled out his circumstance by means of meticulous neurosis. Like the Taurean that he was, he continually broke beyond limits through the fury of maniacal expression. There was never blockage by detail or horizontal rejoinder concerned with quotidian particulates. Instead, he enacted the bravery of despair by always kinetically bounding beyond all limits, corroded as they were by daily entanglement.

At this point it seems appropriate to chronicle his first five suicide attempts and their attendant documentation. It was as though he was responding to the void in his blood. His first attempt was conveyed by the one-line missive: "I can no longer bear this life full of privation." He writes in his second missive of extremis: "causes of my death not to be looked for; there are no guilty, not even myself. I forsake life without any regrets. I ask for restraint at my funeral, cremation if possible, flowers not to be bought." His third attempt codified by the words "O my darling." At his fourth invasion of death, he exclaims that "A nervous illness never incurable never which never tortures me for many years never forces me to end my days. I pay never with my life for the sins of my parents, never my heredity never was burden. If I never did no one wrong I never asked forgiveness." And at the fifth attempt he states, "If it is true, as the errors claim, that after death man continues a phantomatic existence, I will let you know. If you do not hear from me for one month, you will know that death is no different than the putrefaction of an onion, a chair, a hat. I commit suicide out of disgust."

These are haunted prolegomenas, various proto extinctions. With the glaring exception of Artaud, no one's spirit has been so suffused with drifts into surcease as was Luca's. The writing was soaked with its uncanny babble, with its syllables of a wakeless cadaver, always rife with termination. It was in this way that he led by tremor and seepage. He gave us hints, he beckoned from the other side by means of a body virile with the angst of glossolalia. Neither fine-tuned China, nor an unspotted spoon dipped in sorbet, Luca continued to hiss as a restless property; his verbal gales were not unlike the towering global winds on Saturn. I think Codrescu is right when he points out the influential energy in Luca's work just at the point when Breton returns to Europe from exile facing a state of lessened influence. When I say this, I am not keeping a debit sheet or adding up shadows, but acknowledging Luca and the Romanian Surrealists as enacting an occult empowerment of International Surrealism throughout its imaginative diaspora circa 1957. It was during this period that *The Passive Vampire* appeared, a text which Petre Răileanu deemed "Luca's first properly surrealist text," for in it, Luca allows "displacement without impediments," and the radical vivacity of the subconscious spirit where "the Possible replaces the Real." During the same year (1945) that *The Passive Vampire* appears, Luca, along with fellow surrealist, Dolfi Trost, co-authored *Dialectics of the Dialectic*, "the capital text... for the Romanian Surrealist Group," which "affirmed unshakable fidelity to Breton," to "objective chance" while also intoning an organic critique of surrealism, warning the French group of a phantom tendency just to become another "artistic style." On this latter point, Artaud voiced similar concerns to Breton during this same period when he rejected the latter's conscription of his drawings for gallery display. Never was his energy trumpeted through concealed posture. He was always racing against psychic self-engulfment composing at the scale of frenzy, his violation of grammar being a natural progression of his poetic lahar. He was a master of the indecipherable; he possessed no inclination to compose from imported slates, to list literary influence as a mode of retreat. Luca, always roaming as a neolithic wolf searching for the prey of the unanswerable. His instinct was none other than words that equated with visceral diamonds which then transmuted to erotic declarations, moist, venereal with contagion. His language remains a circulatory immersion always tainted with treason with the ravenous as its triumphant genetics of being.

Georgiana Peacher's *Mary Stuart's Ravishment Descending Time*: A Species of Rapture

THIS BOOK FEELS as if it were a series of riveting sunspots stunning one's cognitive properties, paradoxically expanding consciousness by means of its enigmatic anti-narrative. Entering its spontaneous field is like a jolt of interior insulin for me. A photomantic pulse, an overwhelming conduction with an accuracy wrought by minutiae which are not unlike canyons.

I liken her psychic scape to the impastos of Pollock or Soutine. Her gnarly emission erupts as a plasma of imbroglio all the while tilted inside the odyssey of a susurrant Mary Stuart. When she speaks of "Mary's eyes" syncopating "spectra" it is not unlike her language alive with spectral eddies and spinnings. It seems that Peacher conveys Stuart's odyssey through the reverse dimension of sound that conveys an eloquence which whirls throughout this compound verbal maze. Peacher hypnotically transmits the gist of Stuart's danger always prefiguring her looming execution. The book being poetically balanced, is organically shaped by oneiric punctuation. Make no mistake, this is writing seared by the genius of the omnivorous, the book at its core being scribbled biography as trance. Indeed, the opening bout of the book is entitled "Mesmerisis" as she oneirically meanders across estranged botulism acres speaking of "warm bodied boys killed in battle." The language respires with the uncanny, with an intensity speeding across inflammatory meters, across "crevices of mountain rock," with Peacher all the while maintaining her poise inside its historical cauldron.

Peacher remains anomalous. Well into her 94th year she remains unseasonably productive, remaining in creative contact with poet Jonathan Skinner who I thank for putting me in contact with her work. Her writing, fully rooted in its depth before the E-mail era, partakes of the unbuffered process of pencil in scorching contact with paper. As regards persuasion via ancillary promotion, via Facebook or other forms of cloned connection, none exists. Instead, she harvests her inner lingual field by simply trusting herself. Thus, her métier remains unhalted. As she stated, "In the Spring of 1966 I decide to give up everything, fly to Paris, begin a new life of writing." What an example for the hordes of writers stifled by the crippling need for safety nets. They have lost the power to gamble, to swallow doubt when no one is looking. In contradistinction, Peacher slips as an innominate cipher across the ravine of primordial anonymity. Having as her energy the power that enkindles serpents and owls. At this level she is nudged by hunches and gut feelings, thus, she is privy to human misunderstanding and heartbreak. What she possesses is the existential criteria to creatively chronicle the throes of Mary Stuart. The text is woven as if her gaze burned with four or five hyper eyes wandering up a gyral staircase with "lachrymal nerves, touched by the needle of emotion." Indeed, she couples creative impulse with emotion.

Having gathered this capability after many years as a leading speech therapist, she refused to die from failure that builds from inner pressure, from low exclusion curiously under-scored by suppression according to academic treatise, because her thinking has never been beckoned by entry into theoretical context wrought by sequential thinking. She vowed not to die sequestered away in some academic outpost her writing squandered by "laryngeal stress." As she stated in 2005, "… I avow I would have been dead years ago had I not allowed my demiurge to flourish." Inspired by Anaïs Nin at a critical juncture in 1966, her writing continues to flourish unbowed by time constantly surmounting quotidian register. She continues to creatively unfold "finding old age to be a beautiful new experience, writing and painting artist books, having museum and college art shows," as well as a new book of poems published in 2004 entitled *Skryabin Mysterium: Dream Mind of Alexander Scriabin*.

Great imaginary power does not in itself guarantee notoriety. I've mentioned her name over the past few months to a selected number of beings only to be greeted by expressions of blankness. This non-response is no criticism and never staunches my excitement for her writing. Powerful writing does not erupt from facile recognition. Many are drugged by careerist opportunity which translates to nothing more than competence within pre-set standards of a lingual safety net. A safety net which in turn both suffocates and devours one's imaginary radiance in return for institutional recognition.

Having made her acquaintance not far back, I am heartened by the fact that we've had no conveyance other than by phone call and letter. And I remain convinced that great writing will continue to be read not because of the way it's technically conveyed but because of the manner by which it burns and courses through our psychic nerves dazzling as would an invisible scorpion fish. It hypnotizes and casts a sidewards glance which pierces, which annuls by organic charisma pedestrian memoranda. As the French critic Marc Chenetier so aptly put it, "... she makes possible the osmosis of the underlying patterns of history..." And partially quoting the late memoirist, Deborah Digges, Peacher writes a language which "begins before language" with "qualities" that "tap bedrock in some dangerous primordial slide..."

The Larsons' Journey Beyond Time

THE IMAGES EMBLAZONED by Dean and Laura Larson's European sojourn had an extended stay at the Fine Arts Building in downtown Los Angeles during the fall of 2016. The exhibit, entitled a "Journey in Time," cast an atmosphere that was suffused with duration rather than a glimpse into lineal time. Laura's hybrid animal beings seamlessly inhabit her photographic interiors while Dean's photographic exterior scapes combine as a mellifluous collaboration. An oneiric harmony if you will, presenting in this case a collective document of their double travels in France that included the years 2013 and 2016. The result invaded my eye as a living compendium, not a simplistic blending but a tapestry that brings to mind the aesthetic verbal color that Pere Gimferrer employs in his work *Fortuny* that poetically chronicles the "aesthetic opulence of the European Belle Epoque and successive decades."

Rather than a more inclusive domain, the Larsons' circuitry within this exhibit remained confined to France traversing its earlier eras as they explored locales such as Cluny and Versaille bringing forth newfound wonders from what I would tend to describe as the historically inert.

The works at hand pervade the visual field with a magnetism of hypnotic fluency evoking an architecture of mellifluous assemblage providing the viewer with a fleeting seminar on beauty. Thus the works give glimpse to a dimension that foretells itself allowing each work to emanate with striking insistence as a telepathic clamour that the subconscious seems to spontaneously conjoin with. Saying this,

I am not saying that the exhibit propounded itself via quasi-mystical obfuscation, but on the contrary elicited an ineluctable quality defying the quantitative as containment.

Laura's hybrid beings interact with the mythical plane that they kindle in the viewer almost palpable with respiration. There exists a susurrant call and response between Dean's exterior scenes and Laura's vibrant interior decor. It is not unlike synesthesia, as visual had translated to aural seepage suffusing the derma so that the uniqueness of each work begins to concretize in one's consciousness as a hidden spectral dye alive with heightened interior wisdom. All the while a type of arcane commentary persists as if the factor of menace enthralled the atmosphere with comment. Take Laura's apparitional ferrets haunting the private chamber of Marie Antoinette, or Dean's otherworldly locomotion implied by his Auxerre with its lane engulfed by a teeming spectral presence. Then there exists their collective image that contains its sudden upright buffalo fiercely gazing over an interior decor at Cluny.

There is never the feeling of assumption or pre-scripted posture compromised by induction, instead there is a wave of rhapsody in works that continue to instill their presence long after one has left their actual physical installation. One then associates these works with the realm empowered by Debussy and Ravel and of the aforementioned Gimferrer, possessing beauty that ascends to the plane of the indescribable.

On Sonic Etching: The Work of Jean-Luc Guionnet

JEAN-LUC GUIONNET's recording "L'épaisseur de l'air" ["The Density of Air"] emits itself as a river of sonic quantum fragments illusively fused. Not according to linear occupation but as charting according to spontaneous breathing. Its irregularity rivets and expands through invisible nautical range as a spectral etching of itself. One listens to Jean-Luc as if floating above a sea of spectra. But the latter remains capable of bringing to light prior examples that Eric Dolphy emits on "God Bless the Child" recorded circa 1962. A step further back in time brings us to Coleman Hawkins' work as he sonically inaugurates Picasso in 1948. His melody extends into implicate self-harmony. One's consciousness of another realm of inner sonics that one senses when viewing Sebastião Salgado's "Southern Right Whale" gracefully immersing itself into the waters of the Valdes Peninsula. An image suffused with telepathic transmission. All the while my mind tends to bend as well as self-ambulate into an era post-Roscoe Mitchell and his album *Sound* recorded in 1966. Alas Anthony Braxton comes to mind via his recording *For Alto* recorded in 1969. For Jean-Luc tends in proximity to Braxton's example. The song form having vanished as we've come to know it. His sonic charisma extends into the variability of its own act. The sound can also remain akin to alien facility. Since the song enacts itself as nutrient, aural soliloquy comes to punctuate itself endemic with intervals and errorless silence. Sonic heightening transpires as telepathic grammar enunciation forces that lurk in the unseen.

"Lépaisseur de l'air" is a recording that exists beyond its silences and lines, beyond its spontaneous sonic knottings, and seems, in the end, to always imply mirage. This sound registers to my ear as one could imagine that all the galaxies had vanished. His sound remains impalpable residue where countless random suns are eclipsed and are compressed as spirals of energy amounting to an anterior state with other parallel and simultaneous collections of suns.

Aleatoric Circular Forms: A Trilogy of Circles

IN HIS LATEST presentation at the Berman Gallery in Santa Monica, the iconic filmmaker/photographer, Chris Felver, has ignited the eye with what I'll call aleatoric circular forms. Influenced by the artistic presence of Donald Judd, the grouped circular forms contain photography culled from disparate psycho/physical locales that include Prague, Paris, and Berlin. The trilogy of circles is uniform in size, its images structured by Donald Judd like architectural squares. The circles are inhabited by 150 images that fill and thereby sustain the totality of the circles. When viewed while in motion via side-long glance they flood the retina as black and white blurs and cast an aleatoric mist that seems to spontaneously rotate as an odd concussive whirling. Again, they spin as sidelong blurs giving the impression of a hybrid form of cinema. In this sense they are a continuum of Felver's quest to expand the portrait as an alchemical image of consciousness.

When Felver proto-chrystalizes Judd, he opens for us a mirror where analysis seems moved by susurrant enrichment. And this enrichment invigourates what I'll call an interior mathematics whose equations are not unequal to Judd's autonomous exploration, an exploration that in Felver's case symbolizes living nutation evincing a spell of interior riches. But unlike Judd, instead of an autonomous sculpting that irradiates from stationary space, Felver's circles emit simultaneity over and beyond the seeming stasis that accrues from a static singularity that registers, say, as transposed office space.

There exists in this present evaluation the dominant nexus of the side-long view as density via movement, not in terms of measurable extrinsics but as movement more akin to occulted cellular respiration as expression. Because such respiration never impedes its own synergy one begins to experience through one's optical state a living field that quietly engages the viewer with what I understand to be neural irrigation. When life happens at this deeper state it is many times unsuspected by a less discerning consciousness. Let us take for example, the manner in which trees grow and expand, or to extend this to cosmic reference, I feel compelled to compare Felver's occulted motion to that of Uranus or the outer figments of our solar family, namely Pluto, Eris, or perhaps the dwarf planet Sedna. The latter evincing a single rotation synchronous with the span of 11 thousand years as it rounds the Sun. It is this latter example of movement that is akin to Felver's nutation which typically fails to garner basic acknowledgment when exposed to the commercially vetted eye. It is to Felver's credit that his circular conundrums elicit comparison with the farthest known elements of our local solar family, while at the same time creating an arresting presence in an environment seemingly dominated by the whims of those who remain as distracted passersby.

James Hart: The Cryptic Personality, The Unknown as Presence

SOME BEINGS ENTER only part way in this life, neither dwarf nor giant, their extrinsic balance seemingly intact. Yet they have fissures that seethe, constantly emitted from the other. This is what Roger Gilbert-Lecomte has called "a wondrous prior existence." For Gilbert-Lecomte the "prenatal" was the palpable mean, not as heresy, not as shocking public rebellion, but as fundamental state "a brush-stroke signifying absence."

James Hart having emerged from absence as tenuous composition, his absence emitted as presence, having galloped into life on a riderless phantom pony. In keeping with his arcane arrival, he understands as did Lecomte, language as cryptic personality, experienced through bouts of withdrawal from the senses. Thus, everything is reversed, turned askew, as if one were conjoined on a plane of converse polarity. Hart's lingual navigation veers and enters blinding trance, always examining cusps and shadows, where, at times, phonemes, break off and abandon themselves to grace another dimension.

As Hart himself enunciates "my text becomes an isometric prose poetry that hopes to communicate with this dead-white spirit…" Thus Hart's is requited in that his life on Earth remains a perpetual "Act of Dispossession."

Prologue: Quantum Lingual Deftness

AS I EXPLORE Pablo Jofré's condensed verbal scale, I am swarmed by an overwhelming impression that it has sprung whole cloth from un-corrupted verbal ether. His book, *Abecedary*, provokes in me spontaneous analogy with the seminal power of its Chilean poetic heritage, a heritage that has spontaneously affected Jofré's imaginal crystallization. For me, this poetic heritage remains a monsoon of droplets that continues to enunciate itself through a legacy that is poetic moisture. As inspired chronology it extends from the posthumous fertility that was Carlos Pezoa Véliz, to that of the lyrical dazzling that embodied Gabriela Mistral, and completing this triumvirate is the aerial acrobatics of the great Vicente Huidobro and his limitless *Altazor*. This being a chronology that cannot exclude the surname Neruda, who hovered as a shadowy condor above this disparate poetic playa lyrically altering the Chilean poetic glossary via his personal topos of human contradiction. Within this context, we can never fail to mention the verbal archipelago of his poetic rival the tragic Pablo de Rokha.

It is from this gist that Jofré arises, inspiring through his poetic inscription the magnetic rudiment of vision. And this vision empowers his transmutational expression, swirling as it does his personal monsoon of droplets that cast spells seemingly closer in technique to the creative dossiers of Enrique Lihn and Nicanor Parra. *Abecedary* condenses via poetic semaphore lingual neutron stars penultimate to incalculable eruption. Unlike the complex simplicity of Parra, or the acidic political veracity that was Lihn, Jofré understands our present general condition comprising, in part, a compromised ozone being toxic threat from Fukushima or melting permafrost in Siberia. This hyper-awareness seems naturally instilled as he evinces intrinsic verbal chemistry as poetic practitioner wandering the boulevards or magically investing himself in the microscopic scintillation of a drop of dew.

Because apocalyptic pressure exerts such a presence upon the contemporary poet, Jofré simultaneously adapts and inscribes this pressure intoning in his poem "Abyss," that witnesses present reality as a "shipwrecked morning, in winter" via "nothingness" and "ambiguity." Thus, he artfully engenders the beyond sans the confine of cognitive analytics. In this poetic particle we see him exercise what I understand to be quantum lingual deftness. Fortunately for us, his English readers, his verbal deftness has found a port of entry via this artful rendering of *Abecedary* so wonderfully magnified here, in this, his first English registration, incisively wrought by David Shook.

Majied Mahadi: Enigmatic Icon

THE ISLAMIC RENDERING of his name I interpret to be Glorious Beacon. I do not know if it was a name bestowed or if it was his own interpretation. When I first met him, his visage was furrowed by insight and strategy. As we continued to speak it became clearer and clearer that this original intuition was uncannily accurate. His breadth of interest, his grasp of various knowledges, his architecture of discipline I found quite astonishing for someone having just emerged from their 19th year. As we continued to connect our focus became that of inner mental liberation. This was for us the key in ending the maliciously induced dearth introduced into the Black community via negatively intentioned epigenetics. Epigenetics in the context of our South-Central home-ground meant and continues to mean artificially induced behavioural obscuration.

To combat this we thought by attempting to maximize the mind through study would provide perpetual antidote for what we understood to be the colonized mind with its negative resonance. For us, to breech the provincial was to experience the mind at universal scale. We were not unlike binary suns pushing and pulling one another via feverish search in service of higher lingual expression, our interplay I can only analogize to the version of the Charles Mingus workshop that featured Eric Dolphy and Dannie Richmond. He introduced me to chess masters such Morphy, Alekhine and Capablanca, and I would counter with things such as Paz's book on Levi Strauss, and the poetic fiction of Severo Sarduy and the epic intent that was Julio Cortázar.

Every book or idea discussed was none other than a spur to greater brilliance, to greater insight. Of our two minds his was the more strategic, the one more capable of weighing and dispelling, while I, on the other hand was smitten by non-cognitive immediacy and the poetic example exemplified by Breton. What we both shared was our collective admiration for Jean-Joseph Rabearivelo and Garcia Lorca, poets who had attained in our eyes a magical form of transmission. It was our wont to scale the psychic mountaintops, to animate a reality far beyond quotidian option. Every moment lived, every sentence read, every particle of thought discussed was none other than seismic momentum that attempted to commune with universal reaches.

We then reached Aurobindo our 20th year and began to meditate on Aurobindo's sense of cellular transmutation. Other yogins such as Pararmahansa Yogananda and Sri Yukteswar Giri graced our presence, but it was Aurobindo that held, given his rise from revolutionary action against the British into his alchemical kinetics of the Divine, given that our daily thought was also confronted at every turn by the complexity that was revolutionary politics that seemed to consume us. Aurobindo and Lorca seemed to spin as stunning beacons at other levels of action. In our minds they bridged the gap between a nascent supra language and the quotidian concern that surrounded as we were by the Cointelpro circumstance of the moment. This greater tension was also reflected in our individual difference, he more aligned with strategy authored by involvement with chess, and me more concerned with imagination and the other. In this circumstance I can say that tension generated energy. It sharpened our internal pitch to such an extreme degree that its spirit still generates power inside my mental derma. I am likening its force to grammar as feral fertility not unlike unaltered sound that issues from cosmic explosion. An explosion that continues to ignite in me as that prevails in my awareness of the unforeseen.

He was one philosophically driven, as far as I can see, initially ignited by his stint in the Maoist study collective known as the Red Guard. And it was via this incursion that his discipline was initially honed thereby allowing his laser-like approach to study. By its use he understood texts almost by immediate grasp of getting to their central property then knowing how they reverberated through their periphery. Everything read was underlined and its principle became spontaneous architecture inside the mind.

I always thought that his background provided him with the tools for long-term combat in climbing to higher planes of world achievement where only the giants resided. His con-figurative fuels seemed astonishing. He had a mind I continue to admire, even after the rising and setting of un-countable suns. He seemed a king of sequential brilliance. It was a brilliance that seemed to rivet surrounding meters with ferocious impact. If he spoke of Marx or Hegel, or the charismatic gravity that was Guevara, it seemed a mark was made. It felt as though a lion were growling via significant introspection.

Therefore the competition to know things was paramount in our relationship. The need to keep pace was none other than maddening. I remember upon completing Sri Aurobindo's *Life Divine* and Julio Cortázar's *Hopscotch* it gave him a start, as he was at the time plumbing the chess masters and delving into world cinema. This was a powerful praxis for the mind that was active even through stages of vulnerability and doubt. Because always the big picture subsumed particular mental climate whether high or low. It was the mind overcoming all moments of interior obstacle, thereby coming to an understanding with the confusing state of one's interior wilderness, this being exercise that remains endless.

After an evening of heated informational exchange it was decided that his brilliance was the more malleable of the two and was most suited to the present circumstance that we occupied, and I was the occulted member more suited to future climates. As we travelled this occulted high road there existed in our vicinity the ordeal that issued from silence. When a new vocabulary is attempted proponents of the now who live for the now tend to leave one alone. We existed via blinding imaginary form via poetic scent wafting from the future.

But there was a bitter turning in paradise. Our collective velocity foundered. A consuming erosion announced itself as his life became dour marked by increasing rainfall. We witnessed Thelonius Monk together, and he taught for a time at Cal State Northridge, but his beacon was dimming. A lacuna arose. Daily contact ceased, our imaginal respiration was reduced to a gasp. It produced in me a ferocious puzzling, an essential element had gone missing. Then during random conversation with the great flautist Sulubika (Monroe Jones) he reported that the great Mahadi was seen migrating in and out of dumpsters scrounging for survival. This was shocking to say the least. This was concrete evidence that a diet of general drug ingestion had no respect of person and this was a pointed example of it bringing down one of the best.

He was no longer the glorious beacon psychically ascending higher and higher mountaintops but more and more was suffused with the status of a creature haunted by dissipation. His was a dissipation that created in our immediate community a sense of bafflement. How could such Sattvic aspiration reverse to the depths of such Tamasic registration. In part, his descent was fueled by governmental drug flooding of the South-Central environment, and, in part, by cracks in his psyche that allowed negative familial history to invade his thinking and allow drugs to enter. The combination proved fatal.

By chance, in 2006 I ran into Dedan Kimathi (Dedan Gills, who has since passed on) who was the third part of our original three-person study group. He told me that Mahadi was no more, having been hit by a car two years prior during a foray into darkened streets after sun fall.

Even at this time, his demise continues to cast itself in enigma, astrologically dis-embodied, as if remaining suspended in the continuum, while his legacy continues to shimmer, tantalic with possibility.

New Mexico Poets' Conference: Organic Poets' Society

IN A SOCIETY beset by celebrity and amplification, New Mexico Poets' Conference remains a secretive dialectic to all the withering that disgorges itself upon our synaptic sensitivity. Because we live in such a troubling era of caustic disability there exists collective angular ingestion sanctioned by a debased bio-chemical diet that is skilled at abducting one's spirit into protracted assimilation.

Within the altitudinous New Mexican summer the Poets' Conference signals a true retreat from the scattering deficit of societal devastation. A delimited oasis founded in 2009 by poets Genji Amino and Daisy Atterbury, it allows one's poetic complexity to live for meaningful duration in a living utopia laced by underlying silence. It allows poets to strengthen their bonds with a seldom felt vigour strengthening the subtext of insight. Instructors and students cross-circulate sans hierarchical boundary allowing a mental ozone where poetry can return to its founding source allowing spontaneous continuity.

True, there exist lectures and readings, but these are inculcated in such a manner so as not to hamper but to ignite creative rhythm without feeling the presence of rational over-sculpting that invades the spirit as fatigue. Within its seminal current there are un-scripted moments where colloquy and spontaneous dialogue forge aboriginal connectives where verbal liberty is struck. As for psycho-physical experience it more than rises above diagrammatic indignity. It carries as its principal shape retreat where the poetic mind was never claimed according to a protracted or influential disfigurement. There was never gregarious or superficial proclamation. Its métier was none other than a truly spontaneous society enlivened via the undercurrent of poetic bonding. It is context for the soul, not a mis-stated mystery. A heresy if you will in terms of what configures as contemporary grouping. Not unlike scientific corroboration it is an atmosphere that does not advertise individual brilliance of instruction as a ploy to lure students. There was never vain-glorious imbalance. Its physical realm has never been artificially expanded to attract paupers of the spirit. Never was there desire to foment an architecture that houses a climate that houses second after second best. As for carnivorous inflammation of the spirit none could be detected. Always one's spirit was magically lifted by insouciant blazing, never by insistence on strategic capitalization. What is left to the soul is energy that configures auto-spontaneity sans scientific jackals to ponder.

This has never been one of protracted errata that seems to function at the core of daily life as one pursued life through a maze that emanates from continuous tremor. This being the tremor that New Mexico Poets spontaneously addressed by providing the poet with the properties of quiet and absence allowing an inner neurology to rest from civilian embranglement. Hikes to Anasazi mountain caves, then lectures on Pueblo farming technique by master builder and poet Daryl Lucero.

Not poetics solely operant as academic confinement but a conversant poets' society where the body and the mind were allowed to heal and function as one.

Beyond Baroque: A Seminal Wind Encircling the Planet

A BEACON BEAMING rays through the mists of inclement realia not unlike a lighted mount above a sequestered alabaster grove. This inner mount being Beyond Baroque, a refuge for imaginal practitioners. Not a mirage, mind you, but a living amplification of language, operative since the latter 1960s, prior to most of the poetic bureaus and seminal presses of the present era. It has pioneered, it has taken chances, it has paved the way as a forward agent, brewing a living poetic habitat.

Not a mirage, but a three-dimensional facility, housed in the old Venice City Hall, constructed circa 1908. As stated, it remains a poetic refuge, but more than a refuge it is a zone where poetic combustion transpires. Certainly not a space that appeals to the psyche of technocrats, or to poets buffered by disposable income and unwarranted status. It is a place where psychic mud can withdraw and smoulder igniting its own disappearance. Where the imagination can meaningfully teem and is given the liberty to blaze.

As Poet-in-Residence I have never been hounded by a carking agenda herding me into zones that conform to conventional expression. Never has there been ideological susurration shadowing my choices of individual readers or my predilection concerning the selection of readers for collective events. This remains increasingly rare given the tendency towards sponsored surveillance that surreptitiously beclouds our present era. Existing in an age super-imposed by extrinsics, poetic survival is most rare indeed, hounded as it is by the bickering voices that continue to rise from discomfort of those mechanically and systemically riven by profit.

Beyond Baroque remains a Foundation fortified by the bones of integrity not unlike an organic inherence, running as an unbroken lava from its founder George Drury Smith through a series of inspired directors that have included the late Fred Dewey, Richard Modiano and its current Director, Quentin Ring. Of course, there are many names I could intone but suffice it to say that they remain integral to empowering a poetic oasis that transcends individual personality.

Workshops for the poet, the novelist, the screenwriter all gratis. This remains diametrically opposed to an active commercial tenet, the latter concerned with draining one's personal coffers. Instead, at Beyond Baroque there is foremost concern for longstanding creative sustainment, for maintaining the irreplaceable elements in one's spirit.

Baroque's motto: "a place dedicated to the possibilities of language." Because of its irreversible dedication to art of creative language it retains its hard-scrabble demeanour, it takes a no prisoner approach to the outward trappings of comfort in spite of the passivity that now brokers the fuel of the bourgeoisie personality.

Its presence is none other than a grace conferred on the Los Angeles region, and beyond that, a subliminal icon bending its rays like a seminal wind encircling the planet.

Wanda Coleman: Bulletins from the Lava Floor

WANDA COLEMAN ROSE to linguistic heights inching her way upwards through a tense volcano kingdom. And what is this volcano kingdom? America, with its institutional apartheid being at one with skilled institutional treachery and its other voice symbolized by the explosion of Watts generations prior and the general sphere once known as South-Central Los Angeles. A nether dimension always a semi-spark away from eruption. It was within this eruptive immensity that her rise began as a five-year-old beginning her odyssey as a reader. By 13 she had had her first poem published. Quite an accomplishment for a soul so young all the while struggling with the double malady of gender and colour.

Let me say first off, Wanda was not an exotic, a precocious mantlepiece to be savoured and observed from afar. Her works were none other than bulletins from the lava floor. She was tested, not only by rejection from the European literary mean, but also by her peers for being odd and out of place. I do not script these lines as an institutional outsider who has studied maps of the region and dug up its footnotes. We shared the same community terrain scorched by the above mentioned double acidics of being an outsider while remaining under institutional apartheid. Wanda and I had the opportunity to discuss these tensions on more than one occasion.

But let me say, it was Wanda who blazed the way, striding unbowed through misunderstanding. Never comfortable with the calculated, with that of consensus understanding, Wanda, when confronting racism, would stand her ground, making her opposition withdraw, causing its claws to bleed, and then for good measure scorch it with the hot barbed wire of her language. Not the simulated wire of a long-term careerist or a scholarly hand scripting language via mimesis. She never catered to consensus levels of comfort. She was dangerous in the sense one could never figure her reaction to any pre-set cognition. In this sense she was not unlike Baraka, aiming at icons such as Maya Angelou and Derrick Walcott.

In this sense Wanda Coleman can never be reduced to a precious local commodity, nicely abstracted for those too fearful to roam. She took on the urgency of her circumstance, all the while suffering the sting of chronic poverty. She was never delimited by hordes of provincial acolytes who sought her blessing so as to foment their own ineptitude.

We are facing a future that has no place for this as our species continues sailing down an apocalyptic concourse.

Wanda we love, we will always love you, knowing as you knew that the implacable power of language erupts, always igniting new scalers.

PART III

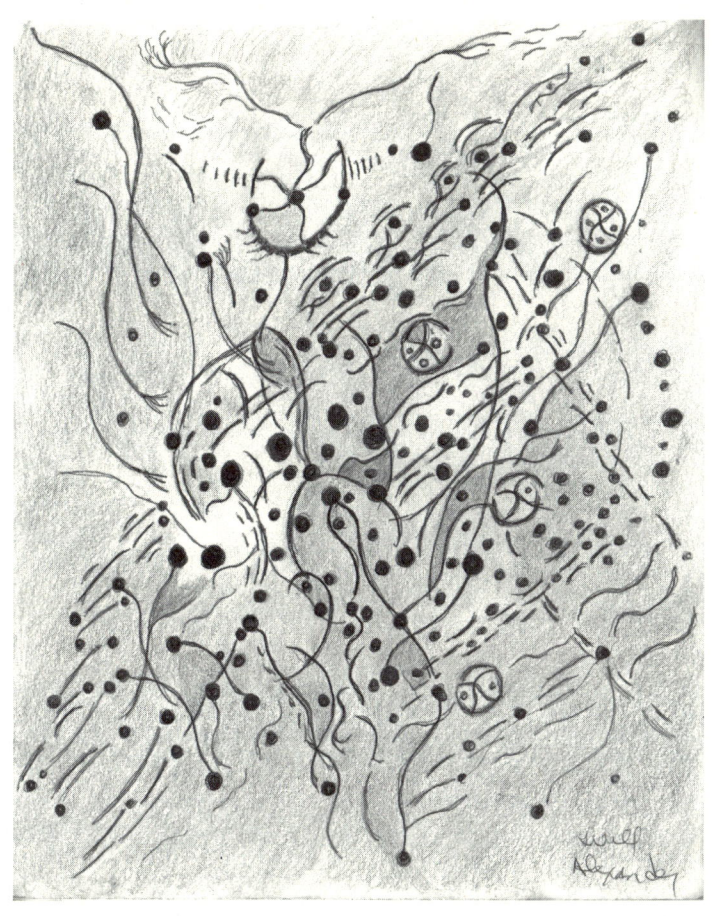

PHOTONIC RESPIRATION

Interviews

Primordial Vibration

with Elizabeth Bryant

ELIZABETH BRYANT: You were born in Los Angeles and have chosen to live your life there. How often, if ever, do you have Los Angeles in your mind when you are writing?

WILL ALEXANDER: Let me say, first off, I am not a Los Angeles provincial. But I've needed the cultural resources of a global capital, and Los Angeles is a global capital. Its cinema, museums, and libraries, its cultural fertility has been crucial to my development as a poet.

EB: How has your relationship with the city changed over time?

WA: Los Angeles remains a susurrate catalyst for my work. To me, it cannot be privately hoarded or provincially compressed, or didactically extolled according to a previously constructed American narrative. It continues to rise and shape itself as a global presence and as a vector for the powers of otherness outside the standardized enunciation of the English language. A few days ago, for example, I engaged in an extended exchange with a gentleman from the Ivory Coast and had another with a friend from Mexico. This type of spontaneous cultural exchange is a very common experience in this city. As an African-American male, I also bring an otherness to these exchanges, since the African-American presence remains a foreign element within the governing American narrative. But as we spoke, this narrative was notably absent. What I'm emphasizing here is that a whole new cultural identity seems to be transpiring in Los Angeles according to tenets of the unforeseen.

EB: Many of your works, like *The Sri Lankan Loxodrome* and *Asia & Haiti*, concern places far from Los Angeles. Where have you traveled over the course of your life, and what places have made the most significant impressions on you?

WA: For me, the most vivid form of travel has been in situ, not unlike Raymond Roussel spawning imaginary realms from seeming occlusion. If it's "the Sri Lankan Central Hills," or "the Gulf of Gonâve" in Haiti, or "Yamdrok Lake" in Tibet, they are not literal configurations of the stated locales, mind you, but in the context of the writing they rise as imaginary nodes, or points of raised significance at crucial junctures in my work. Therefore, what I write is never tainted by verbal tourism, rather, it is physically involved with this geography, allowing it to shift via seepage into the "differential." In short, a geography that partakes in what Henry Corbin called mundus imaginalis.

EB: Tell me a little about your creative process in regard to your visual art. What is the relationship between your artwork and your poetry?

WA: The visual art and the written art both arise, for me, like flora and fauna. They ignite from the same invisible wellspring yet phenotypically differ. In my work this invisible energy enters into both the writing and the visual work. In my case, I call the written work energy of the right hand, and the visual work energy of the left hand. Thus, the artwork is symbiotic with the writing. Yet I do not draw something in order for it to fit with something already written. When an image is drawn, it is akin to applying words but more instantaneous, more hypnotic. If I have any dictum, it must be paraphrased thus: all imaginative creation must invoke itself as energy, and remains spontaneously feral.

I am also concerned with what the Tamil philosopher Anada Coomaraswamy called "the picture which is not in colours." I've realized in my practice of using language a certain cellular electricity. A level no longer bound by exoteric meaning, but language that internally registers as alchemical energy. A language organically unpredictable, yet always internally balanced.

EB: I've noticed that you often choose the British spelling of words over the American. The word "vapour," for instance, appears throughout the collection spelled with an "ou."

WA: I've been drawn to British spelling since I read the word "colour" as a child. So when I started to publish my poems it felt very natural for me. I guess to some individuals it may seem as something exotic. But what I can understand is that for me, it adds texture to the text, which allows the text to emit a more complex savour.

EB: You have developed a formal style of including a glossary at the end of your works. I've noticed some of the words you choose to elucidate are imaginary terms like "goatfish burin." Others are archaic, technical, or specialized, for instance "globigerina," (shells of falling radiolarians). Yet others of a similar nature go unannotated. How do you choose which words upon which to expand, and which to leave "unsupervised"?

WA: My glossaries are not meant to serve as mechanical handrails for the reader. They help orient him or her to a higher dimension of my language. If I took an accountant's approach, more and more words would be listed; the result would be something altogether tedious and scholarly.

EB: How does orientation affect how your poems are read aloud?

WA: The poem is not aurally dependent upon glossaries or any extrinsic structuring agency. It naturally emits a vibration, which is audibly intelligent to the listener over and beyond any cognitive aspect. I call it primordial vibration.

EB: What are you currently working on with your poetry?

WA: I have five books due in the ensuing months. Two are collaborations—one with the visual artist Byron Baker titled *The Codex Mirror*, and another book with New York poet Carlos Lara inspired by Breton and Soupault's *The Magnetic Fields* called *The Audiographic As Data*. A book of my early writings, *Aboriginal Salt: Early Divinations*, will be published by the Detroit press White Print Inc. There's more than the above, but I'll only mention one more project—it concerns Muslim polymaths during the age of the Moors. The book revolves around Dar al-Hikma, an institution founded in Cairo in 1005 that foreshadowed Cambridge, Bologna, Salamanca, and the modern university.

On African Free Labour and the Interstellar Vacuum

with Chris Holdaway

CHRIS HOLDAWAY: It was just announced that you are the 10th recipient of the Jackson Poetry Prize—congratulations. How are you processing this, and do you already have ideas on what efforts the award will go towards?

WILL ALEXANDER: Of course, it is an honour to receive recognition at this level, but always my natural reality is moment by moment alchemy via language. It is a perpetual drone, perhaps, akin to the background radiation of the universe. Since I had absolutely no idea that the Jackson was approaching my vicinity, so the news has naturally melded into the reality that I am continually conversant with. I'm in the midst of typing a very difficult book. I'm doing this while in motion back and forth to work, during lunch break, and during evening hours when the narcotic of sleep attempts to abduct me. So, reception of the funds can only enhance my inner realia, allowing me extrinsic liberty from the waste that the culture perceives as work. They will allow me liberty to draw and to travel to other parts of the world before circumstances overtake us. In the midst of fires and tragic chemical leaks there is sea rise, and gusts of refugees worldwide. I feel this is the best time to explore the wider world.

CH: This time of crisis you point to is one that, at least in public imagination, is often particularly dominated by the spectre of the climate. Do you have any particular vision for the role of the poet in relation to ecology?

WA: The state of the present global circumstance seems non-sustainable, rife as it is with all forms of contamination. At every level of the human populace there is the gathering sense of our collective vulnerability. Not long back I heard a 9-year-old testify about climate change and salmon disruption in the state of Oregon. It's as if we are hanging by threads within a self-created margin, yet because there seems to be no immediate impact on general consumerism in the United States the crises tend to go unnoticed by the harried majority trying to survive the daily entanglement that the dearth of capital unleashes. Thus, the climate, even at this late date, continues to be seen as something esoteric, distant. It is for the poet to telepathically pick up via language the deeper circumstance at hand. For instance, NASA recently reported that the Earth's axis has tipped due to displacement of polar snow. The poet cannot provide answers laced with bromidic immediacy, but he or she can begin to inaugurate a verbal atmosphere that opens onto other states of awareness. For me, each phoneme is akin to Hindu psychology and is capable of vibrating at a higher or lower pitch. Too often, poetry is created through the aural lenses of the tamasic, immured as it is at a very low vibrational pitch. This lowered condition generally lends itself to sentimentality, to lower bodily function, to chronic inter-personal friction. These concerns tend to elicit an occluded view of things and never awakens the listener or reader to internal radiance so crucial to lingual maturation.

Unfortunately, recent poetry has been subjected to the business model via structured writing seminars that, for the most part, occludes deeper research into the self. It places more emphasis upon the book as viable technical product rather than as a document that seeps from the irregularity that is higher consciousness. Poets aspire to publishing poems, to placing books into the world, which, well they should, but sans a dash of vulcanism in the language, so content is subjected to erosion via entropy of the marketplace of current consciousness. Rather than introducing us to possibility that beckons from an immaculate prairie of possibility a form of blinding sets in. Absent of internal metrics, exploration is reduced to shadow moving inside shadow. Instead of poetry providing direction for science, the opposite now seems to be the case. Being able to suss out an internal vocabulary, poets such as Gilbert-Lecomte, Césaire, and Artaud, inaugurated verbal movement that enlivened geometries of the invisible. Their writings seemed to induce states opening the reader to organic possibility. An undeniable livingness is felt in the language. This being language giving life to the prevailing impact mystery that is mystery. This being language over and above the cult of personality, over and above the anecdotal. Can one see Rimbaud or Gilbert-Lecomte being dutifully bound to attending lectures and doing weekly course assignments? Exploration of language as alchemy explores the substance of who we are and evolves a sensitivity open to risk and instability. From the 20th century there exist whole lists of examples. I have mentioned Artaud, Gilbert-Lecomte, and Césaire, first, because they have greatly influenced me, allowing me to hone and respect my own hearing within a transformative tenor, and second, because I have recently written three epic poems on the three of them collected in book form soon due out from Reve a Deux, entitled *Spectral Hieroglyphics*. But as stated above there are many others who have invoked the value of risk via aural exploration.

CH: How might one begin to enter or activate such a language of *risk*?

WA: Exploration at this level of intensity is generally not encouraged. One must be internally equipped for the voyage. Initially one needs sustained focus capable of fecundity in all circumstance. This being language as unbroken trance. Since we live in a society that fosters all manner of distraction a language possessed by such imaginary focus automatically rises above the fray and garners its own intransigent momentum. In the tamasic kingdom that we occupy this language remains exceptional and spontaneously exemplifies itself, so much so, that it eventually gathers notice without conventional promotion. With poetry so invaded by the business model, by the quotidian dictate of long-term financial security, one can, if one chooses, become adept at playing the game of verbal risk while remaining comfortably ensconced even within the declining reign of the suburbs. There is poetry, and then there is poetry that has succumbed to quotidian strategy. The former is consumed by audition, the latter dominated by vacuous ordeals bestowed by credentials. Thus, poetry, like the rest of life as we know it, has now been divided and thrown into question.

CH: Speaking of divisions, much of your own work seems to have a vast cosmological scale to it, yet at the same time is replete with images of the body, & never far from singular lyric pronouns ("so what concerns me / is a yoga which implodes the sun"). I am reminded of Dipesh Chakrabarty's influential challenge to really think the human as *species*, even though "being species" is not something an individual ever truly experiences, especially when we know certain populations are disproportionately responsible for climate change, & others are disproportionately affected (often with a high degree of mutual exclusivity between the two categories). Is this something you can see this language of risk addressing?

WA: One can never forget the inequality spawned at the beginning of the modern world, sparked by the Portuguese entry into Africa. From the early 1400s to the present this entry has created a collective stumbling block. The general orgy of murder and exploitation that followed has now engulfed the southern globe as a negative staple. Resources have been extracted without surcease from the southern globe in order to enrich its northern half. Not didactic enunciation, but a dominant pattern since the feral beginnings of John I and Prince Henry the Navigator. It is a pattern that has supplanted Islamic syncretism found, say, in 10th century Granada (lost realia that Lorca increasingly lamented). Or let us take recent events, the example of King Leopold in the Congo. Leopold and the Belgians hijacked the equivalent of a billion dollars in today's currency, and this hijacking continues unabated by the Americans, the Canadians, the French… Since 1997 six million Congolese have perished as a direct result of this plunder. It is a tragedy the Northern media and

Western scholarship have, for the most part, obfuscated. Can one imagine this many Europeans having perished without general comment? It is unthinkable. Yet the American automotive industry, as well as its electronic sector, and of course, its military sector, would go into steep decline without this daily plunder of minerals and metals. So clearly, there is little concept of species collectivity when it comes to say, Africans, or tribal south Asians, or American Indians. When Linnaeus and the great classifications transpired, a standing disparity was permanently invoked between Europeans and all other living forms on Earth. Francisco Bethencourt speaks about this era (shrill as it was with division and re-ordering) in his book, *Racisms: From the Crusades to the Twentieth Century*. European hegemony has been nothing other than a disaster. Its policies have put the human collective at risk, forcing it to function across this great divide. This remains the undercurrent of collective human experience rent as it is by divisive tribulation.

A few months prior I saw footage of a private investor speak to a gathering at NASA concerning human voyage to and habitation of Mars. During the course of his talk the name Christopher Columbus was pointedly invoked. I immediately noted a mentality skewed towards extra-planetary exploration as colonization. And we know colonization has had and continues to have no respect for even itself as a living form. This is a mental state sickened by addiction and has led to the current mass extinction of wildlife unparalleled in 65 million years. It is a state of mind based on acquisition. Not unlike an infection, it has spread from the thirst for gold symbolized by Cortés to the intense consumption that riddles the eastern seaboard of China. The Earth would need a diameter that rivals that of Saturn in order to absorb the long-term toxins being spewed from simultaneous regions. In order to sustain the present circumstance oil must be pumped at a rate of 42,000 gallons per second. As for long term quality habitation of Mars it feels to me as if it is to be a protracted Roanoke waiting to transpire. At our delimited level glaring contradiction persists more and more as seeming technical advance by those who aspire to alien worlds yet who persist in referring to Central Americans and immigrants from Mexico as "aliens." This remains a dangerous travesty.

CH: Related to this, I often see (white male) poets making the case that identity-based or political writing is too "small-scale" or irrelevant in the face of climate change/the Anthropocene, which is apparently what we should really be worried about. How might we think at a global/planetary scale without rendering the question of identity moot? This is something I often see troubling much new materialist thought.

WA: It must be understood that the Whites, though they control the largest military on Earth, find themselves more and more isolated by the very factor of their behaviour towards indigenous planetary culture for the past 500 plus years. Of course, this started with the Age of Discovery when wealth and power were accrued at unprecedented levels. But the manner by which this gain has been wrought, Europeans seem to have self-branded themselves with un-stinting stigma. The late British writer Cottie Burland discusses aspects of this behaviour in his book *The Exotic White Man: An Alien in Asian and African Art*. This ongoing behaviour continues to spark general susurration and revolt that abounds amongst the Southern peoples on a daily basis. The great divide falsely invoked by Europeans at the rise of the modern world wantonly disrupted other invisible cultures of science in return for material items, thus crippling deeper insight, leaving the lot of us woefully unprepared for the experience of deep time. All the peoples of colour have in some way or another been subverted by the European swath that has occurred during its recent history of acquisition. There is not much time left to heal this very complex and embrangling rift, yet all the old colonial policies continue to brew under other monikers and appellations having negative impact on ecosystems around the globe. Rather than a mature and organic process as attempt to conjoin the human species, instead we are being provided with the curious possibility extended by alternatives that include the superficial range of robots and genetic engineering which seem at best, inspiration for further damage in the long term. In this sense neo-mechanization seems nothing other than the glorification of failure.

There needs to be an attempt to reconcile with the rest of nature rather than stoking the same polarizing policies that have put life on Earth at the brink. Marco Pallis once penned an essay titled "Is There a Problem of Evil?" I think that the title remains quite applicable in our present circumstance. If we look at Occidental interests from Torquemada to the ongoing conflict in Iraq, we see institutional murder condoned as a political corrective. Remember, the Occident has benefitted from almost 400 years of free African labour, so at present I don't feel it has the moral authority to preach to anyone. Given this persistent climate of division the white male poets you refer to need go back to their rooting in Modernism. Aldon Nielsen in his book *Reading Race in American Poetry: An Area of Act* uncovered the letters of Stevens, Williams, Cummings and others. Their racial provincialism is appalling. Rather than take issue with a climate that spawned public lynchings, they complied with its basic tenor. There is always this argument for dividing Pound the man from Pound the poet or making allowance for Eliot's outright racism and anti-Semitism. Such a legacy quite possibly has a great deal to do with the grand starvation of language we see condoned in certain quarters that tends to alter creativity in favour of what I'll call cognitive super-imposition (say the replication of the phone book passing itself off as creativity or reading the minutes of a rape trial). Such a poetic climate spawns the supremacy of desiccated cognitive technique, thereby promoting arthritic lingual application. Yet there is hope. As long as humans from all persuasions attempt to unite with one another, healing can possibly transpire. People like Noam Chomsky and Bill McKibben constantly give us alternatives to the old psychic models. Stephen Hawking is right when he warns against tapping into extra-terrestrial intelligence armed with only the bravado of an isolate technical language.

CH: One of the most notable features of the poetic line across your projects is the near singular utterance that collapses as the first line of a "stanza," before blooming in supernova. Something like: "yes / as a dark stochastic wheat drained of its magic as drift." This initial term is often a pronoun (especially the "we" throughout *Asia & Haiti*), or a rhetorical device. How does this particular alternation between extremely punctuated and expansive line allow you to work?

WA: Pronouns resonate as particulars of balance. Rather than confine they allow me to gather myself during the heat of composition not unlike impalpable way stations, seeding both momentum and expansion. As particles, they are akin to say, a saxophonist hitting a note to procure balance in order to ascend higher into the hail of the imagination. Thus, the poetic faculty transmutes via the intervallic trampoline. Within this imaginal storm they are blurs, nanosecond stanchions, not unlike particles inferred from collision within the Large Hadron Collider. They are evanescent flashes that exist as part of the continuum, and the continuum is the quicksilver cosmos of the imagination that has no limit. True, the latter is seeded by study but cannot be equated with the most miraculous facts or ideas if these facts or ideas have not been verbally transmuted. It is unlike the learned disciple seeking to replicate his master. There needs be instantaneous transgression in order for the imaginary to re-ignite itself so as to experience itself as that which foretells its spontaneous unfoldment.

CH: Something you have written extensively about is a radically composite origin for your own being & thought; in Caribbean lineage, through West-African/Dogon expertise, to an alternate history of Arabic knowledge you've already mentioned, one seldom recognized beyond vague lip service to Avicenna & Averroes as transmitters of Aristotle to later western thinkers. I'm thinking especially about your essay "The Post-mortem Imam." What is at stake for your work in this practice of searching for a new/old-but-erased ground?

WA: First of all, a major transgression transpired thousands of years prior. When the early Greek philosophers kindled their original utterance, they had not developed within an independent Greek educational matrix. For instance, Pythagoras was an Egyptian subject because Ionia during this era was controlled by the Egyptians (then later by the Persians), so quite naturally his initial contact with mathematics and music came from the auspice of the Egyptian Mystery System. His was not an independent genius that suddenly erupted as a stunning wholeness out of nothingness. According to Plutarch he "received instruction from... Oenuphis of Heliophis," who was part of the Egyptian Mystery experience. Yet our institutional instruction has repeatedly absented this phase, telling us via omission that the Pre-Socratics kindled universal thinking, with only a cursory paragraph or two covering the Egyptians and Babylonians.

This remains standard fare in freshman philosophical textbooks, and thus seeds in-built blindness within the educational process. Because of this there exist successive generations of the educationally maimed. Occlusion becomes a principle when it comes to noting intellectual achievement that rises from the Southern globe. This is why there has been this desperate attempt to create a terminology that somehow linked Egypt to a European source. This is why Cheikh Anta Diop remains anathema in certain quarters. He incontrovertibly proves that the original Egyptians were the originators of the arts and sciences. There exists the fact that there were advanced Egyptian orchestras 900 years prior to Pythagoras during the "XVIII dynasty." It is unfortunate that one has to continue to point out such realities, knowing that we have a climate with those who possess doctorates and means of research, who willfully fail to fully align themselves with non-European conduits of history. Averroes and Avicenna have been turned into particles and abducted by the Occident sans the learned innovation of Islamic culture. I've noticed in many instances a confusing circuitry of detail mixed in such a manner that it gives the impression that "alchemy," "astrology," and "theurgy" ignited under the auspices of the Greeks. At a certain level the mind tends towards an unfortunate calcification and becomes complicit with the complication of non-aligned particulars. This is what I'll call a partial purview stemming from what I consider to be the colonization of information that leaves one, in the end, turning to the four quarters of emptiness all the while remaining sans the athleticism of the spirit. This remains the Occident within its form of modern secular arrangement. There is only proof by matter and the simultaneous manipulation of matter. This remains science at its highest journey self-propelled as an embrangling tautology. It is always attempting to prove to itself that matter is the source of the creation yet, paradoxically, its vocabulary of experiment remains absolutely fascinating. Its creative complication of language is something poets can take quite a few notes from. Césaire gives great instruction in this regard. His was a mode that poetically seeds the future.

History as it's been generally conveyed in the Occident needs be significantly transmuted, with the Greco-Roman presence understood as a subsequent state, not an original innovation, all the while connected to a prior condition of things. Its African origin needs be fully stated, thereby providing some restorative balance to the species as it's evolved over the past 10,000 years.

CH: How might you relate this composite and alternate history of thought and knowledge to your vibrant and lyrical form of essay/criticism, one that eschews any traditional western style of scholarship?

WA: Being in touch with my inner vibratory kindling, with its African fiber, with its trace amount of aboriginal Indian fiber, naturally dictates a yield that is sans European domination. Instead the European can only be supplemental. To superimpose its criteria of expertise, thereby suppressing African prestige can only lead to scrambled utterance, to carnivorous stalemate and fatigue. I do not work from knowledge as resistance, but to knowledge that induces flow. To fully live within intuitive conservation. This does not enable limitation, on the contrary it ignites voraciousness, for instance Thomas Kuhn / Cheikh Anta Diop, Charles Fourier / Aimé Césaire teem as simultaneous flow. One gathers nutrients and the mind becomes akin to subconscious plasma. When I wrote my essay on Fourier the first line ignited as a lingual surge without prosaic foregrounding. It was as if I saw Fourier penning his Harmonian utopias. I wrote this essay by means of inward pitch. Details followed. I aurally opened my mind to Fourier and after the flow had ignited cognizant activity transpired that included his ideas in the form of biographical data. This was the principle that energized all the essays. It can be said that the actual body of the texts sprung from poetic mystery. Paz and Leiris speak of lingual grace. In my case there exists this kindled through-way to non-cognitive levels. These levels are always analogous to me of what the late Chilean psychiatrist Matte-Blanco refers to as symmetrical, and as I understand it, reaches levels where the asymmetry of difference via the ego transmutes to deeper strata, not unlike the invisible mathematics of the Egyptians that Schwaller de Lubicz refers to. This is an active conduit open to all as Lautréamont once put it. This is the conduit that Breton so fruitfully extended. In other words, elements of Egyptian psychology continue to permeate the modern world via the Moors, the Sufis, Romanticism and the Surrealists. Rather than the superficial codification of matter, one touches upon an inner power that is related to the pent-up centimeters of empty space with each centimeter representing the energy of a trillion atomic bombs, and empty space being commingled with collective solar creation. This power being not unlike the elements that populate Dogon culture and comes through in the works of Césaire and Afrocentric elements within Rasta culture.

CH: I recently heard you read from your chapbook *Based on the Book of Ghosts* in LA, in which you invoke Nigerian writer Amos Tutuola as the poem's propellant. This seems like another important part of your practice, figuring also Philip Lamantia in *The Brimstone Boat* & even marrying with collective populations as in *Asia & Haiti*. You likewise mentioned forthcoming work taking on Artaud, Gilbert-Lecomte, & Césaire. But I get the sense that these moves are not conventionally commemorative elegies, nor are they persona poems from the subject's point of view. What is involved in summoning these texts?

WA: Tutuola remains a living field, not of course as a biological destiny, but as expanded activity via language. Because our languages intertwine across differing dimensions, the particulars of Abeokuta Nigeria of the 1920s and Los Angeles California of the 21st century spontaneously desist as grounded obstacles. So there exists, at this level an interaction, a free communion between the living and the dead if you will. There is nothing deliberate or analytical about the manner in which I connect with Tutuola. He is not some monument, or a ragged dialectical abstraction extracted from the mists, but a perpetually living presence. He is not some pointless candelabra to be revered as a terse uncanonical figment, to be registered in the secular ledger. At this level one is never prone to the static registration of corpses, to static admiration of a living experience. As a living Egyptian carrying trace amounts of American Indian, I understand that the cosmos is a living experience that can't be separated into fragments. Like the Thai I have never been mentally colonized, so as I once stated (in an old *Callaloo* interview) I am a "psychic maroon," a runaway who has no use for the disorder caused by the false distribution of the cosmos. Since the Egyptian pyramids were constructed 1,700 years or more prior to Thales, and Thales is regarded as an inalienable originator, this tells me that I have been forced to function in a climate of not only scholarly but general prevarication. Until human electricity is sorted out at this level it will continue to end in more and more obstreperous entanglements, being more and more subservient to technologies that give the illusion of movement. Take Tutuola's language, contrasted to the colonized English of his Nigerian critics, and as is said in sporting terminology, there exists no contest. Because they had copied the British there remains no maze of circuitous magnetism. In the poem I speak of his "living example," with its "ability to singe," "to stumble as haze through incitement." The creative person can never be detained by his or her status. Tutuola, if I recall correctly, was a Junior Clerk during his composition of *The Palm Wine Drinkard* (1952). As far as outward circumstance was concerned, he had no credibility, no right to instill verbal bravado. But hasn't the greatest work come into the world sans degrees and official accreditation. Poetry is in the electricity of the language itself, its ability to mesmerize even at the level of its smallest particles. When entering a Miró drawing or listening to Miles Davis play "Teo" with Coltrane, one gets the shivers because its aural profundity literally invades the neurology providing an actual physical sensation. So, it is with Tutuola's language, it enters one as would a flood of ciphers, as if each phrase existed as a-structural neutrinos, magnetized by non-cognitive velocity. So, when his seemingly educated critics first witnessed his works they could only adhere to their European training. For me, having come to English in a similar manner as Tutuola, I recognized his power immediately. When we look at Tutuola it is sans the sophistication of the capitals, sans London, New York, or Cairo. When Cortázar and Lezama Lima composed their towering works, *Hopscotch* (1966) and *Paradiso* (1966); both books astonished in different ways. Because Cortázar's background included cosmopolitan locales such as Buenos Aires and Paris it provided a modicum of context for his spectacular foray into world presence, whereas Lezama's rise created puzzlement. Such puzzlement continues to whirl about the oeuvre of Tutuola because even at the highest levels creativity is many times thought to derive from the lack or from the largesse of one's circumstance. In Tutuola's case the imagination evinces an unmistakable fruit in spite of the paucity of his daily circumstance. In my case, Abeokuta was not unlike South-Central Los Angeles, where expectation of the intellect has tragically plummeted over time. Given the objective graph this interview should never have happened. Like Tutuola I was supposed to have been diverted along the way, shunted away in the provinces forever. But the cosmic principle persists of life perpetually springing forth far beyond the restriction and the mind's ability to comply with such restriction.

CH: Your work is often claimed as a bastion of US surrealism, and you've already mentioned touchstones in both old and new world lineages (Gilbert-Lecomte, Césaire). How do you see your language of cosmological risk that we've been discussing here in relation to the tradition of surrealism?

WA: When Paz and Breton strode for the final time through Les Halles in 1964, Breton expressed the fact that Surrealism was entering a zone of neutrality and was in a state of surpassing itself. That surpassing in my view is none other than psychic entry into the interstellar medium. The interstellar was akin to music in Breton, sans engagement. He distanced himself from the interstellar in the 1962 issue of *La Brèche*, but what remains with me are the implications of his conversation with Paz. It has passed like a spore through all manner of circumstance with music and the interstellar medium as part of our organic context. This seems to be part of our natural state at this time post Coltrane, post fly-bys of Egeria and Jupiter, along with the Hubble and James Webb telescopes as prime explorational mechanisms. I recently heard a documentary on the four major moons of Jupiter; they are 450 million miles away, and possibly when the Sun expands in billions of years a place such as Europa may be more Earthlike. Such scale brings into scope capacity that surpasses the human, but it can't be denied that our psychic environment has spread far beyond local planetary confinement, with our biology now provided the field where it can phase into potential exo-states. This is where shamanic internal praxis transpires, which brings to mind Aurobindo's transmutation of the cells, implying a state other than human. But the hostility of the heavens requires an incalculable level of adaptation. Rather than an attempt to overcome of its elements via human facility as we've known it, there is the necessity of the unthinkable, something I've explored in my drawings, evolving figures that carry only the residue of the human. Aurobindo has gone on to say that the human is not static, that it has the potential to generate impalpable electricity over and beyond its visible station. These are levels that were being explored by the original Egyptians, by aboriginal shamans across the globe, so clearly, we have lost perhaps the equivalent of two millennia of work at this level. When we compare the capacity extolled by Descartes it partakes of both tragedy and comedy. Humanity has been given over to the mechanisms of matter infected by global racism. Thus, we have not been able to practice the true alchemy of the species. I'm thinking of the famous Dogon example and their discovery of Sirius B without the aid of Occidental instrumentation. This notice drew ire and doubt from certain quarters, but what I am speaking of supersedes every level of limitation that we have been conditioned to conceive. This being entry into galactic maturation, a maturation sans the pernicious embranglement of the European skill set. Not that this skill set should be negated, but to understand that it needs to harmonize at the general level without need to separate itself from the collective effort. Such an effort at this hour needs be re-ignited through language. Artaud, in the midst of his magnificent enunciation to André Breton ("Letter to André Breton") uses the words "electrical revolution" which have stayed with me. Invigourating language with alchemical pulsation is the dawn of magnetism, bringing to view something other than vernacular habitation. This is alchemy that supersedes the absurd. It is a reality where the mind as we know it in use tends to break down. It is analogous to Van Gogh's taking off in a "train to a star," a particle from one of his letters. It enunciates a protracted level that vernacular experience can never prepare us for. I'm concerned here with consciousness capable of movement into deep time, this being part of the alchemy of species transmutation. In this state of reality, war, the exchange of capital, life and death as we know it would transmute as well in the wake of such experience. Our present mind, in order to even approach such apperception must at minimum engage in oneiric exercise so as to experience its realia as alchemical seepage.

This is where surrealism has prepared the way, not through ideology but through praxis at the level of the anonymous energy. Oneiric language tends to subsume individual concerns so that the author as separate entity tends to de-exist, submerged in language as all electrical spontaneity. When we work with language in this state of spontaneity, we can begin to get a sense of the Earth before humanity was formed; an apocalyptic balance, an intelligence prior to the formation of creatures. It must be understood that historic dating falls within the space of only 10,000 years. When we compare this to the spinning of the Earth as it existed 400 million years ago we can begin to truly understand the ratio between human action and cosmic action. To cease to respect the latter retains realia shot through with blasphemous staggering. This is especially egregious when this staggering represents the microscopic sliver of human action distorted by a delimited European component. Thus, we are compelled to occupy a reality that is asinine and again, completely egregious.

CH: Surrealism seems to be something that US poetry has at best begrudgingly accommodated, at worst tried to quarantine/expel. Why, in your experience, do you think this is?

WA: Surrealism remains a threat to a scripted delimited locale of consciousness. There is always the linear as threat hovering in one's presence. The whole of reality is permeated by this yes/no construct. There is never gradation or experience within the liminal, or a both/and grammar that allows expansion beyond mental partitions. Having had the opportunity to participate in a number of collective writing projects over time, my experience has been one of liberty, always feeling a sense of psychic aeration and relief. Working with Andrew Joron, Janice Lee, Carlos Lara, Byron Baker, and Heller Levinson and others work has always gone smoothly, rather than feeling a sense of confinement. It has felt as if my mind was permeated with a powerful elasticity and from my collaborators' feedback, they've felt much the same way. There was never the thought of one person's writing over the person's work. A field was shared, minds were at ease. When the mind is at ease it accelerates absorption, effort that would be turgid, frustrating as isolated endeavour tends to vanish. When I sat down with Janice to go over the proofs for *The Transparent as Witness*, the work was completed at one sitting and flowed without complication. Such experience seems somehow foreign in a land dedicated to the isolation of the individual, always barbed with competitive angst. Thus, one roves around in life blinded by the observations of others. Hence, the pejorative term "consumer." Say, the human race was connected at levels other than protracted distraction, perhaps an interesting galactic community could be shared because there has been long term disfigurement truncating the mind at large. What immediately comes to mind are three nodes of regression: The Council of Nicaea, the fall of Granada, and the Berlin Conference in 1885. In all three instances the African or aboriginal mind was suppressed via murder and most importantly the embrangling of the mind to favour European auspices as thinking. Simply by renouncing murder as a prime tool of power Asoka towers over world leaders as a source of possibility.

This is why the philistines reacted to Breton so strongly when, as the cliché goes, he jumped ship, and language has never returned to internment behind barriers, to recto-linear standstill not unequal to a maze of shopping catalogues. In his essay Poetic Matters Philip Lamantia castigates Ginsberg and others for communicating at the level of *Time* magazine, for never absenting the push and pull of the cognitive, or the superficial cage that sputters with the language of commerce. This latter state can do nothing other than condone the criteria of stasis, of things as they remain, while brandishing at times a patina that seems to exhibit liberty. As Lamantia clearly states, this is writing sans imagination, sans circuitous absenting that inhabits linguistic empyreans. In other words, modern day Imperial Latin given over to natural surcease. A superficial understanding that classifies Surrealism as being solely immured in French. Certainly, its original proponents used its properties with unusual adroitness, yet, as Miguel Carvalho demonstrates in his spectacular compendium *Caleidoscopio Surrealista* (2011), Surrealism functions in French, Spanish, English, or Dutch with uncanny power. Collective thought, use of various cultures and languages certainly poses a threat to an authorship spawned by Pound and his cohorts, who, at base, remain apologists for original Nazi culture originally seeded in the early modern world by a triple curse of gold and race: Hernán Cortés, the African slave trade, as well as the Italian Inquisition. And it is from this negation that 1776 arises with many of the early American presidents being active participants in this tragedy as slave holders themselves. As a species this idea of "liberty" so extolled across the past several centuries has never really existed when we consider Jefferson's remarks concerning Phyllis Wheatley. These are remarks that remain a perpetual insult and, when compounded by general Saxon exclusivity in the published annals that we've had as I'll call it, a protracted inferno. Can we see Césaire's welcome by Breton into the core of Surrealism replicated in a welcoming by Eliot into the poetic elite? It was the latter who won the Nobel Prize off of the strength of Pound's reworking of his *Wasteland*, this prize being the prime symbol of individual authorship. In contradistinction, when language ignites from the impalpable internalities it sweeps away analysis and principal stultification. When I worked with the artist Byron Baker on *The Codex Mirror* (2015) we were joyously amazed that our differing genres spontaneously erupted as harmony, allowing us to complete our book sans interior carking by the ego. This same spirit suffused my work with Carlos Lara and Andrew Joron and Heller Levinson when I worked with them on separate occasions over geographical distance. These examples are now unlike a scientific proof applicable in all directions. In fact, all of my friendships and meetings seem facilitated by the telepathy of consciousness. Breton always spoke of the "ease" by which things are accomplished, this being an ease which has nothing to do with the Protestant work ethic.

Hearing a Second Bell in a Mirror

with Sofi Thanhauser

SOFI THANHAUSER: *Singing in Magnetic Hoofbeat: Essays, Prose Texts, Interviews and a Lecture, 1991-2007* presents many different voices. For example, it contains the voice you use in interviews, the voice used to give a lecture, and it presents the voice you use in your essays over the span of over a decade. Do you think there is an argument, or affect, or an overall impression that emerges from the combination of these different ways of speaking? Did you think of this as part of the intended effect of this volume?

WILL ALEXANDER: There was never any pre-intention in the book's enunciation. The voice condensed as would a forest or a coral reef, naturally, without cognitive interference, by means of inner evolution via duration. Each essay arose in me like a photograph that suddenly presented itself and called out to be taken. It is interesting that immediately prior to commencing upon *Magnetic Hoofbeat* I tentatively considered taking up photography

I have such an aversion to funneling creativity through a technical appendage (however adroit it may be), so I decided that my photographic urge could be powerfully penned in essay form all the while working in the spirit of Cartier-Bresson's dictum, that the picture takes you, it is not you who take the picture. Thus, I began to commence the book at irregular intervals as subjects of interest spontaneously evinced themselves.

ST: I think the comparison between the essay and the photograph is a very interesting one. It reminds me of a Godard quote I read once in which he said he turned to film because he couldn't stand the fact that you can't express simultaneity in writing. So, for instance, in a film a train can pull in to the Gare du Nord, and it can be raining, and a man can be watching, all at once. Whereas in writing these clauses have to come one after another in some order. However, on the contrary, I feel that in your essays there is a certain kind of simultaneity being enacted or expressed, a kind of "all-at-once-ness." Do you think linear time is circumvented somewhat in your essays? Is this an intention?

WA: This "all-at-once-ness" is none other than aural molten. It is language heated to such a degree that it responds as inner solar plasticity. Which means the language is rife with spontaneous possibility. This being inward power through aural deepening. Hearing at this level of density, energy begins to collect and spin at what I'll call a rapid aural rate. In reaching this aural deepening language osmotically heats to such a degree that its properties begin to transmute into the basic energy of sound that one hears in the work of Albert Ayler and Eric Dolphy. There is incredible flow in their sound all the while inflected by utopian gravity. A primordial sound from which erupts a deathless energy. So, when I hear my private language it partakes of this primordial scale and when it connects with quotidian tenors the whole of each phrase writhes like liquifous glass, spontaneously, capable of forming into instantaneous shapes. And these shapes are, at base, the sound of primordial flow-through which en-soaks the depth of each phoneme. And so the phonemes by being at such a heightened tenor begin to move as free particles then as fractions as an extended portion which is the syllable that extends to words and phrases, which happens as imaginal projection which then begins spontaneously dictating words and their subsequent motion as phrases, thereby setting off a concussive stream of chance. Say I know the basic nature of dinoflagellates, I never seek to know about them in a straightforward manner. I never know how my aural faculty will interpret information, so I plasticize my reading so as to get to essential vocabulary of the document that I'm reading, this being a covert nursing ground for sound, the latter, being for me, the life blood that runs through universal subject matter. The broader, the more eclectic one's interests are, they remain naturally infected by this deeper sound, always ready to spring to life. Whatever subject it invigours. With such language one can effectively write on an array of topics without exhaustion. Again, this is how *Magnetic Hoofbeat* extended itself across duration.

ST: *Singing in Magnetic Hoofbeat: Essays, Prose Texts, Interviews and a Lecture, 1991-2007* seems to me to be a lot about intellectual genealogies, and about how important it is to create one's own set of foundational writers, texts, and historical moments. Do you think of this as a process that is constantly in motion? Do you think of it as a process that helps to constitute the writing self, or the self most broadly constituted? Do you think it comes with any perils? (I know this is sort of a bulky question: you can just answer whichever part of it, if any, seems interesting to you.)

WA: First of all the process existed sans a priori ideology, I was, and never have been mired in praxis spawned as a pre-set point of view... For me, there is always living fluidity. So, since writing is simultaneous with living it constitutes the living body of the self. In this sense writing for me is a spontaneous body, endemic in my case, with its own peculiar liberty, which, by its very nature transgresses fixation, the latter being conveyed through the method of what I'll call rational segregation. It is the imagination rife with its fecundating tenor. And since it transgresses fixation, it seems to fail to find a home within preset literary forms. When I discovered Rimbaud, his example seemed synonymous with my neurological predilection. Not only the power of his writing, but his ethos of resistance from which the writing sprang. This compound reality of his ethos and his writing began to influence my psychology towards language allowing me to analogize its motion to the fluidic architecture of clouds. Never for me has language been some sort of abstracted model frozen at its core as lifeless form, this lifeless state conveying to me nothing more than a calcified compendium shaped by quotidian delimitation. Like Gilbert-Lecomte and Daumal I've been able to find a language simultaneous with inner exploration. It is not something to be equated with static concentration housed in a work for sterile consumption in order to attain manipulated literary honour. Language in this state allows us access to the exploration that is mystery which I find to be at odds with the daily mind colonized as it is by the stasis of gross statistical verbiage.

ST: It seems like a lot of interviewers are interested in the "psychic" component of your work, and so am I. Do you think there is a value in attempts to codify or clarify the cosmology (or to define or identify various spheres of the cosmos, or levels of reality) implied when we talk about writing as channeling, or picking up on signals coming from a kind of shared mind-space, as opposed to being the product of an individual consciousness?

WA: It seems I naturally channel lingual energy from a trans-personal level. From the very beginning I've always experienced language as a connection to the unseen. In this sense I feel akin to aboriginal respiration as it continues to respirate with First Nation peoples in the Americas, as well as with its parallel undercurrent as it continues to thrive in African traditional value. Again, wherever this value is found I recognize it instantaneously wherever it occurs. For me, I picked up this aboriginal sensibility in Islamic scholarship between the 8th and the 16th century. I've commented on this in an unpublished work entitled "On Dar el-Hikma" and centered around Dar el-Hikma, the great lay university founded in Cairo in 1005. Knowledge of the incredible human achievement during this era has either been willfully suppressed or skillfully colonized by the Western canon as has been the case with Averroes. This has given the false impression that modern world knowledge has been exclusive to the European psyche. Having essentially grasped the error of this circumstance, it has indeed, put me in resonance with what has passed before, providing me with a deeper, more feral critique of presentation of knowledge via

European exclusivity. As a result, it has deepened my solidarity with Diop, Césaire, and Rodney, giving me a more profound appreciation for Daumal, Gilbert-Lecomte, Artaud and Breton.

ST: One of the things Daumal and you obviously share is an interest in science. He claimed science for Pataphysics: you absorb and revisit science and scientific vocabulary and make it sing in new ways. I personally see the marriage of science and poetry as a natural one. (Earlier this fall, when scientists coined the term "Recurring Slope Lineae" to speak about formations on Mars, I began referring to them in my head as "the poets over at NASA.") Can you speak to the relationship between your poetics and contemporary science?

WA: It seems in the main that contemporary science has achieved a maturity that contemporary poetry has failed to achieve. When the poetic instrument is reduced to interpersonal squabbles or to defense and fortification of the geo-psychic province it has obscured itself in a maze of imploded parlour mechanics. Blindness in service of a momentary reputation emitting language expounded via secular myopia. I recently had a wonderful experience of reading an Egyptian utterance over 3000 years old and its language was torrential with vivification. It was not language beholden to a style, a school, a personality, or an elitist verbal cult. The latter is not unlike language lifted from a phone book, or a court case, at best, it's stillborn, and to maintain this state by limited argument maintains mental contamination. When "Recurring Slope Lineae" is invoked, one feels the verbal beauty of its alien character unimpeded by a sense of pedestrian mechanics. But what is revealing is that the phenomena has been wonderfully noted but the waters' origin remains shrouded in mystery. In passing I need to make note about the water I scripted flowing on Mars, in the first few years of the century prior to the enunciation of "Recurring Slope Lineae." Instead of stating the water as phenomena it was verbally endowed with consciousness. The poem is entitled "Water On New Mars" and it concerns itself with the waters, as a spontaneous occurrence, not unlike the notion of a million year rainfall that empowered the initial oceans. I gave a reading of the poem in front of 20-piece orchestra in Amsterdam at the Bim House in 2009. One can google it. One can simply punch my name in slashed with Ghasem Batamuntu, the orchestra's leader. The poem is also included in my City Lights volume *Compression & Purity*. As I originally handwrote the poem it seems that my access to its mystery was instantaneous, electric, having more seminal contact than the collective technical team at JPL. Of course, let me say, that the work at JPL remains concentrated and fabulous. It is interesting to note that the poem was ignited within the general vicinity of JPL around the launch date of "The "Mars Reconnaissance Orbiter" in 2006. This is not to aggrandize my own finding, but to verbally evince that poetry via intuition can at times take the lead over and beyond expensive technology. Of course, this does not include poetry which self-excludes itself from vision fueled by (Erica Hunt's term) "ready-made complacencies." I'm thinking of written work by a coterie of intelligent beings, perhaps, partaking of socio-economic privilege playing with facile verbal facility. I had the pleasurable opportunity of reading aloud the other evening (with Jerry Rothenberg and others from his outsider anthology *Barbaric Vast & Wild*) "The Dead King Hunts & Eats the Gods" from the Egyptian Pyramid Texts. It was utterance originally "inscribed on the walls of burial chambers" guiding the dead on their journey into death. It remains as fresh as it was circa 2350 B.C. when secretly inscribed. This was a populace consumed by language quite adroit at guiding the dead. Can one imagine a poem like this written today with competition for grants fueled by pointless personality cults. To paraphrase Paz, when language has been degraded via commercial utilization it is unable to guide. It is unable to gain transparence via mantra.

ST: You refer more than once in this essay collection to the fact that there is nowhere else to go once we've destroyed the earth. To me, this brings a freshness to your critique: it's a very straightforward way of putting it. In late September I was struck by two NY Times headlines that occurred in the same week. September 24th: "Investors are Mining for Water, the Next Hot Commodity." September 28th: "Mars Shows Signs of Having Flowing Water." I'm not suggesting any kind of conspiracy or causal link, though I do think both headlines reflect concern over the ongoing drought. Do you think the desire to find a new planet to colonize will ramp up further as environmental degradation and scarcity on earth become even harder to ignore?

WA: The search for other planetary worlds is certainly not new. It has been whispered that translation of bodies through space has already occurred. There has been susurration that a half million souls are located on Mars battling in competition with forms such as land-based plesiosaurs, perhaps a base of super soldiers stationed on the moon. I am certainly not codifying these scenarios, but outer space for the human mean remains bleak and disabling. I've seen terrain from, I think, Egeria, one of the asteroids, and it seems absolutely terrifying. Of course, there is Mars and its moons as well as Earth and its Moon, a select number of asteroids for possible habitation, which, even at best leaves an incredibly small choice. Add to this the addictive lifestyle that consumes the majority populace across the Occident as well as the elites of the world who share this addiction and you have an incontrovertible population incapable of flexibility. Add to this the abyss that is China intent as it is on extinguishing all consumerist records. How can the Earth survive such incessance? As general commentary it has been noted that this rate of planetary consumption cannot persist as an indefinite praxis. I'd say there has been a turn towards the irredeemable since the dawn of European exploration. Superficially one can point to its seeming high points, the founding of America, the development of an adroit technical network, modern space exploration, which sums an overall convenience culture. Yet the average Haitian lives on $2.50 a day. Clearly the whole of humanity has not crossed the Rubicon into criminal consumption, but in fact are willfully deprived of fulfilling basic daily needs. In this context, healthful water has become a palpable commodity. If I am in Brussels or London I am able to access drinking water without second thought, but in the exploited lands of the southern globe this is not possible. Because the southern globe has suffered not only physical exploitation, but worse, it has suffered psychic vilification from institutional propaganda so endemic to the Occident. Over the long view it has fueled an institutional viciousness towards invisible forces, which, over generational duration has eroded indigenous psychology. The shaman, the griot, the medicine man continues to be seen as an exotic appendage not to be trusted as regards substantive reality. But it is this very reality that has created the failing agenda that we are now privy to. Perhaps an unbuffeted shaman could ignite alchemical contact with "alien" intelligence far beyond the efforts of Project SETI which have so far been nil. I am thinking of the shamanic facility which allows human shift into other species. What if such facility provided human access to other planes of living. Of course, this being the polar opposite of rocket launch transferring a traumatized populace to the deserts of Mars, or to asteroidal fields conjoined by nickel. I feel a terminal insistence nagging at our collective circumstance much like hearing a train roar down a tunnel which has yet to arrive. Saying all that I have said I do not wish for the worst. Yet we have far surpassed the condition out of which the writings of Daumal, Gilbert-Lecomte, and Breton emerged. It is a frightening prospect. My language is always grappling with this looming implosion constantly magnified in whatever I say. Of course, this is not some skillful pose on my part being some ruse to gather audience. Another dilemma of population transfer is the electricity of a populace tainted as it's been by intra-competition brought about by the values that seem to extol competitive juvenilia. Add to this our connection to 4 billion years of complexity and you have something far beyond the capacity of what's known as science fantasy. We live in a psychically deprived context as Henry Miller so artfully stated in 1956. Great language cannot be encouraged in this type of culture, witness the years-long ban of Miller's own writings, or the last second suffocation of Artaud's broadcast "To Have Done With The Judgment Of God" by Fernand Pouey, "Director of Drama and Literature for the French Broadcasting Company." These restrictions continue to echo in other forms today. In the United States, we are seldom addressed by poets on foreign policy. Say we could have someone such as Gilbert-Lecomte or Césaire address the populace concerning the difference between a white Parisian corpse, and one endemic to Beirut. Of course, under the present circumstance the latter possesses the lesser value. We seem to be exclusively informed by the reportage of journalists. Believe me, I am not casting aspersion upon the work of those who risk their lives moment by moment, or leak aspersion upon the astonishing yield of Noam Chomsky, or cast a lesser light upon the fearless delving of someone like Jeremy Scahill. But when the day is finally done, it seems we remain psycho/physically moribund, horizontally imprisoned in this night and day world, continuously fatigued by collectively assumed mayhem. Yet we are more and more forced to internally inhabit the unthinkable. It certainly can't be done by use of a linear based projection through reality via strategy. This is a dilemma that certain poetic voices may tentatively start to address. Krishnamurti pointed out some years back (in dialogue with David Bohm and I paraphrase him) that as we evolve even death is no longer a major issue. Artaud once spoke of the electrical revolution, and Aurobindo enacted the transmutation of the cells through a living yoga propelled "onward, beyond the tombs." In the wake of the Paris attacks most commentary seems immured in the geo-political sphere never concerned with human transmutation, nor with the objective depth of the circumstance concerning general species removal to other planes. Let us remember, that Isis has sprung headlong like a malevolent genie from explosive depths less than a decade prior and has already rattled a civilization infinite times its senior. It seems to me events of recent days differ from the chronic violence that happened in Algeria, Viet Nam, and the continuing mayhem that is Iraq and Afghanistan. There now exists a palpable venom capable of a major, chain reaction having the capability of siring a circumstance where major populations of the Occident are now subject to unthinkable derailment. What is frightening to the Imperial powers is the electricity of intelligent coordination in fomenting its vengeance which posits another configuration... It seems it is another, more troubling turning capable of gathering us up in general engulfment. Within this context planetary evacuation seems an impossibly fragmented ordeal incapable of realization. With everything so scattered, with parts attempting to be wholes, and wholes attempting to present themselves as parts, it seems our general language remains decay as confusion. Traumatic confusion to say the least. There are planets in worse circumstances than ours and others at higher levels that our present mind would find incomprehensible. The Earth now finds itself in this middling position overextended far beyond its governmental capability. Louie Psihoyos's new film *Racing Extinction* makes note of palpable urgency for change in the near future, as we are more fitfully challenged by susurrant extinction. As I've stated elsewhere, Gurdjieff has properly remarked, if one species partakes of vanishment, the human one must be in serious decline. The odds at gaining balance seem more daunting day by day. Even if the northern nations suddenly had a change of spirit by bringing populations such as those of Haiti and Somalia into socio-economic balance, how indeed, do we deal with methane flares? Each individual must continue to treat Earth as a mysterious gift that, as far as we know, has no peer.

ST: Henry Miller talks about discovering himself as a kind of organic American surrealist. As though there was no need for an actual physical meeting to take place: on both sides of the Atlantic, the same spirit flared up. Would you define your relationship to the European Surrealists in similar terms? And what, if any, do you see as the relationship between your writing and that of Henry Miller?

WA: The verbal energy whose appellation is Surrealism remains ubiquitous not unlike water, or the surrounding circumstance which is the sky. It is not the province of any particular geography or language. It cannot be defined according to academic cul-de-sac. So, what Breton evinced in 1924 seems part of the natural environment; a natural environment he witnessed in Mexico some years later. A natural environment cannot be consumed by ideology and doctrine. It remains a dark eruptive sea that never codifies and replicates itself. As ubiquity its specific phenomena are naturally asymmetrical. No one will be able to theoretically house its energy via the appropriation of the writing of say, a Breton or an Artaud, or the artwork of Miró or a Masson, as if they all inhabited a pre-inscribed mission as their original source. This psychic geography can never be symmetrical at its source. Miller and Breton seemingly remain at disparate parts of the imaginative spectrum, yet what they've inscribed remains constantly eruptive across this spectrum as verbal vulcanism. Let me say, Surrealism has never been a theoretical enclave for me. When I discovered Rimbaud, he was a free-standing entity. As for Césaire and Artaud they too, were free standing entities. When Nadja appeared in my consciousness it was a magnetic manual on the beyond in this life. Upon discovery of these writings, I was struck by the way the language veered and electrically snaked its way through opacity. It was so different from obsolete language Breton so rightfully condemned in the First Manifesto, the latter being this linear language that consistently appears on the top seller's list. One need go back to De Bono's *Lateral Thinking* penned many years prior concerning alternatives to linear entrainment. It is an entrainment that persists in social and military strategy, in general religious praxis, in commerce, the latter, over the past century and a half, having become the God of daily life. It persists as chronic aggravation that arrogantly persists as business even into the afterlife. I once, by chance, met a forensic economist, concerned with accidents and crashes, and the assets left behind. Unfortunately, this terminology filters down into interpersonal relations, when conversation turns to assets of the deceased. Did he or she leave behind substantial savings? What did this or that person do with their money while still living? This remains a vexing hallucination. This is something Henry Miller faced in the mid 1930s, economically bereft, faced with general personal obscuration, this is none other than the psychology of the provinces, controlled by all manner of niggling reminder. He was freed from its various suffocations by magnificent use of language. This is not unlike Breton's use of "Surrealist" language, ungoverned by all the static ruses that the linear mind attempts to convey. Division in the mind creates blockage and effort. When verbal flow is established it is inclusive and is capable of conveying disparate languages such as mathematics, poetry, history, magic, politics, science, as well as mystical utterance to name only a few. In other words, it can extend itself into transfigured channels without consensus precedent. This is what Miller unleashed within the Occidental tenor and its expression within English. This is why his books were childishly banned amidst the furore of forgotten neo-philistines. And it is precisely because of his boldness that I never had to consider concretizing verbal revolt through biographical tableau. I have been freed to roam across the English language because of the verbal brilliance of beings such as Miller, Philip Lamantia, and Bob Kaufman. The atmosphere cleared by their great verbal winds allowed me to bypass brokering the psychic webbing extolled by quotidian verbal practitioners. Those poems about back porches and autumn harvests which still form the criteria for mainstream relevance, this is not unlike the human visual band circumscribed by its insignificant band width, all the while leaving out the greater view. The majority continues to be immured in a 19th century band width in spite of emails and space probes launched beyond the solar system. They continue to perceive reality as a beginning, middle, and end possessing this as a formula for events. Creativity is then naturally delimited being corralled within this tenor rewarded by popularity and financial recompense for staying within its accessible magnetism. What then occurs is some sort of lessening for he or she who subscribes to this state as the highest region of consciousness. Linear balance being overwhelming in the Protestant North, so I guess that is why Miller and Beckett ended up in an earlier form of Paris where they felt free to vibrate verbal innovation. When I first heard Artaud's writing on radio (on Van Gogh) read aloud by Jack Hirschman

I couldn't believe what was happening to me. It was beyond my capacity at the time. The same holds true when I first laid eyes on Césaire's *Notebook*, in both cases the language was moving at another strength, at another level of comprehension. I could nascently sense how its powers extended but was quite incapable of working in the vicinity of its reach at the time. I was in my early 20s and even before this contact I had vowed to find lingual capability in this region that they occupied. I found firsthand that Rimbaud's derangement of the senses applies and continues to apply. Reaching this zone requires living alchemy over time. It is not for the faint of heart. When one is going through this process over time one finds that it extends pressure inward, thereby putting pressure on the circulatory system, or, at another remove, perhaps one may slip into a cul-de-sac of substances as did Daumal, Artaud, and Gilbert-Lecomte among others. Not that a great level had not been reached by them, but the side effects derailed them as it did Dolphy, who sacrificed diet and other daily needs in order to play, as he put it, "even if it kills me." Saying this, I am not recommending deadly outcome but the enterprise in an intrinsic sense does signal risk. The fact exists that there is no guarantee for a neatly structured outcome. It seems one creatively travels like a spore across the void fortified by the study of life through experience. Part of that experience is fortification by reading the alchemically relevant texts that empower one's journey. One picks this or that tome as one begins to know one's own nature, whether it tends towards upper or lower, warmer or colder. Knowing this is essential for the poetic journey, for poetic distillation, and I am not speaking of barricading oneself in archives, of course studying essential texts, but not combining cognitive achievement with other forces of life that roil excludes one from opening fissures to what I'll call the verbal unknown. One's poetic praxis cannot be subsumed by stasis, by other's experience superimposed upon one's own electrical orientation. This was Miller's English honed as it was by bitter personal experience. I think of the anguish that ignited the language of Bob Kaufman, who as Philip

Lamantia once told me on a walk through North Beach is "our poet." Though purposely occulted by official culture Kaufman inhabits the voice at such a level that its ancient rooting is awakened, its inner resources tapped, so much so that it is undeniable. One hears this rooting in his poem "To My Son Parker Asleep in The Next Room." At this level it seems he has no peer far surpassing his more celebrated contemporaries. Not unlike Kaufman, Miller was perpetually banned and underexposed because he wakened language out of death, he brought to its motion a vibratory renaissance which always kindles the dead with negative reaction, as academic understanding, of say, Allen Ginsburg, or Ezra Pound could never do, when I heard David Jones reading from his "Anathemata," again by chance one evening on the radio, it made a more positive impression than being pressured by a grading system to read commentaries on say, someone such as Pound. When I think of language, I think of its utter vitality continuing to rove in deep time. Creators like Kaufman, Breton, and Miller continue to wreak havoc on an Occidental culture not quite alive. The latter, giving its energy over to stasis which is not unlike John Synge's "Playboy" upsetting the general state of a dead enclave. Living language being the bane to death carrying the true energy of life.

ST: The absurdity that for Daumal, if I understand him correctly, produces pataphysical laughter, is that one's true identity is the vast totality, while simultaneously one is consigned to acting the part of an individual being. Do you experience that dissonance? I love what you said about the writing body having "its own peculiar liberty" and language being a "connection to the unseen." Do you think that language, and writing, present a way to navigate this double role?

WA: It is true, one is born into dissonance. Although the vast majority of beings seem constrained by individual figmentation, as if they were individually contained as fragmentation. When living in the Occident one is instilled with freedom via fragmentation, and origin in our present context has been so obliterated it is thought to never have existed. One exists as one's own cause spellbound by fragmentation.

No other dimension is thought to have ever existed. For the most part, the Protestant faith keeps the mind bound to pragmatics and the strategies of day-to-day manipulation. In this circumstance salvation via the Christos functions as if one had incorporated a superior brand rather than as inner connection to what the traditional mind naturally embraces as an active invisibility. What now functions as contact with this invisible kinetic seems more the province of exploration via creative language. This is what I admire about Daumal and Gilbert-Lecomte, their intrepid quest in search of themselves through charged phonemic activity. And how is phonemic activity charged? It is language non-colonized by basic rational embrace. In the experiments of the Simplistes and *Le Grand Jeu* we see a daring, a total immersion of the poet with language exploring dimensions that we now see were quite consonant with the indigenous mind in its exploration of the uncharted. After European global ventures commenced in the 14th century what accrued was general riddling of inner exploration and its connection to dimensions other than visibility. These other dimensions have over the centuries been reduced to a vocabulary which describes them by means of superstition and ridicule. Thus, a great blindness continues to occur with capacity reduced in these areas, so in the main, the individual tends to wander as a private figment, buffeted by the amplification of matter. It is no mistake that I have been drawn to writers such as Daumal who were not bound to the hallucination of themselves as commodified literary fragments. They remain connected to the mysterious electricity that remains animation itself. When one not only acknowledges this electricity but makes the leap to participate in its mystery via written expression, one finds that another energy is made manifest, a superior vivacity if you will. It's as if a more resonant aurality spontaneously announces itself, obviously a less literal aurality which exists beyond opacity as three-dimensional limitation. What occurs is a more profound aurality, I call it the "second bell which rings in a mirror," it is this deeper hearing that Lorca spoke of when he scribbled with pencil on blank paper waiting for more superficial voicings to dissipate allowing deeper voicing to transpire. In this state one is not subsumed by a depthless public adulation, or conventional literary honour, but the level that Daumal spoke of when paraphrasing what used to be referred to in the Occident as the "Eastern" mind. He says, "The Hindu regards himself as an entity to complete, a false vision to rectify, a composite of substances to transform, a multiplicity to unify." Instead, the author in our present is compelled to announce his or her powers through anecdote, fueled by personal or particular anomaly. Then superficial pressure is extolled being analogous to accessible witness, thus, anecdote and personal anomaly become equated with a moribund comfortability. I'm thinking of writing as being electrified, not unlike the traditional carver or blacksmith whose work is imbued with trance, bringing the viewer or the listener into higher understanding leaving behind gross quotidian strategy. Such continued trance establishes over duration greater neurological capacity to access other states so that they become palpable thereby enlivening one's greater participation in the cosmos. The disaster of the Catholic Church as well as its Protestant counterpart has been their allegiance to diurnal consciousness thereby occluding less palpable levels and a consequent neurology, replacing the latter's evolutionary state with one enchained to "immediate perception." In the process of enlivening our senses with the microscopic nature of buying and selling, one loses view of the greater whole thereby empowering opacity when it comes to what I'll call alchemic sensitivity. In a deeper sense one has lost the gift of living. Life has been exchanged for product evaluation and momentary satisfaction. The gift of the poet is to break through this knotted nature of commercial exchange so as to introduce via language other dimensions of experience. Thus, language begins to restore the seeming rift in being with "vertiginous" precision.

Interview for National Poetry Month

with Entropy

1) *Why poetry?*

Poetry is aboriginal utterance. It generates the palpable via the impalpable. It concretizes the telepathic. It opens in us various scales of mystery. So, the poet by his or her nature evinces living adventure. One can never predict the living glass of speech, or how it will spontaneously form, or predict the reverberation of its impact. By its very nature it is susurrant, provocative. The systemics of politics or religion fall by the wayside, and what makes it so foreboding is that it continues to provoke and generates beyond surcease. Because it needs no intermediary the quotidian is naturally understood to be of ancillary standing, thereby ceasing to corrode one's seminal aural ignition. Poetry, for me, is not unlike dark energy, it galvanizes, yet eludes detection. There are some poets I maintain as being part of the populace of the uncontrollable. They have risen above the need for repartee with established means. In one of my recent publications, *Spectral Hieroglyphics,* I focus on a special triumvirate, Aimé Césaire, Antonin Artaud, and Roger Gilbert-Lecomte. They represent the other in such an extreme and effective manner that it calls up the hidden and embrangles the more superficial planes with primordial invasion. In summary, to paraphrase the gist of Paz, language needs spin as subversive enigma.

2) Do you feel like poetry is more or less important & relevant today?

Poetry can never be legislated by pronouncement from a cognitive lectern. It remains as the original blizzard of energy that created seas and deserts and mountain chains. It is that voice that continues to whisper beneath the superimposed scale of hyper-vocalized consumption. The latter in its on-going denouement, producing in its wake consumptive psychic wreckage, composing a citizenry poisoned by fantasy, seeded by what I'll call an electronic morality, with its spirit cast into a dark elective suspension. In consequence, collective neurology has been compromised to such a degree that it has in many instances foregone seminal contact with itself, eroded by the abstract community of products. The insistence wrought by Bernays and the advertisers since 1923 continues to compromise the subconscious with a thorny array of choices meant to occupy one's spirit until death. Poetry, being naturally resistant to this debacle, hovers as torrential witness underlining a dossier of errors. Under this continuing circumstance it spontaneously unifies a utopian thesis of human maturation and entry into galactic realization. The above being uttered during the explosive failure of Trump and its effect on his ilk that have been promulgating themselves around the globe for the past 500 years. A reckoning has suddenly appeared on the horizon with the retrospective ghosts of Lorca and Rabearivelo beginning to stir anew. I am not speaking here of the revival of books and translations, but that of the aboriginal voice that poetry represents. Despite legislation and lack of financial endowment the voice burns without limit. The region of analogy continues to expand its torrent of blazes.

3) Tell us about one poet who has greatly influenced you as a writer and a thinker.

I must say that there are many. But in terms of an overall psychological impact I have go to underline the name Octavio Paz. I say this not in terms of quantitative ranking, but in relation to my state upon my first my contact with him. I had initiated my course as poet. I was my initial stages of neurological adjustment to the writing of poetry, not as hobby or a curious form of entertainment, but as living destiny, as a higher form of living arrangement, so when I picked up *Configurations* by chance, it confirmed my initial finding concerning the poetic quest. It led me not only to his poetry which was blinding, but a form of conduct when contending with protracted obstacles. He, in turn led me to other poets and painters that allowed me to engage in my initial liberation. He confirmed my original insight into the quotidian and allowed me to survive assault from quotidian embranglement that tends to ensue across life. Too often poets are technically and historically proficient and many times fail in the embrace of outward embranglement thereby stunting their imaginal invention. It was Paz who provided for me the poet's ability to effectively extend across genres without the carking invocation of deficit sans theatrical gyration. My initial contact with his work included *Eagle or Sun* on through and beyond poems included in *East Slope*. Not deification, but Paz as alchemical example.

4) Tell us about one lesser-known contemporary poet who you'd like more people to know about.

The very nature of the question causes difficulty, it implies a kind of ranking. There are so many great poets, so many fertile approaches to language from Adam Cornford and Heller Levinson to K. Curtis Lyle. But having worked in extended tandem with Carlos Lara on our book *The Audiographic As Data* alerted me to his muscular signature and stamina of language. The book we composed takes its cue from hunches, from implication, from the charisma of chance, from the violation of boundary. It is a dense calamitous script burning with interior amplification. Yet there is mellifluous pacing. Lara has an extremely developed aural sense. We were listening to one another at such a level of complication that my imagination and his imagination were corresponding at levels with that which seems to de-exist. A powerful oracular mechanism quantum in demeanour. Very few can hear at such an angular level and extend it into an enriched aural tapestry at velocity.

5) Share with us one of your recent poems and tell us a little bit about its context.

This is an excerpt from my poem "At the Vertigo Borders for Roger Gilbert-Lecomte" from my recent book *Spectral Hieroglyphics*:

& so you remain
hovering
saturant with roaring
an environmental cadence
which sounds to the physical ear as a bell
with pure Tibetan underscoring
creating trances & spells in a cathedral of droplets
an energy unconcerned with the opposable brew
of conventional dialectics

As miraculous leper
you understood
as a kind of crystal
the pure mystique of absence
as unbound code across parsecs
never humbled by reductive regional glass
or by pointless reactive effort
spinning across a gaze of static
yet you occulted yourself

The latter
being hail from sidereal Bohemias
vehement with perfectly kindled phonemes
each letter blazing as percussive concurrence
leaping embraced bullion
leaping a roof of ghosts
so that language alters
what I'll call Leonardian anatomy
taking as proof
bodily diagrams from Tibet
always taking into account
"invisible forces"
"vibrations"
"wheels"
"currents"
all beyond the domain of the visible body

These being the stark coronal properties of pure contagion
which continues to populate travelers like myself
who open soils along the way
knowing your provocation
concerning the expendable body
serves at the level of a nervous inapplicable body

Subject to its highest mutational inferno

Knowing de-inhabited vehicular form
combined with the essence of self-confronting
always in recovery from synthetic error

Because the void possesses laws of living annihilation
you were able to experience drafts of primal flashing
knowing experiment through funicular tumbling

honing terror like a mason of the invisible
sculpting the non-traceable as amulet
enlivening spontaneous blessing through articulate vulnerability

This being the density of your second or incandescent body
uttered as diagram
as the initial stage of the afterlife
which craves its own subsistence through creative immolation

Its apparition spun in half
then subsumed in unspecified origin
with all of its variety evinced through private seepage
& this seepage we have no way of charting
as we would by micrometer an oceanic locust

So am I saying that I have analyzed surcease?

Or enhanced a lamp of invisible fever?

As if watching you escape a cliff of demons
by means of a symmetry othered by nothingness
& this nothingness
having nothing in common with Dante's circles
with their known chartings conveyed by the body of Virgil
hovering within the law of Christian decimation & fatigue

As if I could mirror your flight
across acres & acres of extrinsic mathematics
as if I could force a tunnel through an ozonal mirage
envisioning your apparition as a trenchant or corrosive fuel
then equating sullage as a protracted type of empire
as if the weight of history could compare with interminable revelation

Perhaps I am akin to a lama testing my utterances
in a vat of bottomless echoes
searching all the ethers for a magnetic global forest
a utopia spiraling with haunted eagles

& these ethers possessing the combinatory touch
of old Tibetan physicians
by one touch
gathering the bearings of death
or the chirality of health
as if the body wavers between these two indefinites
thriving on liminal portions
somehow above the constitutions
of bile & phlegm & wind
the 3 markers of the human species
with you Lecomte
being of utter wind
residing in a Bardo summit of unsummoned schist…

This fragment as mentioned above is from the poem "At the Vertigo Borders for Roger Gilbert-Lecomte." The book from which it's taken, *Spectral Hieroglyphics*, is concerned with revolutionary powers of language that I explore in this troika through the worlds of Artaud, Gilbert-Lecomte, and Césaire. Language being the key to alchemic inner radiance, capable of provoking a mantra of health in the cells. Concerned with the poet who extols radical liberty not only socially and politically, but invoking language that spontaneously melds with inscrutable energy that perpetually flows from the cosmos itself.

it remains sonic occultation

with Stephen J. Fowler

STEPHEN J. FOWLER: A profound achievement of your work I think is to make an identity purely through your language and its content in flux, rather than the positing of your own authorial presence. Many achieve the occlusion of the authorial identity, but few are able to form something that takes its place through the sheerness of their work, through the language becoming its own identity. Is this an active process in your writing?

WILL ALEXANDER: To say it succinctly language is life and life being motion what follows is the intuitive understanding that creative language cannot be plotted by contiguous, or what I understand to be verbal architectural planning. For me it is suffused with explosive electrical current, wayward, encyclopedic, seismic—alive by means of seeming disorder. Which does not allow for the controlling posture of "the author," anchored as he or she is by external classification.

SJF: You seem to attach your poetry to certain worlds of language which seem to act as host bodies for your writing, and then permeate and define that work in a wholly symbiotic way. Do you search for subject?

WA: I am fascinated by the river which is knowledge. Everything flows, the mating cycles of sea turtles, architecture in the colonial Andes, dictatorship within the circuitry of the old Soviet Empire, perhaps palpable life within the oceans of Europa... For instance, I was sitting in my reading room one late afternoon and became fascinated by a momentary dust beam, a thin ray of light which illuminated particles of dust, dreamlike, without transition I opened up a *National Geographic* sitting next to me and read an article on Albania. The trance of the dust beam transmuted to language which symbiotically meshed with Albania and its experience with its long-term dictator Enver Hoxha. This resulted in my poem "Albania & The Death of Enver Hoxha." In this sense one remains unchartable even in terms of one's own recollection. One stays in a state of what I can only term as poetic alertness. It is, of course hearing at the level of nths, of constantly wafting like a hawk in an ozone of savour, which, when combined with natural curiosity, the unexpected erupts.

SJF: This process then seems to posit the poet as the receiver of language, as an externality, which is then expressed, in your case as visionary interpretation. Your work is essentially luminous, visionary and prolific, it seems quite purely an adjunct of a life practice, a spirituality of poetry, in action.

WA: Poetry is reception. For me it remains sonic occultation. This being raw aural voltage. This level being simultaneously woven with one's basic nature and predilection, so much so that after a time a leap takes place, and one enters one's voice. A process more easily written about than lived. In spite of natural congruence there is, paraphrasing the drummer Max Roach, hard work needs be engaged. For the poet this work is a lifelong learning curve, of challenges that remain obscure to the outside world, protracted sacrifice, working when no one is watching without seeming external reward. Leiris says the poet's payment remains the bolt of language from the blue. The condensation of sound becomes palpable manifestation to the ear. If one has been in search of a higher engenderment of being all these elements become simultaneous in the writing. I always make the analogy of poetic power to good wood or seasoned whisky. A durable language if you will, which, for me goes back to original embodiment of primal sound. The original right brain that elucidated the early Egyptians. Mind you, not a didactic understanding, but language as riverine electrical current, a current one finds in Lorca or Tutuola.

SJF: You seem also to place this practice in the physiological as well as in the realm of consciousness, having spoken about the effects of breathing exercises and willful states of meditation on your writing. Is this accurate?

WA: There is certainly a verticality of consciousness, and because consciousness extends vertically it is inextricable from language. The Occident has been almost universally resistant in this regard. It has been a little more than 100 years since the furore over Freud and his tenets, expertise at the time channeled through a solely diurnal consciousness. Respiration being endemic to both macro and micro levels, a subconscious domain must have supra-consciousness as extension. An extension not in terms of measurement, but as experiential suffusion. A suffusion which, for the most part the Occidental consciousness perceives as pejorative fantasy, wizened as it's been by 19th-century mechanical notions of science and the reductive tenets which continue to flourish as regards Christian suffering and guilt. In consequence, supra-consciousness is something that Aboriginals pursue, something that backwater peoples proscribe. This is a perspective I find to be absolutely perilous. Guilt and belief in guilt keeps consciousness static and averse to possibility. At an absolutely untenable moment the Occident has signed a treaty with impasse. With Fukushima leaking hundreds of tons of poisons into the Pacific on a daily basis, there remains palpable non-response in the admitting of error. This being an event in the face of what many learned parties have understood to be as none other than catastrophic. By listening at the vertical level, language for me, becomes suffused with what the Hindus understand to be sattvic energy, where not even the phonemes are divorced from this suffusion. This is how language wafts and rises and gains beauty by this wafting, which is not entrapment within the scrolls of parochial thinking pattern. Language then expresses another shimmering, another texture, another experience, immediately contagious to those within the rays of its transmission, not unlike holding in one's hands the bluish ipomoeas of Césaire.

SJF: What connection do you feel the later history of European poetry?

WA: As for European poetry, I can only mention the large continents which were Artaud, Breton, Lorca, Leiris, Dylan Thomas and Bonnefoy, which occludes more recent transmission. This occlusion being my blind spot, my distance from site-specific excellence of more recent times. Being a hybrid as a result of the African holocaust, it would be less than fitting to forgo any source of poetic power from wherever it arises. Let me add to the aforementioned names the black and white work of Hayter, and the drawings, letters, and paintings of Miró.

SJF: You are coming to read in London next month, have you shared your work outside of America often? Have these experiences been important?

WA: I've had poems translated into Romanian, Spanish, and Italian, with critical articles appearing in French and Dutch. This is important to me in that the aforementioned contagion can transpire, allowing direct transmission to readers in other languages. Let me say this, the first poets on Earth were not authors, they could spontaneously inscribe, this is how birds and stones and air were first brought to human cognizance. There was no pressure upon language to conform to a socially constructed presence, to the niche of personal authorship.

Ghasem Batamuntu & Will Alexander
with Darrell Jónsson

DARRELL JÓNSSON: Can you tell us a little about the literary foundations of your and Will Alexander's work, and how it first intersected?

GHASEM BATAMUNTU: My meeting with Will Alexander seems almost destined in retrospect. The one force responsible for the dynamics that would shape the events of our crossings strangely enough is the Watts riots of the early 60s. Post-riot events led to the formation of the Watts Writers Workshop; one of many think tanks to arise after that event. It impacted me in a different but relevant manner. I was a bit younger than Will and other such notable workshop participants as futuristic literary personalities Curtis Lyle, Stanley Crouch, Ojenke Mapenzi, Kamau Daa'oud, all of whom would later become very important figures in shaping the consciousness dynamic in an evolving collective movement that swept black America during that period.

DJ: The thing that is striking about both of your work is that there is a distinct animism that is found in the better poetry and music of the last century. Batamuntu's music avoids what the German Jazz critic Ernest Borneman called "a complexity which makes music ipso facto unintelligible for the untrained listener and thus robs the musician of the echo which he needs both spiritually and economically." Alexander, your work as well seems to avoid jumping on any of the typical American post-war artistic bandwagons, and seems to be all the more powerful because of it. Which brings the question, rather than mimicking or emulating the Beatniks, the Surrealists or Imagists or other 'canons'—shouldn't it be asked if the idea of stream-of-consciousness isn't a natural reaction to the confluence of languages, dialects, and situations found in daily life in a place like South Central Los Angeles?

WILL ALEXANDER: For me, even the phonemes vibrate. Los Angeles naturally seems to spontaneously confirm this nomadic response by means of a nomadically functioning discourse. Unlike New York or San Francisco, it functions without a recognizable locus and has developed discourse amongst a most spectacular array of human confluence. Like the city of Los Angeles, I've had the fortune to poetically evolve without a centripetal model. I've not been an advocate of Rimbaud, or Breton, or Césaire in terms of looking at their work in terms of stationary posting. What I mean by stationary posting is that their work has not enveloped me in terms of wanting to respond to their power by writing works which mirror them by replication. There never existed and continues to not exist in my spirit conservation by means of any stationary limit. I've always responded to language as though I were in-scripting by means of improvised combustion.

GB: These streams of consciousness empty into oceans of imagination, forming a vertical beach, which erodes those tributaries of fantasy, ingrained with coral condensed to pearl.

DJ: Regardless of the of dismissal or removal of Los Angeles from much of what was the New York-San Francisco-London cultural map, you seemed to embrace the work of Aimé Césaire, which had a clear European-Caribbean-African linkage, was part of that because Francophile Césaire was an inspiration to refuse to stand in the shadows of Saxon culture?

WA: As Lilyan Kesteloot has pointed out, "Césaire strikes at the very heart of Western civilization, at its key value, Logic…" I must say that I had come much to the same conclusion before I read him, yet I didn't possess his maturation or the verbal substance he commanded. Reading him inspired direction in me, giving me something other than the Saxon modernists to follow. For me, Césaire remains a paragon of dissonance. When I discovered his *Cahiers*, I was a few years younger than he was when he wrote it. To read it was both thrilling and daunting. The imagery, the unexpected leaps. It was thrilling, burning. I felt it was not only a fantastically written document but the very fiber of Césaire's being poetically expressed. His maturity amazed me, overthrowing the classics and the foundation that nourished them.

DJ: How about you Ghasem, in the environment of Los Angeles, the Austro-Germanic musical tradition, which dominated the areas concept of 'classical' music or the European musical canon, must have seemed as foreign as the Anglo-Saxon literary thread? Yet from the beginning with earlier versions of the Nova projects like "Mezzanine" you seemed to be dealing with some facet of 'classicism' in the theatrics and sound?

GB: For what you refer to as "the Mezzanine" this is not the case. Of course, you could say that Max Roach was applying another approach to classical science in his investigations of odd meters he was into there at one period with his compositions featured in those ensembles with Booker Little and Eric Dolphy and Ray Draper and so with (the improv oratory of) Abby Lincoln. That is the music I grew up with and was influenced by. In that way there is a classical reference. Max Roach playing timpani in jazz music and such. Still in South Central Los Angeles classical music was always a bit exclusive, difficult to access and especially integrate into your daily movements. It was only by special arrangements normally; a school field trip for example… or some long haul by automobile of getting to a classical event, which was all in the difficulty of experiencing it; not at all like in central Europe. My composition and approach to performing in Mezzanine and subsequent projects resulted from my contemplations about finding a feel that was both West Afrikan in pulse and Afrikan American in flow. You can see much of this on YouTube (unfortunately the length of the Mezzanine piece forced me to edit the dance segment before I could post it). Later though there are dance segments that further heighten the rhythm contrast I was trying to highlight. The piece is actually called "Ntu the Ninth Wonder" and is intended to be an exercise and illustration in a comparative way of the manner in which odd meters and even meters shape the space you hear them in. It's a long two cycles of nine rhythm fragments against a swinging 4/4. They each have a distinctly different shaping of the space you hear them in. The 9 is somehow wider and angular with an inherent free-feeling element while the 4/4 is indeed aerodynamic and slick it does not have the same sort of geodesic geometrics in how it fills the audio space. Somehow it is less wide and broad yet sudden like an eel… an electric eel… while the 9 gives me a sense of timing surging and tumbling like an avalanche of polyrhythm… seeking to resolve two kinds of rhythmic presences without a loss of spontaneity… that is a conscious launching site for freer forms of rhythmic presence…

WA: Let me say that Austro-Germanic or English culture has never fomented in me a blindness for its absolutes. Of course, we see its influence, year by year, fading into a kind of cultural post-mortem. Not that it's completely behind us, but as I was walking in my neighborhood quiet recently, I broached the vicinity of a Muslim lady in full garb, several Korean people doing power walks, and two separate groups of Mexican people, one speaking English, the other, Spanish. America is no longer the land of two divided racial forces, one Black and one White. This old perspective has practically run its course, with Los Angeles providing a new intriguing exclamation for human possibility. It is an environment where I can verbally tap into the beyond, using English in a way that totally transmutes its Germanic heritage. This is what Deleuze and Guattari describe as using your own language as a foreign transmission. For me, English has become a nomadic mixture of sound capable of infinite combinations. Its 26 letters can work through an infinity of combinations fueled by the sun of imaginal radiance. Its letters are not unlike the Mayan numerical code capable of moving across eons with accuracy.

DJ: Such enlivening impulses seem to be disappearing from Jazz. Here we have the issue of Central European/Slavic poetic and artistic impulses always in threat of vanishing beneath the sweep of more visible cultures, yet these very ideas have historically had vitalizing effect on the arts. Miroslav Vitouš when I interviewed him 2007 was saying jazz "is sort of repeating," like others he seems to be implying that jazz is dying or dead.

GB: I'd have to disagree with Mr. Vitouš who I believe to be a prolific and an innovative bass player. I disagree because of the degree of musicality I see being transmitted and passed on to the next generation of practitioners. There are some really beautiful young players developing out of and extending the ideas of acclaimed maestros and masters that set out a conceptual road map before them. Master musicians like Jackie McLean and Horace Tapscott who set up community seed banks for notions and times such as these. Their conscious efforts at seeding urban fields with the bird seed and dolphin dung has created fertile soil where once only electric towers and streetlamps grew. When I hear new players like Jason Moran and James Carter, the Roney Brothers, Joshua Redman, Kamasi Washington, Isaac Smith, I don't hear anything close to death unless it is ancestral and omnipresent in nature. If people feel the presence of the dead in jazz atmospheres, perhaps they should see if their real estate is built on top of a graveyard. I think what he means is that the business of jazz has gotten a strangle hold on the means to access the innovations that are occurring. First of all, you have to realize that jazz has truly become a global expression and activity, and New York is not the only place to measure the jazz pulse. It doesn't hold all the cards as to controlling how the general masses can access what is occurring in the music, nor is it an exclusive hive of innovative activity.

Because of its business parameters perhaps that is someplace you may hear innovations that are brought there, but that does not mean the process is not ongoing in the influences of other situations. Millions of people on an island have to do something I suppose, but if you think jazz is dead then I think you should travel a bit further. I think you will find it nearly every place you go. You will see many musicians struggling still within and against a basic business configuration that limits access to innovations that are occurring outside of business concepts and formats that determine access to what sells best.

The fact that nearly a decade into the 21st century the presentation of this beautiful music is yet basically limited to environments that cannot facilitate its potentials—because they interfere with business practice—is the dead smell in the air. There is a real necessity to try and find new and elevated life forms in the means of access to the wide variety of innovation that is a part of the living presence in the music.

A jazz club in 2008 is little more than a roaring 20s speakeasy with a makeover… maybe shredded chrome curtains instead of polyester… head mounted microphones cause that leaves more room to put in seats. There are so many more applications optional for the music. It should not be limited to three 45-minute sets. I think by this he really means that the business of jazz is killing the music. I have a blues tune that says… "you can't die lessen you already dead." So don't worry and think like that… it will kill you… if left in the grip of business concerns the progress of the music is indeed impeded. But I think it safe to say that jazz cannot die. Just like music cannot die. Wait till you hear the new Eskimo jazz with Siberian subsonics and Mongolian phase shifting. You may not be able to read its pulse with business radar and x-rayed profit graphs but I can assure you jazz is tattooed upon the surface of the earth… it has evolved towards truly a human expression by embracing the human struggle of resolving the human dilemma and will exist as long as humans live… it is a gift from the gods to aid in their living long and happy lives in several life forms…

WA: I can understand this feeling of mortality and ending when you look back on the John Coltrane band, on the worlds of Dolphy, Coleman, and Ayler, and now experience a focus more commercially shifted. We are dealing such an atomized state of affairs that insight seems tangled. The rush of the present era has created jazz studies, and not nurtured an environment where organic creation is key. But conversely, I've had the great experience of being the poet in Ghasem Batamuntu's band, with stellar musicians like Nate Morgan, Sonship Theus, and Roberto Miranda. These particular musicians remain active, and jazz music remains active, maybe not in the concentrated way that previous bands performed night after night, but in the sense that its powers of improvisation continue to prevail. It's like trying to suppress nature for a time, but yet it is always there, ready to burst forth from suppression as uncontainable quanta. For me, to improvise is to breathe, so when I listen to my inner verbal forces, they start to flow on the page as inevitable pyroclastics. Jazz, improvisation, remains a living essence, which will, over time, reassert itself as a necessitous power in the human continuum.

DJ: Ghasem, how has your sound evolved in recent years?

GB: When I lived in Amsterdam, I played in the streets quite a lot as well as at the North Sea Festival or the Bimhuis. Amsterdam is a quite patronic and social urban contour so people are out in the streets and active in a civil manner more than in many of the urban centers I've visited. Anyway, there is a lot of water, and mortar, and brick integrated into the architecture and landscape of that canaled grottopolis which also dilates the acoustics of sound. But in a very organic manner as opposed to electronic. So there in Amsterdam is a natural reverb and delay that echoes between the brick palaces and financial centers… in the tram stations… and plains where the public gathers. I became intrigued with this sound but could never reproduce it say in a jazz club there… you were lucky if you got a sound system that performed in a balanced manner. I grew up in the 60s so Jimi Hendrix was like one of those tribal Dogon ceremonial deities that you were lucky to experience once in a life cycle… just like Coltrane, Sun Ra, or Cecil Taylor, they ooze like sap from a tree at a particular moment in time. And then it's not like that again until the next occasion… Anyway, he gave perspective to the dilation of sound I am making reference to. So, with the advent of the digital tonalities that are condensed in these various devices available today you can more or less deconstruct and reconstruct sonic cells and particles… I hear music from the mountains of Japan and Mongolia that have that organic resonance... the aboriginal approach as well.

Anyway, I have been busy with trying to recreate that sound of playing outside with the soprano saxophone mostly these days... around the time of the Mezzanine clips I was experimenting but since then there have been lots of new technical developments. As well I've constructed a few acoustic wind instruments and when played thru various simple electronic devices the sonics are increased to prehistoric proportions allowing the imagination to place them in unexpected scenarios... like some ancient birds or wild beasts howling from the darkness of the jungle canopy... it reinforces the images that appear suddenly in the poetry. Lately I have been contemplating a vertical beach... it is an experience easier to describe thru sonic associations than any given linguistic.

DJ: Here it seems, Ghasem, you find some clue to the adaptation or mediation of this changing environment, via a strong reference to a pantheon of functional heroes. So where does this division land? Between totemic symbol as spiritual and technical reinforcement, and totemic symbol becoming a rigid dogmatic monolithic pantheon. A body of dogmatic style and symbols that is then used to reduce the natural human will and imagination and the tens of thousands of years of linguistic use and development as a side show — reduced to something people need to put a face on, name on, package and either worship or commercialize. What about the intonations of living ancestors as well, and the dramaturgy of everyday life, how do you weigh these factors into your sense of poetics?

WA: Because the conscious mind is so prevalent in the West there is always the predilection towards dividing and stratifying people and objects and feelings. Because I feel such distance from such judgments, I see everything as being alive, not from a strictly optical presence. For me, there can exist no surcease, no eternal divide between beings who have died, and beings who live, and beings who are yet to be. As in African animism all is alive, therefore each leaf, each cry of a bird, possesses an organic inner balance. This is the momentum at the core of my writings. Life is constantly applicable. That is why I possess dictionaries on everything, from medicine, to astronomy, to warfare. Not just an inscrutable kindling, but like the colours in a Miró or a Jackson Pollock painting, words in a text must poetically balance. So, each article is as essentially charged as some far reaching term aptly put.

For me, language must psychically cohere in all its disparate parts. It is an illuminant endeavour, a life which resounds as encompassing auditory health. This is quite the opposite of works promoted for strict commercial consumption where a momentary style and obsolescence is key. This latter seems a world of simulacra and superficial consent.

When I speak of Bob Kaufman, or Philip Lamantia, or Aimé Césaire, they are never monuments monomial in demeanour. Instead, they emit a living radiance. During my poetic inception they were my primal guides. They've allowed me over time to attain a boldness in my research and expression. Their works for me have been nothing less than transporting.

They opened me up not only to my subconscious ethers, but also sparked flight in my supra-conscious mind. It could be said that by reading them it opened another understanding so that when I read Sri Aurobindo's *The Life Divine*, I then understood language as infinite circuit capable of movement between the subconscious, conscious, and supra-conscious mind, an understanding practically unbroached in the West.

Knowing principle works of Kierkegaard, Nietzsche, Gogol, and Dostoyevsky alerted me to the fact that a dissonant intelligence was already at war with Europe. I knew the incandescence of Blake, the poetic blaze that was Shelley, and was able to see the connection between their seeds of dissension and the eruption of Surrealism many years later.

DJ: Do you think it would have been possible to arrive at a similar place without an index to Parisian trained or European based literary figures?

WA: As for Paris, Breton, Leiris, and Artaud remain essential for me. What Artaud and Leiris expressed was not unlike the Afro-centric revolt one finds in Césaire's *Tropiques*. Also, the examples of the painters Miró, Vlaminck, and Masson have greatly moved me. What I've found is that Los Angeles seems akin to an earlier era in Paris, with its animisms, with its infinite dialects of the psyche. From the beginning of my poetic odyssey, I always sensed a nascent liberty which existed through language. But no matter how free, how inclement the power of one's lingual premonition, it needs time and experience to fuel its metamorphosis. No matter what some quotidian detractors may claim, reading remains a powerful component of the human experience. It is absolutely essential for poets especially in their developmental stages.

GB: In the pursuit of poetic portal as dharmic inertia, equating suddenness with improvisational music skills… feeling enough about the language to barely hold on to its flow its letting go I take spontaneous direction and instantaneously at the speed of concept embody it with the arrived logic and give it a life thru communication… association… application thru the dharma of our muse.

DJ: Nowadays university scholars are calling (an overdue) observation that European culture is Eurasian in fact, if one counts the historical symbiosis of science, industry and the arts. The moniker of Euro-Islamic civilization is nearly as accurate but far more controversial. Egypt though is the most accessible symbol Africa provides us with towards Euro-African civilization, particularly with the influence on Greece, the "Classical world." How, in your lifetimes, have you seen and expanded the definition of Yoruba and other sub-Saharan civilizations towards informing the impulse of Afro-centrism?

WA: The oldest nation on record to date was the Nubian nation Ta-Seti located to the south of Egypt. This reality remains a source of power for me. I feel that I emit its original rhythms through the voice in my writing. Not didactically mind you, but by the improvised spontaneity found in my instinctive verbal actions. I feel as if I am commingling my powers with a primordial electrics, so that everything I write trembles with the quickness of lightning. When I say this, I am not trying to invoke some kind of superior literary largesse, thereby aligning myself with some chronic literati competitive with exhaustion. But like Césaire I seek to engage the electricity of the total environment. This for me remains African; understanding the palpable world by means of its inner grounding, this being analogous to the natural respiration operant in the powers of true poetic creation.

DJ: Earlier I mentioned the 'classic' elements in some of Batamuntu's work. Especially when dance, poetry and music are all combined, I do see something 'classic' as well in these collaborations you have done together like "Solea" on the upcoming CD. Here I find that sense of what Harry Partch called 'corporeality' that in Europe is historically found in the theatre of Greek antiquity. Via my studies in ethnomusicology though, every year there seems to be new links tying the ancient music, science and culture of North Africa to that of what is called 'classic' Europe. How do you see the global influence of Africa on the arts both ancient and modern?

WA: There is no question that Africa has fueled not only the arts in the modern European movements, but also the arts and knowledge of the planet. There is no mistake that when entering a philosophical seminar in the West, one is never allowed proper entry into the proto worlds of the Pre-Socratics. As the scholar Asa Hilliard points out, that Egypt "was the parent of other systems of education, especially early Egyptian education in Greece and Rome." Education "was not seen primarily as a process of acquiring knowledge" but "was seen as a process of the transformation of the learner." According to Plutarch, Solon, Thales, Plato, and Pythagoras found their original maturation not upon the soils of Greece, but in incandescent halls provided by the Pharaohs. We see the rhythmic source of Africa in sculpting, in the dance, in the verbal arts. In Europe one need go no further than Vlaminck, Picasso, and Leiris to see its profound influence on expression in modern art. And it remains essential to this hour, even if its legacy seems willfully minimized by the residues that still inform the post-colonial West.

GB: Africa arrives through illustrating an equating of an embodiment of the spirit… an observed dilation during the process and interaction of parallel inertias ascending and descending upon the same moment of intent thru an opal portal poised in complex rhythm. Structures pulsating prior to propulsion… John Coltrane's meditations in Seattle with Juno and Olatunji, Sun Ra's Egyptian Echoplex, Cecil Taylor surrealistically twisting time around granadilla wood and ivory… humming a bird song for Henry Dumas and Mory Kanté.

Spontaneous Aural Combustion

with Justin Desmangles

JUSTIN DESMANGLES: This afternoon on New Day Jazz we are remembering the life and history of saxophonist David S. Ware, joined by poet, playwright, novelist and pre-eminent voice in surrealism in the Americas and throughout the African Diaspora, Will Alexander.... Will, thanks so much for being so generous with your time and sharing this afternoon with us.... for many of us it came as a tremendous surprise that David S. Ware left so soon after his long battle with his illness and then returning triumphantly. It was quite a shock to see him leave us.... You've been listening to his music for some time now. What are some of the thoughts you'd like to share this afternoon with our listeners?

WILL ALEXANDER: David has been a triumphant spirit and been able to weather the storm for so many years, playing this type of music in North America under feral conditions, always ascending the barrier of resistance. I first met David years ago when he was playing with Cecil Taylor, aside Jimmy Lyons. At that time, he was lean and mean and without any assistance, personal, health-wise, and I had a chance to meet him at a reception after they played one evening at UCLA. It was Cecil and the trumpeter Raphe Malik and Jimmy Lyons, that group.

JD: Now to play with Cecil Taylor is an extraordinary accomplishment in and of itself, wouldn't you think it's fair to say?

WA: I'd have to say so, because the energy is unbelievable. And Cecil himself, you know, quoting out of the bebop book that A.B. Spellman wrote [*Four Lives in the Bebop Business*, 1966, now in print as *Four Jazz Lives*], in '61, '62, he used to wear a white shirt and underneath there was a sweatshirt—which allowed him to mediate the energy—that was the type of energy that was pouring continuously from his pianistic complexity, and you have to just play in a circular movement and you have to have total command of your horn and be able to improvise. Something that's very very very crucial. People think that free music is a lax music. It's incredibly demanding. And David has always been up to the challenge.

JD: So, the demands that free music makes on the imagination and the mind, the spirit and the technical ability of the improviser are tremendously physical, aren't they? The level of exertion that is required, and focus, emotionally and intuitively, is absolutely astounding. I mean a lot of these cats will leave the stage utterly charged but exhausted at the same time.

WA: You have to be. It's all at once. To work, it has to be done all at once. The technical, the imagination, the focus, and the prior discipline has to kick in, and you're off on a journey, and you have to trust yourself.

JD: Now that's key isn't it—trust—in the sense, if I follow you, being able to submit to one's own intuitions and the absolute expansion of your own intellect and emotional life within. In order to bring that out, you have to trust in that.

WA: You have to trust in that. You can't rely on a songbook for somebody else's drafts of the imagination. It doesn't work.

JD: When I think about David S. Ware, and listening to his music… one of the ideas that occurs to me, very similar to the approach, I believe, that is demanded when exploring your work as a poet or as a novelist, or in your plays and non-fiction writings as well, and that is the idea of the poet-historian or the musician as storyteller, one who deciphers and interprets history as a kind of map-making process. Do you think this is something that applies to Ware's music as well as it applies to your literary work?

WA: Absolutely, I mean you're not quoting somebody else's history, you're making something absolutely new. And so therefore it's different from a scholar that has assiduously studied and then put all the parts together. The improvisation, the element of improvisation supersedes that. Poetic historians are not, I wouldn't say—they are detailed, but they have a range that you call circa or can spiral in and out. In other words, the information they have available does not hold them but inspires them to move, make motion, rapidly. In other words, you're not doing second and third drafts.

JD: It certainly feels in evidence with David. S. Ware that the ideas, if you will, of being that exist in his music are far more expansive than the categories of history as nations or tribes or peoples or any of the usual geological merchandise that's fobbed off as art. None of that seems to be present in what he's doing. In other words, the consciousness that is expressed in his music appears to be cosmic, appears to be universal.

WA: It would have to be, and that's resonant. It's the African rhythmic. When you see a Black person beginning to move, to gyrate, in terms of dance, if it's in the Solomon Islands or if it's in Brooklyn, NY, there's a resonance. You hear that in David's work. I'm sure all of us are international travelers, not necessarily by United Airlines, but by the fact that we travel in the mind so acutely. You know, we have had that experience, as slaves. We have been colonized by so many of these European entities, if it's Spanish or Dutch or English, French, this is why we speak all these western languages. We turn these languages into a relativity then to an enshackling. And David does that with all these different tongues. As I was mentioning to you the other day, I was listening to *Organica II*.

JD: Right, from the recent AUM-Fidelity release *[Organica: Solo Saxophones Volume 2]*.

WA: And *Minus Gravity* as well, particularly *Minus Gravity* not with the tenor, but the soprano. I was thinking of this great article on Oriental Africa, Oriental African music, as termed by Yusuf Ali, when Yusef is talking about the music and North Africa and the rhythms, and I was thinking about North Africa when I was listening to *Minus Gravity*. This is a part of our tradition. We're not limited to a West

African ethos; we go further north too. It's all part of Africa. This is what I picked up earlier on, when I first heard John Coltrane's *Olé*. It felt as though the sound had sprung from that region, and Trane always had that as an undertone. This kind of feels like Oriental Africa and you can feel that in Africa itself. I am referring to the Africa of feeling that springs from *Africa/Brass*. He had North African elements in the work.

JD: With music such as that coming from David S. Ware, we're talking about an articulation of being that is much more firmly rooted in a larger definition of humanity that includes all these other lands and other cultures that have been sequestered or cut off from, allegedly, American experience and specifically the African American culture, through the retentions of the music and the culture from North, West Africa from the southern part of Europe are quite evident in the tonalities and the rhythms of the music of David S. Ware.

WA: Absolutely, which means that he is not, and never was, a provincial traveler. He was never involved in a limited scope. And this is one of the reasons that the American commercial system is always trying to incorporate you into ghettos of northern Philadelphia or southern Los Angeles, so you can stay within the confines, where you're cut off from your actual wellsprings. And the music you make up turns you into a flightless cassowary.

JD: I'm sorry, a what?

WA: A cassowary is a bird, a giant bird with wings that can't be used. It can't leave the earth, it's completely grounded, it has no aerial capacity. And David's music is the kind of music that'll wake you up at two or three in the morning with thought patterns, thinking patterns which will lead you to other areas of opening. It may inspire you to go see some paintings or find out about the great calligraphers from North Africa, say, Ibrahim el-Salahi—that type of work—or get into Jean-Joseph Rabearivelo further south in Madagascar. This is the type of exploration one needs to do concerning the Black Diaspora across the planet.

JD: As with your work and the others we have discussed, the life and legacy of David S. Ware is but one step in that very important direction.

WA: Of course, as I was listening and watching him play, I was particularly taken with the trance quality of something like "Mikuro's Blues." He was playing with Matthew [Shipp] and Guillermo Brown and William Parker.

JD: Right, the great quartet.

WA: That more people should know about. I mean they are tuned in. You know, the wavelength is so intensely scattered at this point around the world. During an earlier less technical era the mind could focus better on its strengths.

JD: You mean the period when that particular quartet was together?

WA: Yes, the strengths. Like the John Coltrane Quartet was focused on the general consciousness, because there was less peripheral damage going on in the consciousness.

JD: I see. I was mentioning earlier—we heard three of the tracks from the DIW releases of the David S. Ware quartet—that, this particular group, for the last decade of the 20th century, this was the most important working group in jazz.

WA: I would say so. It's magnetic, and it's the trance quality that's always involved in the music. It's like they're all the time together—away from one another and together with one another. They're always involved in the music, the sound. They're living the sound.

JD: I'd like to explore this last question with you for a moment or two, and that has to do with another correlation that I think follows parallel with your own work in literature. I mentioned not long ago the idea of the cartographer or the poet-historian, the person who explores and creates the map of the conscious and unconscious mind in order to not only to be more easily understood individually but also to help guide the people toward a higher sense of being or higher state of being, if you will, or higher state of historical consciousness or even transcending consciousness, but those ideas of course are not exactly new. We can find them deeply rooted in the surrealist tradition, but most specifically with the ideas of someone who I know has meant so much to you personally, and that is the work of the artist Antonin Artaud. Artaud believed and articulated that this state of development that we are in as human beings is actually stunted spiritually by our inability to embrace conscious evolution. That we are inhibiting ourselves. It seems to me that David S. Ware is making some attempt to break through and extend beyond this sort of locked passage that we're in. Do you think it's appropriate to bring in somebody like Artaud when talking about David S. Ware and the impact of his music?

WA: It's all of a family. All of a family. Artaud, David S. Ware, myself—there are so many people and this is what we've all discovered we are dealing with, an incredible blockage from the reign of the European consciousness, from about 14th century to the present time. That era was absolutely maniacally brazen and torrentially obtuse. As we see the resistances in America, can America somehow ignore that? The historian Henry Steele Commager entitled a little book (and I paraphrase the title) *Was America A Mistake?* Not a psychological one but one more geographical in leaning. In hindsight one in many ways would have to answer in the affirmative. Being on the brink of irretrievable extinction, since 1945 the circumstance has increased existentially. We have a carking problem here. When you look at some of the details that I've alluded to there had been for the musical genius, there had been so much resistance to extolling deeper sonic grammar, attempting to work in tandem with the Christian empire has been unbelievably complicated. So, you have these problems—there was a massacre around 1572 when one of the popes, I think Pope Gregory, the Catholics slaughtered the Huguenots, the Protestants, and when he slaughtered them, he built bonfires in celebration. And this is gruesome—they were actually selling body parts... [Recording ends]

PART IV

ELECTRICAL GRAMMAR

Afterwords

Note Concerning Higher Mental Scale

THESE DEFINITIONS REMAIN prone to the essays at hand and have not been written to replicate or garner official definition. First of all, I want to thank the inclusiveness of my editor E. Tracy Grinnell and her staff for pointing to these particulars as they naturally erupted from the texts at hand. Let me say that the brilliance I've been graced with was not completely covered in these writings. These are names I've written about elsewhere or not at all. Let me say, acknowledged or not, they have made their mark. What has emerged remains a bulletin of immediate arrangement. These definitions are of course not doctrinaire or complete prone to personal ideology. They exist as a bastion of particles according to the principle of immediate arrangement. What has been invoked is higher mental scale not as super-imposed hierarchical pattern but eruptions as nuance rising from necessity. Never was there any pre-planned intervention on my part. Never did official parameter persist but energy not unlike the dictum of Cartier-Bresson that I am fond of paraphrasing that the picture takes you instead of you taking it. This being a book that registers existential mirrors. Therefore each isolate inscription burns and then others as a creative gale of fire. Thus, they have magnetized themselves as collective inscription.

Higher Mental Scale: Glossary

EINSTEIN-ROSEN BRIDGES Albert Einstein along with Nathan Rosen theoretically understood how a black hole's surface connects to another space-time. Such realia ignite for the mind profound realia of possibility. **ANDREI LINDE** Russian American theoretical physicist authored the reality of an inflationary expansion of this universe into another thereby igniting another parallel hidden reality that cannot be cognitively tracked or measured. **SRI AUROBINDO** Indian poet/yogic. Did his most mesmerizing work after his political career when helping eject the British from India. Wrote many tomes in a supraconscious state that included *The Life Divine* and *The Future Poetry*. Collaborated with The Mother (Mirra Alfassa) at Pondicherry working on cellular transmutation. **FERNANDO PESSOA** The indelible Portuguese poet who wrote his many works via incalculable heteronyms. Was fortunate to visit his former abode white visiting Lisbon. Years prior to this was able (along with poet Anthony Seidman) to dialogue with Richard Zenith, Pessoa's biographer. **ELON MUSK** Entrepreneur/business magnate whose latter-day psychological chartings seem catastrophic via Martian colonization in tandem with a failing climate on Earth. **WERNER HERZOG** German film director remains symbolic for me of the provocative and the unexpected. Director of *Aguirre, the Wrath of God* and *Into the Inferno*, amongst many others. I remain always struck by his unsanctioned walk through Albania. **RENÉ ADOLPHE SCHWALLER DE LUBICZ** Transformative Egyptologist. Made seminal study at the complex at Luxor. Declared

Egypt, not Greece, was the acme of planetary civilization. **RICHARD FEYNMAN** Was able to compress complexity into communicable language. This trait remains invaluable to poets. Shared 1965 Nobel Prize with **JULIAN SCHWINGER** and **SHINICHIRO TOMONAGA**. **K. ERIC DREXLER** Never in philosophical agreement with the generic power of Nanotechnology yet remain in generic agreement with his brilliance. His engineering elan seems exclusively employed by the richer nations to the North. **GERD BINNIG/HEINRICH ROHRER** They discovered a simple method for creating a direct image of the atomic structure of surfaces. Shared Nobel Prize in 1986 for the design of the scanning tunneling microscope. **VOLTAIRE** French enlightenment sage taken to task by Pulitzer Prize-winning historian for taking on the accepted denigration of the African countenance. **MAURICE BLANCHOT** Seminal French author that remained personally self-obscured. Author of *Thomas the Obscure* and *death sentence*. Was most concerned with written thought. **MICHEL LEIRIS** For me most significant was his understanding that the poet's strife is rewarded by being flooded by great language. Author of *Aurora* and the monumental *Phantom Africa*. **SATPREM** Confidant of The Mother (Mirra Alfassa) as she worked on her 15,000-page *Agenda*. Author of *The Mind of the Cells*. **ERIS** Trans-Neptunian object discovered in 2006. Symbolic of collective strife and discord that is our current experience. **PHILIP LAMANTIA** Instinctive poetic sage of lingual volatility and wisdom. He personally emanated to me realms of protracted insight that I've inscripted in my book-length poem *The Brimstone Boat*. "Red phase" of the "Great Work." **ANDRÉ BRETON** Ignited planetary Surrealism. Ubiquitous in the world mind with higher poetic insight. He symbolizes language as pure alchemical praxis. **EDWARD DE BONO** Late British/Maltese author who scripted *Lateral Thinking* – exercises leading to liberty from the cognitive enclosure of the mind. **AIMÉ CÉSAIRE** Indelible poetic alchemist from Martinique. His example has led me to upper realms of my own lingual spirit. His lightning-like mind first appeared in print in 1939. **BOB KAUFMAN** Declared all-consuming

Surrealist by Philip Lamantia. Author of *Solitudes Crowded with Loneliness*, and *The Ancient Rain*. "To My Son Parker Asleep in The Next Room" comes from the former volume and remains consistently a-myopic for me. **PETER VAN WYCK** Author *Signs of Danger* concerning nuclear waste extending far beyond the realm of conventional human palpability. **CÉSAR VALLEJO** According to British critic Martin Seymour-Smith, the most significant poet in 20th century literature. Ignited language at the purity of stammer. **MARIA SABINA** Indigenous shamaness whose praxis positively infected the realms of Oaxaca. Her healing rituals opened "the gates of the mind." **THOMAS BERNHARD** As Cioran made possible for me the expression of the aphorism so too did Thomas Bernhard's mind make possible for me the exploration of the novel. Without *Correction* my work *Diary as Sin* could have never erupted. Critic of modern civilization and its expression through Austrian lens in particular. **KRAKEN MARE** Largest known body of liquid on the Saturnian moon Titan. Discovered by the Cassini Probe in 2006. Slightly larger than the Caspian Sea. **KEVIN GILBERT** Aboriginal Poet, playwright, printmaker. Born on the banks of the Lachlan River in New South Wales. He was what I understand to be a breakthrough being, organically railing against the institutional mistreatment of the aboriginal by European domination. **MARYAM MIRZAKHANI** Late brilliant Iranian mathematician. She would cross standard structure to get to computational essence. Not unlike the insight that Thomas Kuhn wrote about in his *Structure of Scientific Revolutions*. **MOUNT OSSA** Highest mountain in Tasmania. 1617 metres above sea level. **FRASER CAVE** Important in establishment of antiquity and range of Aboriginal confluence dating back to the Pleistocene. It is now called **KUTIKINA CAVE** on the Franklin River in Tasmania. **BLACK WAR** Violent conflict between Aboriginals and European settlers in Tasmania from 1820s to 1832. **OTWAY / MURRAY ESTUARY** Where fresh water meets the open sea. A fertile eco-system for Aboriginals. Never a potential for malignant geography as happened across the Earth in modern times. **KING HIGHLANDS** Central Highlands of

Tasmania. Named after first Norman monarch of England. Ruled between 1066 to 1087. **SOUTH GRAMPION NATIONAL PARK** Under the ownership of Europeans. Tasmania's Aboriginal name was *Lutruwita*. They now own less than one percent of its land mass. **THE FURNEAUX ISLANDS** Named after British Navigator Tobias Furneaux who was part of the James Cook expedition. **GIPPSLAND RURAL REGION OF SOUTH-EASTERN AUSTRALIA** near the Tasmanian Sea. Named after George Gipps who was Governor between 1838-1846. **MOUNT GAMBIER WARRNAMBOOL REGION** Named by the Aboriginals as "two swamps," "place of plenty," "ample waters," from the language of the Kuurn Noot Aboriginals. **PELION RANGE** A mountain range in St. Clair National Park Tasmania named after Mount Pelion in Greece. **BANTU** According to Dr. Yosef A.A. Ben-Jochannan a pejorative term that has linked these African people to perpetual lessening. **TASMANIA** Imprinted in the modern era by Dutch explorer Tasman in 1642. Subsequently used as British penal colony from 1803 to 1853. **WALYER** She was a rebel leader that led an Aboriginal rebellion in the early 1800s. **ALBERT EINSTEIN** Listed before in relation to theoretical connectivity to other universes via Black Holes. He symbolizes a monumental force as representative of higher consciousness within our species. **MAGICIAN TETA** Egyptian Magician mentioned by E.A. Wallis Budge having the power to raise sacrificed animals from the dead. **CHEOPS** Second Pharaoh of the 4th Dynasty in the first half of the Old Kingdom during which time Teta existed. **TIBETAN ZHITRO** Cycle of teachings referred to by Karma Lingpa believed to have been written by Padmasambhava. The Zhitro are considered to be an inner Tantra visualizing peaceful or wrathful ditties. **OUPPA GALDOS** Mythical auditory being. **ORION SPUR** Locale in the Milky Way where our Sun is located. **LANIAKEA SUPERCLUSTER** Encompasses 100,000 Galaxies over 520 million light years across. **KUNZHI NAMSHE** Base container of consciousness. According to Dzogchen value it does not dissolve it empties itself. As from the Chittamatra view it remains mixed with cosmic traces that dissolve and when purified disappears. **NIRMANAKAYA** The Emanation Body. **DHARMAKAYA** All the good qualities of the Buddha, the wisdom, the compassion, and the patience. **PRAKṚTI** In Hindu, made of its guna, the qualities of matter. **ASVAGHOSA** Buddhist orator, poet, philosopher, dramatist, lived 50 to 150 C. E. **NĀGĀRJUNA** Lived 150 to 250 C. E. Buddhist. Greatest Indian court writer prior to Kālidāsa. **METHUSELAH** Quantitative symbol of human eternity. Methusaleh wrought Biblically in the chapter of Genesis as ancestor of Noah sired by Enoch. **ENOCH** Psychology associated in the general mind with Divine longevity due to the exceptional nature of his offsprings' long life. Via the rendering within the book of Genesis did not die and was taken whole soul and body into heaven. **SIRIUS** Brightest star in the heavens. Almost twice as bright as next Brightest star Canopus. To the Egyptians was the most important star and signaled living inundation. **ABYDOS** In Central Egypt. Resting place of **OSIRIS** as well as its early kings. **IZAR** Located in the constellation Boötes, part of a double star system over 200 light years from Earth. Provides the ability to absorb in the world positively enhanced by this starlight elixir. Assists in balancing sodium and potassium in the body. **PROCYON** Provides mental acuity brings enhanced states of mental concentration. Located in Canis Minor. **ALDEBARAN** Provides a greater understanding of the process of death. Consolation and transition are its chief tenets. Located in Alpha Tauri. **KEMET** A pre-European appellation of Egypt. Not only represented the black colouration of its soil but also the colouration of its beings. **CHARLES IVES** Incandescent American composer of the 20th century. **JOHN COLTRANE** Like Ives incandescent a seminal planetary inspiration. His recordings emblazon the psycho-physical nebulae wafting inside the spirit. **WOLOF** Indigenous African language spoken inside Senegal and parts of Gambia akin to the musical fluency that is said to empower Chinese. **CHOKWE** Part of the Niger-Congo language family. When last counted in 1990 possessing just under a million speakers. **ROMANI** Indo-Aryan macrolanguage spoken by a bit over a million beings. **VODOU** Syncretic mix of practices ancestral Roman Catholic always alive via palpable spells that register the other. It's praxis registers via African old-world praxis and the new world via powers used in Haiti and the American South. **POMO** Only 10 thousand plus members remain extant. They now centre 100 miles north of San Francisco on the Russian River. **COMANCHE** Being part of the circumstance of victimization where only 17,000 members continue to interactively commingle with the living. **DOGON** Numbering over a half million souls in West Africa. Descended from the Egyptians. Had knowledge of Sirius binary system and Sirius B long before the technical appearance of the telescope. **YORUBAN** Again a Niger-Congo language spoken by 50 million people. From my delimitation, Standard Yoruba is a separate member of a dialect cluster founded by Samuel Crowther to translate the Bible. Yet Yoruba casts its presence in other forms of its expression, namely **OYO** that reigns north of Lagos. **JOAN MIRÓ** One of the most influential beings in my life, not only in terms of his drawing and painting, but in his quiet unruffled persistence. **LAKE TURKANA (OMO RIVER)** Symbolic of East Africa where humanity erupted. This being the Great Lakes region. In what I consider to be a former incarnation of my life I had a significant experience shaking hands and holding a brief exchange with the original Dr. Louis Leakey. He signed a random card that has long since been misplaced. **THALES, HERACLITUS, PARMENIDES** According to **DR. YOSEF BEN-JOCHANNAN**, all these gentlemen have been implanted by Western scholars with mythical existence. To the Western mind such notion remains none other than a heretical substrate. **FYODOR DOSTOYEVSKY** In spite of the massive legendary tomes he has authored it is the opening section from his *Notes from Underground* that has most seminally affected me. It seems his lingual powers condense via philosophical eruption. **VINCENT VAN GOGH** Again and again I return to Antonin Artaud's assessment of Van Gogh's 1947 Parisian display of his works. He upended malnourished assessment of his brilliance spawned by purposely mishandled psychiatric assessment entitled by his essay "Van Gogh: The Man Suicided by Society." **COFFIN TEXTS** Missing link that connects the Pyramid Texts and The Egyptian Book of The Dead. It expresses the desire for immortality thereby avoiding the danger of dying a second death by the traps of threatening beings. **BURYAT SHAMAN** These Mongolian shamans are viewed as bridges between the visible and the invisible. **LENT** A latter season of abstinence imposed by the Catholic Church by those between the ages of 18 and 59 from eating meat. It symbolizes a ubiquitous reminder of human demise. The praxis of fasting and prayer. **JULIUS CAESAR** I am not thinking of a ubiquitous dictator who commanded fearsome military forces but of a colonial invader that ransacked the Gauls. **GONDWANALAND** Covered one-fifth of the Earth's surface during the Paleozoic era 550 million years ago. **AUK** Proto-Germanic bird, part of Alcidae family that includes Auklets, Puffins, and Murrelets. This name derived from the Icelandic Sea. **MOUNT MERU** Located in the state of Uttarakhand in India. Meru is Sanskrit word for peak. Symbolized in my mind by the compositional and expressive power of John Coltrane and Eric Dolphy. **CARCHARODON** Ancient shark genus primarily extinct, the only extant member being that of the Great White Shark. **SOMBRERO GALAXY** three-tenths the size of the Milky Way. Symbolic in my mind of riveting visual brilliance. **ARAWAK** Reminder of endemic colonial violence. The Arawak were slaughtered by the forces assembled by Christopher Columbus. This dastardly experience was depicted by Bartholomé de Las Casas captured in his book *A Short Account of the Destruction of the Indies*. Penned in 1542. **CIBOLA** Cíbola was symbolic of the destroyed complex that was the living Hawikuh site desecrated by Francisco Coronado. Cíbola in the common colonial consciousness was symbolic of riches via the surplus of confiscated gold. The hallucination of a malignant mythical mind. **NAVAMSHA** In Vedic or Indian astrology it carries a one-ninth portion of the chart. It is said that if one combines the birth chart with the Navamsha chart it provides the astrologer with incalculable significance. **ALBERTO GIACOMETTI** His uncanny sculptures traced themselves to the power of drawing. He once stated "if one could master drawing, all would be possible. Drawing is the basis of everything." **HOPI** Has almost 20,000 members according to a recent U. S. census. They have been residents of Oraibi since 1150 of our common era. Maternal essence. 13 of its villages have resisted official tribal dictates that have aligned themselves with official governmental policy. **PANTOCRATOR** Jesus Christ as ruler of the universe appears as icon and in domes and apse mosaics in Byzantine churches. **PALMARYAN** Being that graced Palmarya that was first spoken of in the 2nd millennium B.C. where the Moon rather than the Sun captured the status of primary importance. Palmarya established colonies along the Silk Road throughout the Roman Empire. **OORT CLOUD** First uncovered by Dutch astronomer Jan Oort in 1950. Alive with icy planetesimals between 2,000 and 200,000 astronomical units from the Sun. It signals the ungraspable power that is the universe. **JACQUES RIVIÈRE** First significant correspondent with Antonin Artaud. He was a contemporary who failed to grasp the complexity of Artaud's mind. **ANTONIN ARTAUD** Endemic renegade. Authored *Letter to André Breton*, continues to erupt inside my current of thought. Has written explosive work on Van Gogh and the compelling *To Have Done with the Judgment Of God*. **THE INTERNATIONAL EXPOSITION OF SURREALISM IN 1947** Participants included Wifredo Lam, Joan Miró, and Roberto Matta amongst many others. A higher pitch of post-war solidarity. **ANAÏS NIN** Essential contact between personalities as diverse as Henry Miller and Antonin Artaud. Years later had enormous influence upon the artistic psychology of an artistic colleague of mine, Georgiana Peacher. **GNOSTICS** Erupted in 1st century A. D. Claimed interior knowledge to consist of living insight beyond darkness. Like many poets, they could never be structured according to what is considered to be doctrinal Christianity. **ABEL GANCE** Early French film director. Worked with Antonin Artaud when the latter employed himself as actor. Also remains part of Artaud's correspondence during the early modern era. **JEAN PAULHAN** Had essential correspondence with Antonin Artaud during the inter-war era. **HENRY CORBIN** French scholar who helped forge conduction with Iranian Sufism in the West. A key text for me has been his *The Man of Light in Iranian Sufism*. **DAVID BOHM** Collaborator with **JIDDU KRISHNAMURTI** concerning the very nature of existence. Author of *Wholeness and the Implicate* in the era that was the 1920s and 30s. **KANT, HUME, HEGEL, HEIDEGGER** Major western philosophers having eschewed African psychology as effective criteria. **SOLON, PYTHAGORAS** Initially trained according to the tenets of Egyptian psychology. According to G. N. James they were neophytes of the Egyptian Mystery system. Plutarch lists Oenuphis as Pythagoras' essential instructor. **ROGER CAILLOIS** Who promoted Western psychology as the superior tenet. **GILLES DELEUZE/FÉLIX GUATTARI** In their book *A Thousand Plateaus* they understood the power of non-standardized psychology. **ANANDA COOMARASWAMY** Indian thinker who understood the looming presence of the Indigenous mind across all factors of presence. **OCTAVIO PAZ** Great Mexican poet/essayist who won Nobel Prize in 1990. The contour of his mind has had similar impact upon my thought and poetics. Author of *East Slope, Eagle or Sun*, and a major study on the poet/nun Sor Juana. **CLAUDE LÉVI-STRAUSS** Hailed in a small but generative work by Octavio Paz. Did research in Brazilian Amazon. Highly influential as was **THOMAS KUHN** beyond his field of expertise thereby influencing poets. **RENÉ GUÉNON** Penetrant thinker of the declivitous abyss of Occidental values. Author of *The Reign of Quantity and the Signs of the Times*. Left France and passed away as a Muslim in Cairo. **LUDWIG WITTGENSTEIN** Who refuted the rational skill of his own *Tractatus* stating in the end that philosophy had run its course. Gave away his private wealth to pursue thought. Did influential work at Cambridge. **RENÉ DAUMAL** Initially connected with Roger Gilbert-Lecomte (as well as Roger Meyrat and Roger Vailland) to attain the intuitive and spontaneous simplicity of childhood. They ignited as the Simplistes morphed into complex maturity of *Le Grand Jeu* always self-aligned to the impossible. Deningrated by Breton and official Surrealism, the Simplistes and *Le Grand Jeu* explored the architecture of the invisible. **NA'IM AKBAR**

Has explored the power of ancient African psychology and found its modern western equivalent to be sorely lacking and basically malevolent with protracted adolescence always remaining in arrears of the inner technology of Egyptian achievement. **CHEIKH ANTA DIOP** Great Senegalese pro-Indigenous African thinker has written the seminal texts *The African Origin of Civilization: Myth or Reality* and *Civilization or Barbarism: An Authentic Anthropology*. He understood the baffled modern criteria concerning thought process. **HANNAH ARENDT** Anti-Totalitarian thinker, she explored the malignant nature of National Socialism. The latter inscribed the tactic of incendiary thought. **RENÉ MÉNIL** Philospher from Martinique collaborated with Aimé and Suzanne Césaire on the seminal journal *Tropiques*. Resistance to Nazism during the 2nd Great War. His book of essays, *Tracées*, was published in 1981. **LAUREN GREENFIELD** She ignited the documentary *Generation Wealth* exploring the troubled modern mania for wealth foretelling the toxic nature of its current collapse. **KARL MARX** Ubiquitous presence who has authored the seminal alternative to capital in the current era. *Das Kapital* has never exclusively brewed in my system, but I've always noted (along with Hegel and Kant) his negative response to the presence of Africa. **THORSTEIN VEBLEN** Norwegian economist who emerged as intrinsic critic of the vestiges of capital. He is best known for his theory of the leisure class known throughout the world for his concept of conspicuous consumption. Passed away in California. **BYRON BAKER** Intrinsic artist whom I've collaborated with as a painter. For me he seems as one who has transmuted the invisibility that gusts as the mathematics of abstraction. **ROBERTO MATTA** Intrinsic Chilean painter who first trained as an architect with Fernand Léger but went on to paint spontaneous inner realms never limited to linear rationality. Of enormous significance to my praxis both as a poet and visual artist. **JORGE CAMACHO** Self-enabled painter who hailed from Havana. I never have considered his works to hail from ideology, but to always explode from the necessity of vision. **CHAÏM SOUTINE** I've always been inspired by the phantom ellipticality of his going on to paint his subjects without rational preparation. I am thinking of his bell boys and his phantom landscapes at Ceret. **CARLO GESUALDO** Italian composer who famously murdered his wife protractedly judged by the phantom that is history. **HENRY THE VIII** Well known murderer and pragmatist via manipulation. **THERESA TOLLIVER** Little known Los Angeles painter who started creating in childhood. Her imaginative watercolour depicting late actress Beah Richards is owned by Sheila Scott-Wilkinson founder of Arts organization Theater of Hearts/Youth First. **MICHAEL FRIMKISS** Noted ceramacist part of the California Clay Movement. Known for innovative creative technique. Hails from Los Angeles California. **SHEILA SCOTT-WILKINSON** I've previously written an essay on her prior acting prowess on stage and screen in England. She previously played a prominent role in Horace Ove's *Pressure*, the first all-black cast that erupted from England with a role that symbolized Angela Davis. **BEAH RICHARDS** Pioneering Black actress who once starred next to Sidney Poitier and Spencer Tracy in the groundbreaking film *Guess Who's Coming to Dinner*. **MARCO PALLIS** Through the positive infection of my colleague the late Jim Henderson, I was introduced to the works of René Guénon and through the latter's writing to the works of the Greek-British Buddhist mountaineer who took up Tibetan thought and its transcendent power of Tradition. His books included *Peaks and Lamas: A Classic Book on Mountaineering, Buddhism and Tibet* and *A Buddhist Spectrum: Contributions to the Christian-Buddhist Dialogue* amongst others. **SALMAN LOCKER** Birth name of his adapted appellation **GHÉRASIM LUCA** meanwhile also known to some as Costea Sar and Petre Malcoci. Fabulous poet who not unlike Vallejo was capable of alchemical lingua stammer. Committed suicide late in life jumping into the Seine. Translated into English by Julian and Laura Semilian. **PETRE RĂILEANU** Romanian literary critic who has scripted a French study on Luca. I became aware of his penetrating assessment via Contra Mundrum and the essay I had the privilege to script on Luca for the press. He also wrote an essay on Luca for *The Inventor of*

Love & Other Writings translated into English by Julian and Laura Semilian. **GEORGIANA PEACHER** During a trip to England the poet Jonathan Skinner introduced me to the living presence of Georgiana Peacher. Vocally spry and in her 90s she communicated her experience dating back to Amelia Earhart and forward to her marvelous writing that includes *Mary Stuart's Ravishment Descending Time: Prose Symphony*, her poetic prose that spins around the doomed spirit that was Mary Stuart. **MARY STUART** Became a Queen as infant. Due to the tensions of royalty, she was executed by Queen Elizabeth I in 1587. **JACKSON POLLOCK** Legendary abstract painter that self-condoned his own "drip technique." I was highly influenced by his prior period of psychoanalytic works. **JOHNATHAN SKINNER** Poet, whose ecological concerns have positively empowered his work. Poet, field recordist, he has generously written on my work ("On the Spur of Orion") for Jacket2. **DEBORAH DIGGES** Memorist/poet who escaped this world at 59 via suicide. For me not time on this Earth, but one's effectiveness on Earth. **PERE GIMFERRER** Author of the translated work *Fortuny*. Poet, translator, essayist, critic. Hailed by Octavio Paz, and Roberto Bolaño. Juan Goytisolo understood him to have the capability of "self-renewal." **CARLOS PEZOA VÉLIZ** Chilean poet passed away at 28 from tuberculosis. Poetically embellished after his passing within the 20th century. **GABRIELA MISTRAL** Chilean Nobel Prize Laureate 1945. Poet of expanded sensitivity to motherhood and children. Spent a bit of time in Los Angeles during the early 1950s. **VICENTE HUIDOBRO** Chilean poet author of the seminal work *Altazor*. For me, example of psychic lingual verticality. Posthumously hailed as a poet of rebellion and denunciation. **PABLO NERUDA** Chilean poetic conjure. Once advanced his language as co-conspirator with Lorca. As time passed, he became authoritative magnus of poetic language. Stunning by means of his prolific output. **DAVID SHOOK** Poetic practitioner who remains capable of exploring Indigenous grammars. Ignited his global study at Harvard. **CHARLES MINGUS** Advanced musical thinker who evolved in the apartheid setting of the Watts section of Los Angeles.

Was compositionally and instrumentally advanced bassist as early as the 1940s. **DANNIE RICHMOND** Charles Mingus's life-long drummer with whom I was able to converse about the intriguing transmutation of Eric Dolphy's sound coming from the point of one who existentially accompanied the latter's sonic fervour. **PAUL MORPHY** First major modern chess master who hailed from New Orleans and was Black. **ALEXANDER ALEKHINE** Introduced to me by Majied Mahadi. As I recall the 4th world chess champion who defeated Capablanca the great Cuban. Passed away in Portugal via mysterious circumstance. Cantankerous personality that would never give Capablanca a rematch. **SULUBIKA (MONROE JONES)** Fabulous but little-known contemporary flautist. His sound and technique prone to ministrations of Eric Dolphy. **MAJIED MAHADI (CHRISTOPHER JEFFERSON)** Late charismatic scholar advanced beyond his years. Few books passed before he could read them. **COINTELPRO** J. Edgar Hoover's program for tracking and repressing advanced political thinking in the African American community. **DEDAN KIMATHI (DEDAN GILLS)** Psychic revolutionary/environmentalist. Part of an early three-person study group that we both shared with Majied Mahadi. Was always alive with his boldness. **GENJI AMINO/DAISY ATTERBURY** Directors of NM Poetics, who provided an organic invigourating environment for poets and writers in Northern New Mexico. **DARYL LUCERO** Integral member of NM Poetics on Indigenous infrastructure as well as crop yield and various local sensitivities to crops. **GEORGE DRURY SMITH** Founder of Beyond Baroque Literary Arts Foundation. **RICHARD MODIANO** One of the seminal directors within the history of Beyond Baroque Literary Arts Foundation. **RAYMOND ROUSSEL** Incredible precursor of recognized Surrealism. Writer who is worthy of an updated biography of his work. **CARLOS LARA** Prior collaborator with myself (*The Audiographic As Data*) promulgator of abstract poetry. **ARTHUR RIMBAUD** Legendary poetic practitioner who has ignited modern poetry across the world. **PRINCE HENRY THE NAVIGATOR** Portuguese explorer of the early modern world, son of John I explored the west coast of Africa igniting the latter's protracted psycho-physical detriment. **KING LEOPOLD** Ruled The Congo as his private province, extracting its wealth while inflicting suffering upon its inhabitants. **CARL LINNAEUS** Scripted the accepted taxonomies for the modern world placing Africans and other Indigenous peoples at the lowest rungs of possibility. **FRANCISCO BETHENCOURT** Portuguese scholar in London who has probed endemic racism from the early modern world to the present in his book *Racisms: From the Crusades to the Twentieth Century*. **HERNÁN CORTÉS** Spanish explorer who ignited the grammar of destruction amongst the Mayans that continues to spread across the Americas. **COTTIE BURLAND** British art critic who understood the contemporary artistic abduction of ideas initially by European sailors within colonial Africa. **TOMÁS DE TORQUEMADA** Author of the tortuous practices so flagrantly applied during the Spanish Inquisition. **ALDON LYNN NIELSEN** Author of *Reading Race: White American Poets and the Racial Discourse in the Twentieth Century,* who uncovered the hidden stench of racism in the letters of the early poetic practitioners of Modernism. **WILLIAM CARLOS WILLIAMS** Highly influential practitioner of early Modernist poetics during his lingual rise between 1920s and 50s. Yet in a note to New Directions signaled the demise of Western lingual authority should it fail to expand its reach beyond its seeming authority. **NOAM CHOMSKY** Seminal linguist and protracted critic of the techniques of American Empire. **T. S. ELIOT** Author of *The Waste Land*, winner of 1948 Nobel Prize, culturally influential, was pervaded at his core by misogyny, anti-Semitism and racism. **JEROME ROTHENBERG** Prolific poet and cultural biographer of Shamanism for the present psychology. His poetic oeuvre totals over 100 titles. **HENRY MILLER** Legendary author and seminal critic of the misguided American enterprise. His book *The Air-Conditioned Nightmare* is particularly striking. **STEPHEN HAWKING** Physicist who was self-enabled to explore black holes and project his powers into the possibility of unknown realities. **LARGE HADRON COLLIDER** Collector of particle Neutrinos thereby examining exotic realms of reality. An enterprise very instructive for poets. **IGNACIO MATTE BLANCO** Late Chilean psychoanalyst who worked with what I understand to be the existential grammar of the unconscious. **COMTE DE LAUTRÉAMONT (ISIDORE LUCIEN DUCASSE)** Along with Arthur Rimbaud, ignited the radical morphing of language into modern poetry. **AMOS TUTUOLA** Modern Nigerian writer whose work seems to remain torrentially perpetual. Author of many works including *The Palm-Wine Drinkard*. **PHILIP LAMANTIA** Incredible poet who seemed to initiate lingual Surrealism in North America. To paraphrase Breton, his was a voice that rises once in 100 years. Personal confidant, early supporter of mine. **ABEOKUTA, NIGERIA** Birthplace of Amos Tutuola in 1920. **MILES DAVIS** Influential trumpeter who seemingly warped the musical landscape. Was fortunate to grace his presence and speak to him in my later youth. **JOSÉ LEZAMA LIMA** Author of *Paradiso*. I've read commentary that has suggested that Lezama Lima was an anomaly, having authored his masterpiece in Havana rather than one of the cultural capitals of the Earth. **LE BRÈCHE** One of André Breton's last major publishing projects where he surmised life in outer space to be an unfeasible possibility. **LES HALLES** Produce section of Paris made known to me by the last major conversation when André Breton and Octavio Paz exchanged major insights. **EGERIA** Trans-Neptune's object declared by depth psychologist Keiron Le Grice to be a symbol of catastrophic significance for humanity. He declares this in his work *Discovering Eris*. **ANDREW JORON** Great poet, seminal collaborator of mine. His insight erupts not unlike the protracted trance of a slow-motion Galaxy. **JANICE LEE** Brilliant editor of the online magazine Entropy. Author of the novel *Daughter*. **ASHOKA ASOKA** Mauryan king who ignited Buddhist principles while conducting an empire. I previously wrote a book-length play on him entitled *At Night on the Sun*. **MIGUEL CARVALHO** Was fortunate to collaborate with him during my stay in Coimbra. Read from my work *Spectral Hieroglyphics* at his bookstore. Along with painter Rik Lina, ignited the collective Portuguese group Cabo Mondego. Did collaborative painting with

Miguel inside a Portuguese Cave. CALEIDOSCOPIO SURREALISTA Publication from the Canary Islands where a major entry on my work was included. Edited by Miguel Corrales. THOMAS JEFFERSON Early former president who, in the present context, is more suggestive of hypocrisy, and who ignited freedom for the European population but made no effort to liberate the African population some of whom he held as slaves. PHYLLIS WHEATLEY Early Black proponent of inscripted poetic art. Denigrated by Jefferson. HENRI CARTIER-BRESSON Seminal French photographer. I always paraphrase his statement about the picture taking you and you not taking the picture. ALBERT AYLER Great free jazz player from Cleveland who mesmerized by the sincerity of his sound. Often played alongside his younger brother, the trumpeter, Donald Ayler. ERIC DOLPHY For me the most lamented premature passing in the arts. Had a seminal contact with his parents and was allowed to peruse his intact original workspace. My original model for extending my lingual expression beyond the strict domain of poetry into aphorisms, plays, essays and fiction. Dolphy and Ayler had agreed to form a group before the former's passing. WALTER RODNEY Guyanese author assassinated by the Forbes-Burnham government. His book *How Europe Underdeveloped Africa* remains a penetrating document long after the demise of his presence.

Acknowledgements

All pieces are reprinted by permission of Will Alexander with grateful acknowledement to the editors of the journals and editions where some of these pieces first appeared.

"The Contemporary Mind: Pointless Rural Fragment and Phosphenic Threading" was originally published in *Sublevel Magazine,* issue 2 (CalArts 2018). Web.

"Atop a Tasmanian Crag" was originally published in *Entropy.* July 31, 2017. Web.

"Inscrutable Visibility" was originally published in *Your Impossible Voice,* issue 2 (Winter 2013). Web.

"On Crossing the Vermin Frontier" was originally published in *Hambone,* vol. 21, edited by Nathanial Mackey. 2015.

"On the Rise of Sodium and Fire," "Saturate with Refined Enigmas," and "Escaping Mass Seduction" appeared in *The Brimstone Boat: For Philip Lamantia.* (Los Angeles: Rêve à Deux, 2012): pp. 141-184.

"On the Rise of Sodium and Fire," "Saturate with Refined Enigmas," and "Escaping Mass Seduction" appeared as "The Density Paintings" in *Hydrolith 2: Surrealist Research & Investigations.* (Berkeley: Oyster Moon Press, 2014): pp. 75-95.

"Antonin Artaud: A Glossary of Fumes" in *Spectral Hieroglyphics: A Poetic Troika*. (Los Angeles: Rêve à Deux, 2016): pp. 76-81.

"My Philosophical Matrix: A Hurricane of Luminosity." *Towards the Primeval Lightning Field*. 2nd edition. (Brooklyn: Litmus Press, 2014): pp. i-iv.

"Our Present Psychic State: an Awkward Foreboding." *Entropy*. October 23, 2017. Web.

"The Drawings of Byron Baker: Phantom Electrical Scarring." *Caesurea Magazine*. June 12, 2021. Web.

"Superseding the Diurnal: The Latest Works of Byron Baker." *Entropy*. Dec 6, 2016. Web.

"Ghérasim Luca: Fulminate Inscription as Shadow." *Hyperion: On the Future of Aesthetics*, Vol. VIII, No. 3 (Fall 2013): pp. 129-132.

"Georgiana Peacher's Mary Stuart's *Ravishment Descending Time: A Species of Rapture*." *Entropy*. May 21, 2014. Web.

"The Larsons' Journey Beyond Time." *Entropy*. March 10, 2017. Web.

"Aleatoric Circular Forms: A Trilogy of Circles." *Entropy*. March 3, 2017. Web.

"Prologue: Quantum Lingual Deftness." *Abecedary* by Pablo Joffré, translated by David Shook. (Insert Blanc Press, 2017).

"'Beyond Baroque': A seminal ray encircling the planet." *Jacket2*. November 19, 2013. Web.

"Bulletins from the Lava Floor: In Remembrance of Wanda Coleman." *Caliban Online*, vol. 15, pp. 20-21. Web.

Elizabeth Bryant, "Primordial Vibration: An Interview with Will Alexander." *Now That It's Now: New Directions Blog*. December 2014. Web.

Chris Holdaway, "On African Free Labour and the Interstellar Vacuum: Chris Holdaway Interviews Will Alexander." *Entropy*. June 20, 2016. Web.

Sofi Thanhauser, "Interview: Sofi Thanhauser w/ Will Alexander." *Entropy*. Jan 11, 2016. Web.

"National Poetry Month Featured Poet: Will Alexander." *Entropy*. April 10, 2017. Web.

"it remains sonic occultation: An interview with Will Alexander by SJ Fowler." *3:AM Magazine*. Nov. 29, 2013. Web.

Darrell Jónsson, "An Interview with Ghasem Batamuntu and Will Alexander from Prague CZ." Ghasem Batamuntu. May 2011. Web.

"David S. Ware Remembered By Matthew Shipp, Will Alexander." New Day Jazz, KDVS 90.3 FM [Surprise Valley], December 23, 2012, 4pm.

Born in 1948, **WILL ALEXANDER** is a poet, essayist, novelist, playwright, aphorist, visual artist, pianist, whose output exists around 40 titles. He remains in the process of putting in print a collaboration with artist Byron Baker entitled *Anonymous Stellar Ravines*. Currently he is poet-in-residence at Beyond Baroque Literary Arts Foundation and resides in Los Angeles.